CW00589821

The War on Hospital Ships
1914 – 1918

This book is dedicated to the memory of
Claire Louise McGreal

Eternal Father, strong to save,
Whose arm hath bound the restless wave
Who biddest the mighty ocean deep
Its own appointed limits keep;
Oh, hear us when we cry to Thee,
For those in peril on the sea!

William Whiting 1860

The War on Hospital Ships

1914 – 1918

Stephen McGreal

Pen & Sword
MARITIME

First published in Great Britain in 2008 by

PEN & SWORD MARITIME
an imprint of
Pen & Sword Books Limited
47 Church Street
Barnsley
South Yorkshire
S70 2AS

ISBN 978 1 84415 858 4

A CIP catalogue record for this book is
available from the British Library.

Printed and bound in England by
Biddles Ltd.

Pen & Sword Books Ltd incorporates the imprints of
Pen & Sword Aviation, Pen & Sword Maritime,
Pen & Sword Military, Wharncliffe Local History
Pen & Sword Select, Pen & Sword Military Classics
and Leo Cooper

For a complete list of Pen & Sword titles please contact:
PEN & SWORD BOOKS LIMITED
47 Church Street, Barnsley, South Yorkshire, S70 2AS, England.
E-mail: enquiries@pen-and-sword.co.uk
Website: www.pen-and-sword.co.uk

Contents

Introduction

During the early seventies while working as an apprentice shipwright within Cammell Laird Shipbuilders and Engineers I first became aware of men who, while serving in the merchant navy, survived an attack by torpedo. In this instance an unlikely-looking veteran of the Second World War had sailed as a carpenter on merchant ships running the gauntlet of the U-boat packs. In my youthful innocence the man appeared rather old, forgetful and occasionally confused. His workmates explained his demeanour in whispered tones 'His ship was torpedoed while he was securing cargo in the hold. He managed to scale the hold escape ladders with the sea water lapping at his heels and never quite recovered from the experience'. He was evidently suffering from what we now term Post Traumatic Stress Disorder, something I would again become acquainted with during a stint as a carpenter in the merchant navy.

In the 1970s ageing veterans of the Second World War Atlantic convoys still abounded in an ever shrinking British-staffed merchant navy; they, like so many former veterans, shied away from discussing their wartime experiences. However, one individual routinely kept his cabin light off during the night, so as not to show a light to submarines! During the war his tanker was torpedoed off the Caribbean island of Curaçao, and whenever our tramp tanker approached the island he suffered flashbacks, packed a valise and prepared to go to hospital. Three decades later the consequences of the term 'ship torpedoed' took on a new meaning as I witnessed at first hand, the trauma revisit an ageing seaman. It is a sobering thought indeed to imagine the fear and anxiety experienced by the merchant navy personnel as they determinedly maintained the United Kingdom's essential food and materials lifeline. The fourth service depended on women and men like my maternal great-grandfather who survived a torpedo attack off the Irish coast; family legend maintains he returned home, still in his wet clothes. To add insult to injury when a vessel sank, the shipping companies automatically ceased paying wages to the crew. Denied an income, the seafarer generally signed on the next outward bound ship; faced with the starvation of their families most took to the sea, to worry about the U-boats another day. During the great recruitment drive for the army, volunteers officially had to be aged between eighteen and forty-one years old, extended upwards in 1918 to fifty-one. The Mercantile Marine had no such confines, exemplified by Mrs Bridget Trenerry, a sixty-five-year-old stewardess drowned on *Asturias*. If a person's past life flashes by in the seconds before death, seventeen-year-old Henry George Taylor's must have passed in the blink of an eye, as he drowned trapped in the bowels of the *Dover Castle*. Their status as non-combatants meant little during the merciless war at sea.

As a keen amateur military historian, occasionally my research into a Great War combatant abruptly halted, with the sinking of what I imagined to be a troopship or leave boat. Occasionally further research revealed the torpedoed or mined vessel was actually a hospital ship. It seemed perverse that any belligerent should torpedo a vessel fulfilling a humanitarian role, yet history records numerous deliberate instances. Perhaps after the wars everyone decided to 'let sleeping dogs lie', for although the First World War press used the hospital ship losses as a powerful anti-Germanic propaganda weapon, evocative books on this still controversial subject are scarce. Internet forums abound with questions and answers appertaining to the demise of this or that hospital ship. Despite the immunity of the Geneva Red Cross the hospital ships became 'fair game', in a theatre of war largely overlooked by people whose modern perception of the First World War is one of trench warfare.

Intrigued by this relatively unrecognised aspect of the First World War and remembering my experiences with torpedoed veterans, I pondered on how much worse the situation may have been for those incapacitated on a rapidly sinking hospital ship. While searching for first hand survivor accounts within archives my enquiries revealed a startlingly overlooked chapter of maritime history fought by belligerents with an intensity to equal the war of attrition waged on the Western Front. In the post-armistice years the vessels of the Mercantile Marine resumed their usual service, past glories eventually faded into obscurity, as did the crews who faded away. This work attempts to again bring to the fore the terrible price paid by the heroic men and women of the Mercantile Marine and medical services who served on the Commonwealth hospital ships.

Acknowledgements

Throughout the compilation of this book my working day has been enlightened by the occasional arrival of information, or photographs of individuals and vessels connected with the war on the hospital ships. With the assistance of the following people this project has greatly benefited from the assorted images sent by email or snail mail to my overflowing desk, and for this I would like to thank the following. Rather than list the contributors in any specific order I have elected to list the names alphabetically.

Stanley Amos for shipping images. Bryan Bidwell, for information relating to Private E Bamford. Pat Cartmell for the *Dover Castle* survivors image. Mike Carty for images. Jennifer Marrack Cohen, for the photograph of Alice May Swaffield Milward VAD. Jonathan Collins. George Donnison. Pamela Eustice of Southern Australia, for the image and details of Robert Sharp. Angela Hamilton. Barbara Head of the Trinity House Corporation. P Jones for the copy of *With a camera in my pocket*. Stephanie Levitt for a photograph of the Hollybrook Memorial. Mair and Dennis Miller for the images of Private Huws and *Warilda*. Gina Parsons. Paul Robinson. Joyce Stevenson, for her *Warilda* information and the image of Walter Long. Myra Thomas. Peter Threlfall for various images. Mike Whiteford, for the photograph of Private W A Boggis.

With regards to the publication of this work three people deserve special mention. Roni Wilkinson of Pen and Sword for his customary advice and invaluable support, while producing the finished work. My daughter Gemma, as ever has proved invaluable in the production of the manuscript, tirelessly assisting the author in the more complex and bewildering computer tasks. Not forgetting Ann for tolerating her husband's incredibly time-consuming pastime, researching, writing and commemorating the self-sacrifice of a past generation, 'Lest we forget'.

It is customary in a work of this nature to find a rightly justified acknowledgement to the Commonwealth War Graves Commission. Words fail to express the invaluable contribution Derek Butler of the Commission records section has contributed to the extensive roll of honour. Due to his input the comprehensive roll of honour is accurate and possibly the only privately published listing on the subject. Two of the memorial photographs are also kindly provided by the Commission.

In 1975 a First World War veteran of the Royal Army Medical Corps, John Henry Plumridge published his book *Hospital Ships and Ambulance Trains*. His work contains two appendices, listing military hospital ships and ambulance transports in the First World War. One appendix contains the period of service of most of the vessels deployed during the war; various omissions are now included. As the author is unable to establish contact with the defunct publisher or family of the late John Henry Plumridge, I wish to specifically acknowledge the use of the appendix within this book.

Bibliography

Barnaby, K C. *Some ship disasters and their causes*. Hutchinson & Co., London. 1970.
Carver, Field Marshal Lord. *Turkish Front 1914-18*. Pan Books. London. 2004.
Coles, Alan. *Slaughter at sea*. Robert Hale, London. 1986.
Haws, Duncan. *Merchant Fleets, Royal Mail Line*. Planet Press Ltd., Sussex. 1982.
Hoehling, A A. *The Great War at sea*. Arthur Baker Ltd., London. 1965.
Jarvis, SD & DB. *The cross of sacrifice* Vol IV. Roberts, Reading. 1996.
Keegan, John. *The face of battle*. Barrie & Jenkins, London. 1988.
Knight, E F. *Union Castle & the war 1914-19*. Union Castle Mail SS Co. Ltd., London. 1920.
Laffin, John. *Damn the Dardenelles*. Osprey Publishing Limited, Stroud, Glos. 1980.
Massie, Robert K. *Castles of steel*. Pimlico, London. 2005.
McDonald, Lynne. *The Roses of No Mans Land*, MacMillan Publishing. London. 1984.
McGreal, Stephen. *Zeebrugge & Ostend Raids*. Pen & Sword Books. Barnsley, S. Yorks. 2007.
Mollet, Joyce. *With a Camera in My Pocket*. Baddeley Books, Wales. 2005.
Mullins, Claude. *The Leipzig trials*. H F & G Witherby, London. 1921.
Plumridge, John H. *Hospital ships and ambulance trains*. Seeley, Service & Co. Ltd., London. 1975.
Pratt, E A. *British Railways and the Great War*. Official History, 1916 Volume One. J E Edmonds.
Smith, Eugene W. *Passenger ships of the world, Past and present*. 1963.
Tennent, A J. *British merchant ships sunk by U Boats in the 1914-1918 war*. Starling Press, Gwent. 1990.
Woodward Llewellyn, Sir. *Great Britain & the war of 1914-1918*. Methuen & Co. Ltd., London. 1967.

Newspapers and Periodicals

Birkenhead News.
Birmingham Weekly Post, The.
Daily Mirror.
Liverpool Daily Post and Courier.
Liverpool Echo.
New York Times, The.
Times history of the war, The.
Wallasey News.

National Archives

3 Wing Records. Air 1/115/15/39/51 and Air 1/648/17/122/397.
Foreign Office Prisoner of War and Aliens Department. FO383/281, FO383/280 and 1906 FO383/149.
Inquiry into the loss of HMHS *Glenart Castle*. ADM 137/3253 and ADM 137/3424.
Admiralty Transport Department conveyance of personnel and stores onboard HMHS *Britannic*. MT 23/593.
Explanation of the difference between a hospital carrier and hospital ship. MT 23/446.
Admiralty and Supreme Court prize papers concerning the seized *Ophelia*.
Admiralty Transport Department. Correspondence relating to ship and crew of HMHS *Garth Castle*. MT 23/472.
Admiralty Transport Department. Statement of Master and crew regarding the enemy torpedo fired at HMHS *Asturias*. MT23/364. Several more files were consulted, however their index numbers were omitted by the researcher.
Baralong Papers, The. ADM 137/385

Other Archives

Letitia File, The. RG 42 Wreck Commissioners Court. Department of Marine & Fisheries. RG 42 Series C 3A, Volume 595.

Monuments and Memorials

Tower Hill Memorial, London.
Hollybrook Memorial, Southampton.
The Commonwealth War Graves Commission. [CWGC]

Museums

Imperial War Museum. For the extracts from the Diary of Nurse Ada Garland.

Chapter One

1914. Those in Peril on the Sea

The former passenger liner rolled on a lazy swell as she steamed through the chilly February night. High above the brightly illuminated hospital ship, a myriad of stars twinkled from distant constellations; their magnificence ignored by the ship's watchkeeper whose rasping cough shattered the air of serendipity. He stamped his cold feet on the bridge wing deck, in an effort to restore some circulation; in ten minutes' time his watch ended and he could head aft for a welcome hot mug of sugary tea. In the meantime he remained on vigil, scanning the sea surface for the telltale wake produced by a submarine periscope. It was a nerve-wracking business, for each white horse took on the appearance of the briefest of wakes. The odds on him noticing a protruding periscope in the vast expanse of sea before him were slim. Nonetheless, he knew the Western Approaches were no place for complacency even if the steam ship sailing emblazoned with the sign of the International Red Cross had, in accordance with the Geneva Convention, immunity from attack.

Within her accommodation 300 wounded servicemen, many of whom were confined to bed, felt reassured by the Red Cross flag fluttering from the vessel's mast, in the mistaken belief that they were free from attack. Their thoughts were contrary to the nearby submerged U-boat, whose commander, frustrated by the lack of any kills on this now almost completed patrol, watched through his periscope the passing hospital ship. He briefly wrestled with his conscience knowing all too well the consequences of a torpedo strike on any ship, never mind one conveying wounded. As German naval chiefs insisted the British carried munitions on such vessels, he reasoned he was justified in making an attack.

He called out a course which would position his craft at right angles to the hospital ship, torpedoes were loaded and their range set. His first torpedo struck the liner amidships; simultaneously to the explosion, the ship's lighting failed. Minutes later, the first lifeboats laden with people, mostly wounded, were lowered onto the sea, to be gradually joined by others. The bows of the mortally wounded steamer settled deeper into the sea, raising her stern up above the sea's surface, and displaying her now slowly revolving phosphor bronze propellers. She lay there as if frozen in time, before an almighty internal rumble emanated, and she plunged to the sea bed. Apart from wreckage, and a cluster of lifeboats, no visible sign of the hospital ship remained. The war at sea had reached a new level of barbarity, where Germany would attempt to succeed and almost managed to drive the Red Cross from the high seas.

In 1859 a Swiss merchant named Henry Dunant witnessed the aftermath of a long and bloody battle, fought among the hills around the Italian village of Solferino. The French forces lost 17,000 men, against Austrian losses of some 22,000. Thousands of wounded soldiers lay helpless and abandoned throughout the hills, waiting to succumb to their wounds. Moved by the tragic experience Dunant suggested the establishment of volunteer units, skilled in administrating basic medical aid to the casualties of war. To provide the skilled staff, he recommended they be trained in peace time, in preparation for deployment in times of war.

At an unofficial 1863 international conference, Henry Dunant orchestrated an agreement between nations. Consequently each country agreed to form a humanitarian relief society to assist their Army Medical Corps during conflicts. This agreement became the foundation stone of the Red Cross.

A year later the Swiss Government convened a Diplomatic Conference, where a dozen European countries became signatories to the Geneva Convention for the amelioration of the condition of the wounded in the field. It was the first treaty of international humanitarian law. The agreement ensured in future wars that the sick and wounded soldiers of any nationality were to be treated by belligerents as non-combatants and afforded medical attention. Any hospitals, medical personnel or ambulances displaying a red cross upon a white background were to be treated as neutrals. The first international conference of the Red Cross occurred in 1867.

The Hague Conventions of 1899 amended the agreement, to incorporate the laws and customs of war on land. A third convention added prisoners of war, and the inclusion of maritime warfare to the articles first raised in the 1864 Geneva Convention.

On 6 July 1906 the Geneva Convention revised the convention of 29 July 1899 with a further twenty-eight articles having a particular emphasis on hospital ships. The first five of these are the most significant.

Article One: Military hospital ships, that is to say, ships constructed or fitted out by states especially and solely with a view to assisting the wounded, sick and shipwrecked, the names of which have been communicated to the belligerent powers at the commencement of hostilities, and in any case before they are employed, shall be respected and cannot be captured while hostilities last. These ships, moreover, are not on the same footing as ships of war as regards their stay in a neutral port.

Article Two: Hospital ships, equipped wholly or in part at the expense of private individuals or officially recognised relief societies, shall likewise be respected and exempt from capture, if the belligerent power, to wholly they belong, has given them official commission and has notified their names to the adverse power at the commencement of or during hostilities, and in any case before they are employed. These ships must be provided with a certificate from the competent authorities declaring that the ships have been under their control while fitting out and on final departure.

Article Three: Hospital ships, equipped wholly or partly at the expense of private individuals or officially recognised societies of neutral countries, shall be respected and exempt from capture, on condition they are placed under the control of one of the belligerents, with the consent of their own Government and with the authorisation of the belligerent himself, and that the later has notified their name to his adversary at the commencement of or during hostilities, and in any case before they are employed.

Article Four: The ships mentioned in Articles one, two and three shall afford relief and assistance to the wounded, sick and shipwrecked of the belligerents without distinction of nationality. The Governments undertake not to use these ships for any military purpose. These ships must not in any way hamper the movements of combatants. During and after an engagement they will act at their own risk and peril. The belligerents shall have the right to control and search them, they can refuse their assistance, order them off, make them take a certain course, and put a commissioner on board, and they can even detain them, if the gravity of the circumstances requires it. As far as possible, the belligerents shall enter into the log of the hospital ships the orders which they give them.

Article Five: Military hospital ships shall be distinguished by being painted white outside with a horizontal band of green about a metre and a half in breadth. The ships mentioned in Articles two and three shall be distinguished by being painted white outside with a horizontal band of red about a metre and a half in breadth. The boats of the hospital ships and also small craft which may be used for hospital work shall be distinguished by similar painting. All hospital ships shall make themselves known by hoisting with their national flag, the white flag with a red cross issued by the Geneva Convention, and further, if they belong to a neutral state, by flying at the mainmast the national flag of the belligerent under whose control they are placed...

Nothing within the convention entitled a belligerent to sink an opponent's hospital ship. The first real test of the Geneva Convention arose during the 1904–05 Russo-Japanese war. Both parties had ratified the convention and mainly adhered to their agreements. However, the Russians alleged the Japanese deliberately fired at Russian hospital ships, during the May 1904 siege of Port Arthur. The Japanese denied such allegations. In June of the following year Japan seized the Russian hospital ships *Kostramas*, and *Mongolia* which they later released. A third hospital ship the *Orel* allegedly carried able-bodied prisoners of war and military equipment. A Japanese prize court condemned the use of *Orel* 'for signalling and providing other non medical services to the Russian fleet in ways that amounted to use for military purposes'.

As a result of the Russo-Japanese war the Geneva Convention gathered in October 1907, to add numerous amendments to all previous agreements. Two of the additions have particular relevance to this account of maritime disasters.

Article One: It is forbidden to lay anchored automatic contact mines, except when constructed as to become harmless one hour at most, after the person who laid them ceases to control them. Also to lay anchored automatic contact mines which do not become harmless as soon as they have broken from their moorings. Belligerents should not use torpedoes which do not become harmless when they miss their mark.

Article Two: It is forbidden to lay automatic contact mines off the coast and ports of the enemy, with the sole object of intercepting commercial shipping.

The Geneva Convention essentially is a recommended listing of dos and do nots to ensure fair play between foes in times of war, but, a great deal depended on how an enemy interpreted a particular section of the code of conduct. Events later proved some sections allowed sufficient leeway for unscrupulous manipulation of various sections. It would appear nobody considered a large deployment of hospital ships in any future wars, as the only caveat appears to be the insistence 'These ships must not in any way hamper the movements of combatants' [by sailing into the line of fire]. The article alludes to the hospital ships' traditional role of remaining on the fringes of the fleet during a naval engagement.

For centuries hospital ships had accompanied fleets in battle; some academics believe the ancient Greek and Roman fleets contained hospital ships. They base their assumption on the knowledge that the Greek Athenian fleet contained the *Therapeia* [Therapy] while the Roman fleet included an *Aesculpius*, named after the ancient god of medicine. His symbol, an aesculpis, a rod bearing an entwined snake, now represents the symbol of physicians throughout the globe, and is also the central motif in the Royal Army Medical Corps [RAMC] cap badge. The sixteenth-century Spanish Armada fleet is considered to have contained fifteen hospital ships. The first recorded British hospital ship *Goodwill* joined the Mediterranean Fleet in 1620. Her medical complement consisted of one surgeon, a surgeon's mate and three attendants. In 1805 the Admiralty implemented a suggestion that every warship should have its own sick-berth compartment. These were normally positioned in a forward position, capable of benefiting from the warmth generated by the ships galley. As the years passed numerous vessels served briefly as hospital and store ships but their numbers were negligible from 1793 to 1854 the navy lists contain twenty-nine names of vessels used as hospital ships. On average they served for a period of seven years each. As naval battles were fought in coastal waters, it was relatively easy to return the sick or wounded to Britain. Shore-based hospitals had a dreadful reputation and treatment on the hospital ships may have been only marginally better. Two hospital ships were permanently at Plymouth, three at Portsmouth, one in the Thames near the Tower, and another anchored at Cork. The hospital ships which accompanied the fleet during naval actions, took up station beyond the range of gunfire. Immediately after the engagement ceased, the ship ventured into the flotsam and jetsam to rescue the maimed and dying.

During the 1841–42 Chinese Opium War HMS *Minden* served as the hospital ship for the British fleet. Throughout the Crimean War of 1853–56, hospital transport ships sailed for the Crimea loaded with stores. On the return leg to Britain they carried approximately 100,000 sick and wounded servicemen. By 1833 Sick Berth Attendants appear in ships' muster papers as a recognised category of a naval rating. The 1873–74 month-long Ashanti war, fought on the African Gold Coast, produced a high level of sick and diseased troops, particularly among the naval contingent. HMS *Victor Emmanuel* and HMS *Simon* acted as base hospital ships for the succour of the sick and wounded patients during the campaign. In time, the wooden-walled sailing ships gradually disappeared and sail gave way to steam. The revolutionary Dreadnought class of warship ushered in a new era of naval firepower, but the vessels still required manning, and crews still succumbed to illness or sustained

RMS *Mauretania.*

injury in battle. The onset of the South African war in the twilight years of Queen Victoria's reign saw the introduction of hospital ships steaming from the African cape to Britain. Vessels such as *Dunera*, *Nubia*, *Orotava*, *Canada*, *Bavarian*, *Roslin Castle*, *Syria, Plassey,* the privately financed *Maine* and many more were drafted in to convey the wounded and sick home. However, there was no appreciable expansion of the British hospital fleet until the onset of the First World War.

The storm clouds gather

By the beginning of August 1914, the international situation had deteriorated to such an extent that war seemed inevitable. German companies delayed the sailings of their vessels, prior to issuing an order to make for the nearest neutral port. When the East African liner *Prinz Regent* from Hamburg called at Southampton, the captain received a secret message, and he proceeded immediately without picking up passengers or mails. The Great Central Railway Company abandoned all sailings to Hamburg, Amsterdam and Rotterdam, immediately paying off their crews. Undeterred by the impending world crisis, on Saturday 1 August the White Star liner *Laurentic* and the Cunard liner *Mauretania* left Liverpool for Canada and New York respectively. A few days prior to the declaration of war the German naval authorities seized a British steamer, laden with a cargo of coal. The Wilson liner *Castro* had no passengers on board for the voyage to Brunsbuttel on the Kiel coast; she was captured on the Kiel Canal, and ordered to Hamburg. German diplomats explained for security reasons her presence was unwanted in the Kiel Canal; her cargo of 600 tons of coal, originally intended for commercial use, was procured for the military. Meanwhile the Ostend steamer *Marie Henrietta* with 700 passengers on board, gave cause for concern, until she arrived two hours later than usual at Dover. Her delay was due to her interception off Dunkirk, where the vessel was stopped by gunfire and inspected before being allowed to proceed.

On 4 August 1914, Britain declared war on Germany and unwittingly plunged into the abyss of the Great War for Civilisation, which many prominent leaders predicted would reach a satisfactory conclusion by Christmas. Twenty German vessels within United Kingdom ports were immediately captured. The *Belgia* seized at Newport had a cargo of foodstuffs on board, including a significant amount of cheese. The cargo had a value of two hundred thousand pounds sterling, small change compared to the value of one vessel taking evasive action off the American coast. The North German Lloyd 'gold ship' *Kronzprinzessin Cecilie* had left New York bound for Plymouth before hostilities were announced; she had a cargo of two million pounds in specie. Fearing interception by French or British cruisers, the captain altered the vessel's appearance as much as possible with paint and canvas. She doubled back on her tracks, and returned to the neutral waters of the United States. After a four-day run at full speed she arrived at Bar Harbour, Maine. Unperturbed by Admiralty warnings of the German cruiser SMS *Dresden* cruising off New York, possibly intending to intercept the *Lusitania,* she sailed, after a rousing waterfront send-off by crowds singing 'God save the King'. She left New York at midnight on 5 August, and with lights out, proceeded on a course different from the usual route. Nevertheless she was seen and chased by the *Dresden*, but thanks to her speed managed to get away safely.

As an island race we relied heavily upon the Royal Navy to safeguard our shores from invasion, yet the world's first superpower had a comparably small army. Despite the professional army of 1914, consisting of highly skilled men, who had learnt the art of soldiering from the parade squares of Aldershot to the South African veldt, it was of insufficient strength for a prolonged continental war. When the troops of Kaiser Wilhelm invaded France, swiftly followed by neutral Belgium, the British Government issued an ultimatum to Germany, and demanded the withdrawal of her army from invaded territory. No such reassurances were received and at 11.00 pm on 4 August 1914, Great Britain declared war on Germany, for violating Belgian sovereignty.

Shipping companies who had previously operated their sailings with almost

HMS *Amphion.*

military precision faced considerable disruption. The British cross-Atlantic service continued despite disquieting press reports of the *Mauretania* and *Lusitania* being pursued by attackers, who were soon left in their wake. Germany certainly wasted no time in disrupting maritime commerce with the indiscriminate laying of sea mines. At noon on 5 August, the cruiser HMS *Amphion* and the Third Torpedo Flotilla sank the German mine-layer *Konigen Luise*. The 2,163 gross registered tonnage[1] vessel of the Hamburg-America line, had a top speed of twenty knots, and was specially fitted out as a mine-layer. At six-thirty the next morning while steaming at twenty knots off the Thames estuary, the cruiser *Amphion* struck a mine, probably laid by the *Konigen Luise*. The mine exploded under the bridge. Shortly after, the three-year-old vessel was abandoned; the magazine exploded, making her the first Great War loss of the Royal Navy. Her commander Captain Cecil Fox later recalled seeing a six-inch gun belonging to his wrecked command turning over and over in the air like a baby's toy. The captain, sixteen officers and 135 men were saved, but 131 died. Ironically over twenty enemy personnel rescued from the sunken mine-layer also perished, for mines cannot determine whether their victim be friend or foe.

When Britain mobilised her forces, a well-rehearsed military plan swung into action. All Reservists and Territorials were summoned to their regiments and a hastily assembled British Expeditionary Force [BEF] of 160,000 men safely crossed the Channel, between 9 and 22 August under the watchful eyes of the Royal Navy. Unlike his peers, Lord Kitchener warned of a prolonged war, and called for the raising of a volunteer army of 100,000 men. In a wave of patriotism, men rushed to the colours, but it would take time to turn these raw recruits into proficient soldiers, and equip them with weapons and uniform. Many recruits considered the war would have terminated before they had an opportunity to join the great adventure, unaware four nightmarish years of mechanised warfare lay in the future. As Britain strove to amass men and weaponry to prosecute the war, the British Expeditionary Force made a stand near the Belgian town of Mons; though hopelessly outnumbered they successfully halted the German advance, and allowed the bulk of the BEF to retire unmolested. There then followed a rearguard action. German commanders were unnerved by the effectiveness of the British riflemen, who the Kaiser reputedly dismissed as a 'Contemptible little army'. Expert riflemen scythed down the advancing hoards of field grey clad infantry, with such a withering rate of fire, the enemy thought they were under machine-gun fire. As the resistance to the invader intensified, the casualties mounted, and the advance began to lose headway. The armies eventually ground to a halt, and converted shell holes into trenches, as protection from shell and bullet. These positions were consolidated and gradually linked together, to become a continuous barrier known as the Western Front.

The onset of a modern mechanised war produced an unprecedented amount of battle casualties; the battle of Mons provided powerful evidence of the consequences of modern artillery firepower. On 31 August the British casualties were announced for the period 23–26 August: killed 163; wounded 686; missing 4,278. Overwhelmed by the scale of wounded personnel the members of the Royal Army Medical Corps [RAMC] stoically tended the wounded as best they could. Although hospital trains were used in the South African war, the British army had not made provision for any ambulance rolling stock for the use of the BEF. Instead the Royal Army Medical Corps used whatever rolling stock came to hand. There was a preponderance of livestock goods wagons of the infamous '8 *Chevaux* – 40 *Hommes*' variety used to despatch eight horses or forty men to the front areas. On their return journey to the Channel base ports, some of the cleaned and scrubbed empty wagons received the wounded. The seriously wounded often lay on the wagon floor covered with freshly lain forage, the more able-bodied men stood as the goods train rumbled through the countryside. During the opening weeks of the war it was not unusual for a wounded man to arrive at the coast, his wounds still bound in the field service pack, or a fractured leg bound in an improvised splint formed by two rifles.

As the enemy pushed hard towards the prized asset of Paris, the safety of the hospital bases established at Havre [now Le Harve] and Rouen were jeopardised, and staff expected an imminent call for the evacuation of both sites. The position at Havre became increasingly untenable resulting in the temporary evacuation of the hospital base by sea to St Nazaire. The rail journey to the new location added days to the journey of the wounded, with catastrophic results. Unknowingly the wounded faced an invisible but equally deadly hazard to shot or shell, which increased the death toll and significantly raised the level of amputations. For centuries the French farmers boosted the fertility of their soil by the use of animal manure as a fertiliser. This highly fertile soil contained the tetanus [lockjaw] virus and gaseous gangrene germs which soon infected wounds received upon the battlefield. The protracted rail journey allowed the infections to take hold, many soldiers lost their lives or limbs due to the inadequate medical facilities. The long trains of wounded soldiers hissed into stations bustling with military trains despatching troops destined for the front, waved off by cheering spectators. On adjacent platforms the goods trucks containing the wounded continually rolled in; they lacked a proper braking system and when the locomotive halted, the wagons bumped together with a clanking sound, which noise was punctuated with the groans of wounded men. The disembarkation of the wounded made a sad spectacle, as they were loaded into motor and horse-drawn ambulances to convey them in what seemed unending columns to the hospital ships or base hospital.

At the outbreak of war the Admiralty ordered the conversion of three ocean-going liners into naval hospital ships, strictly for the use of naval personnel; a further six were added as the war progressed. The two-funnelled *China*

HMHS *China*.

requisitioned by the Admiralty on 4 August became hospital ship number six; she was evidently highly regarded with great affection by passengers in the halcyon days of ocean travel. Her conversion merited an article and photographic feature in the 3rd September 1914 edition of the *Daily Mirror*.

The P and O Company's liner China *has been turned into a Royal Naval Hospital ship and has left for an unknown destination. Some little time ago I had the pleasure of making a voyage in* China. *It was perhaps the happiest voyage I have made.*

The ship was so luxurious, a sort of floating summer palace: the passengers had been so companionable, the women so pretty and the men such good fellows. My days on the China *slipped away in one swift round of enjoyment. One day last week I paid my old pleasure palace of the sea a return visit, but the* China *I had known was no more.*

The China *is no longer of silken ease for the rich travellers of ocean deserts. She is the White Ship for the wounded, and she sails today under the Red Cross flag. She has been painted white inside and out, and on each side of her are inscribed huge red crosses which it would be quite impossible for any hostile vessel not to see at a great distance.*

The transformation has been so complete that I found it difficult to realise that the good White Ship had once been the China *of pleasant memories. Here were the saloons in which I had lounged for so many hours of charming idleness. Today they are clean and comfortable hospital wards, fitted with curtained cots for the sick and wounded. All the cabins and saloons too, below decks have been transformed into wards, fitted with 220 swinging cots, so contrived as to give to every movement to the ship. The less serious cases can be accommodated in hammocks to the number of 120 or more.*

I found also, two operating theatres, with white tiled floors, these being connected with preparation rooms, which are fitted with every possible thing modern science can devise. There is also a room for X-Rays examinations. Fleet Surgeon Bolster, RN, aided by a staff of eminent doctors, who hold surgeons' commissions in the Royal Naval Reserve, has charge of the entire equipment and personnel.

As I wandered through the wards I could not fail to observe the absolute thoroughness with which the medical department of the Admiralty has equipped the ship. If this is typical of the many hospital ships which the Admiralty possesses the country may feel confident their wounded will be very well looked after. The stores contain every conceivable luxury, nothing has been forgotten, not even the many boxes of games, including dominoes and draughts, and a special soda water plant has been added. The wounded will also be cheered by the presence of four nursing sisters from the Royal Naval Hospital, and for their comfort they have a charming little saloon, where they may rest.

As in her days of peace and pleasure, the China *will be thorough in all arrangements for the comfort of her passengers. The wounded will be lowered from the decks to the wards by means of lifts. They will be transported from the battleships by motor boats. And once upon the good White Ship, those who can walk will be able to do so without fear of hurting any wounded limb, for every sharp corner of the vessel has been rounded off and padded.*

A trio of 2,500 tonnage sister ships, the *St Andrew*, *St David* and *St Patrick* during peace time operated on the Fishguard to Rosslare passenger service on behalf of the Great Western Railway Company. On 19 August the trio were requisitioned as hospital ships; initially painted in a drab slate grey colour, they later adopted the accepted hospital ship livery. Based at Southampton, the Clyde built steamers each provided a cross-Channel service for the recovery of 180 stretcher or cot case patients, from the hospital bases at Rouen and Havre. The vessels operated in this role until 1919, possibly repatriating wounded Allied and former enemy personnel. The largest cross-Channel hospital *Asturias* of the Royal Mail Line was requisitioned on 28 August, and arrived at St Nazaire on 10 September to receive patients. However, the demand for hospital ships became insatiable and within a fortnight five vessels from the Union Castle line became hospital ships. The *Carisbrook Castle* arrived at the beginning of September; by the end of the month *Glengorm Castle*, *Guildford Castle*, *Gloucester Castle* and *Glenart Castle* had arrived to bolster the hospital ship service. The Union Castle line played a significant role in casualty evacuation

The *St George* was built in 1906 for Great Western Railway and sold to Canadian Pacific Railway Co. in 1913; she was commissioned as a hospital ship in 7 May 1915 and served to 4 December 1917.

throughout the Great War. At the close of hostilities, the hospital ships of the Southampton based company had brought 331,404 British wounded officers and men home, and, in addition, landed 8,279 enemy wounded. In order to keep up with the demands placed upon the hospital ships, by December 1914, twenty-two hospital ships were in operation.

The military quickly revised the system and their care of the ill or wounded, paying particular care to the reduction in tetanus and gas gangrene cases. At the first opportunity, patients were injected with an anti-tetanus serum prior to being sent from the front. Shell wounds were treated with antiseptic, and when necessary amputations were carried out at the front, in order to prevent the contraction of gangrene or tetanus. The introduction of booths containing dressing stations at wayside railway stations allowed the opportunity to tend the seriously wounded on the ambulance trains, thereby lowering the mortality rate. At the forefront of this work stood the British Red Cross Society and the Order of St John, whose combined efforts greatly assisted the medical services provided by the RAMC. As near to the front as safety allowed, hospitals were established and equipped within large abandoned buildings or churches. The improvements reduced the death toll, however a considerable number of men, whose incapacity rendered them no longer fit for military service or who required an extensive period of recuperation, were ultimately destined for evacuation back to Blighty [British army slang for Britain]. As the war progressed, a not too serious Blighty wound became the yearned for injury of homesick and war weary military personnel.

Due to the improvements in the medical service, the wounded from the First Battle of Ypres [30 October to 24 November 1914] stood a far greater chance of survival than those wounded at Mons. Assorted goods wagons and carriages procured from the French railways were divided into three ambulance trains.

The wagons were thoroughly cleaned and disinfected, and four sets of a patent steel stretcher-carrying apparatus were installed in each wagon. Thus the sets of three-tier racking allowed twelve lying patients to be carried in each wagon. The stretcher supports were suspended from springs, thereby minimising the severe jolts produced by the brakeless wagons. Converted passenger carriages were converted to hospital wards, surgical dressing wards or dispensaries. The restaurant cars underwent transformation by the addition of ovens and stoves capable of feeding 700 patients. Disinfection apparatus, water storage tanks and ice-making apparatus were also installed. The first three of these ambulance trains entered service in late August, a fourth train made from third-class carriages with the seating removed, entered service a week later. By December eleven hospital trains operated, including one to which the British Red Cross society donated almost £4,000 towards the running costs. The goods carriages were gradually replaced by first and second-class carriages combed from throughout the French rail network; each train could now carry 800 patients.

The first properly designed ambulance train 'Number 12' arrived from England on 12 November 1914. Each of the new coaches had a central walkway, flanked by hospital beds supported on racks, facilitating administering care to the wounded. The next arrival for reasons of superstition avoided the use of the reputedly unlucky thirteen, opting instead for the number fourteen. The number gradually expanded and by 1918 approximately forty British standard ambulance trains operated in France and Belgium.

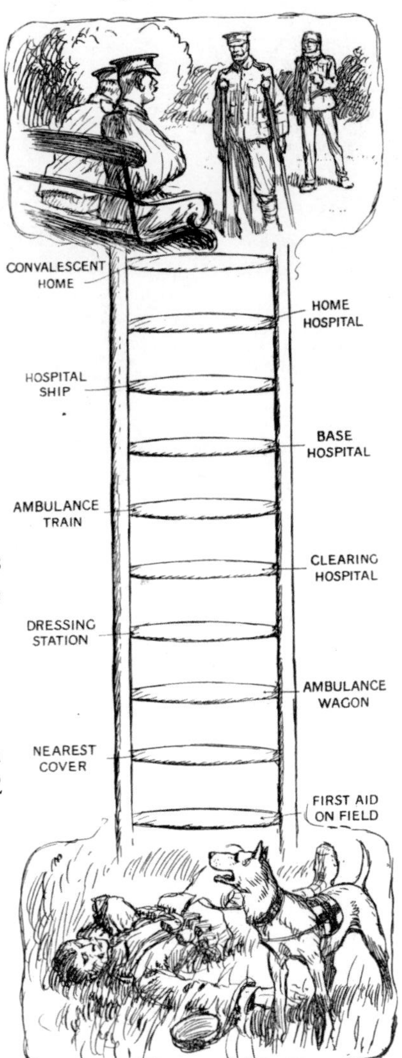

Ladder of good progress.

Each infantryman was issued with a sterile field dressing, for use in the event of receiving a slight wound. If he managed to staunch the blood loss, the walking wounded then set off for the Regimental Aid Post. The more severely wounded, when possible gained the comparative shelter of a shell-hole, to await the arrival of the stretcher bearers. Usually a battalion

Inside an ambulance train.

had thirty-two stretcher-bearers capable, on good terrain, of extricating sixteen wounded between them; it was an arduous and extremely dangerous role, usually carried out under shell and small-arms fire. To the rear of the lines lay the Regimental Aid Post, where the battalion medical officers separated the mortally wounded from those with a chance of recovery, or administered first aid to the lightly wounded, who then returned to the fighting line. The less fortunate were then conveyed by stretcher, ambulance or lorry, via the Advanced Dressing Station, to the Divisional Collecting Station. Motor vehicles then carried the patients to the large Casualty Clearing Stations, positioned beyond the range of artillery. Here, the military surgeons operated a 'triage' system, originally instituted by the French army. The patients were separated into three groups; the dying were placed in a moribund ward, where the sedated unfortunates received unlimited attention, possibly ignorant of their approaching death. A second category, received the attention of the military surgeons who when in doubt amputated. Those patients deemed capable of enduring further travel would progress, usually by ambulance train, to the base hospital located at a sea port. The legacies of the hospitals remain in the form of neat rows of Portland stone headstones belonging to service personnel who succumbed to their wounds. Thousands more would return by sea to the United Kingdom for recuperation, treatment or medical discharge; they may have thought their war was over yet many would face a watery grave, as a result of a mine or torpedo attack.

An army nursing sister wrote:

> *The boat seems so oddly quiet this voyage, after the work and crowded state it was in for the last voyage with our 150 sick and wounded. I never saw a braver, more uncomplaining set of men. Their first demand was for a smoke, then something to drink, and then food and sleep, more sleep.*

The French port of Le Havre became the main port for embarking the wounded from the killing fields of France and Belgium. The port, excluding a brief interval in 1914, remained in Allied hands throughout the conflict. Known as Number One Base, by the end of May 1917 two stationary hospitals, three general hospitals and four convalescent hospitals received a steady flow of patients. Scores of other hospitals were scattered throughout the base areas, and not all patients merited transporting home for treatment or convalescence. Dover and Southampton became the principal ports for disembarking casualties; however, most sea ports received patients. From February 1915 to February 1919, Dover dealt with 1,260,506 casualties, unloaded 4,076 boats and loaded 7,781 ambulance trains. Southampton handled 1,234,248 casualties from 24 August 1914 to 31 December 1918 requiring the use of 7,822 ambulance trains. The patients were then dispersed throughout the country on one of the twenty-strong home service ambulance trains to one of the 196

The start for Blighty

receiving stations. From the rail station volunteers frequently provided an invaluable service, by conveying the invalids in their publicly funded motor ambulances. During the journey home a Royal Army Medical Corps orderly generally asked for the name of the patient's home town. When possible they transferred the man to a hospital near home.

The first trickle of wounded soldiers arrived at Southampton on 24 August 1914, the day when 107 patients entrained for Netley military hospital. The *ad hoc* hospital carriages were war department coaches and ordinary corridor rolling stock, however purpose-built railway carriages soon entered service. The first example from the Great Central railway company's Duckinfields' works also rolled into Southampton on 24 August. The train departed four days later destined for Netley hospital carrying sixty-two cot cases and 125 sitting patients. Eventually the War Office sent thirty ambulance trains to the military forces overseas; the majority operated in France and Flanders. The standard ambulance train comprised sixteen carriages; the number included a pharmacy carriage, two kitchens, a personnel carriage and a stores and brake carriage. Each train had the capacity for 400 lying and sitting patients plus the RAMC staff and locomotive crew. Each overseas ward carriage contained thirty-six beds in racks of three, while home duty rolling stock had tiers of two.

In peacetime Britain had 7,000 beds available in military hospitals; by June 1916 the figure had risen to 200,000 beds. A year later 300,000 beds were available and by November 1918, precisely 364,133 hospital beds in the British Isles were provided for military patients. These figures excluded the number of hospital beds used by the various expeditionary forces. At the time of the Armistice the number of patients with the various expeditionary forces numbered: France 150,096; Egypt 49,177; Salonica 26,141; Malta 5,178; Italy 6,142; Mesopotamia 7,815 and North Russia [Murmansk-Archangel] 283.[2] The figures give an indication of the scale of the problem facing the Government departments responsible for the evacuation of patients from the various theatres of war, and the need for a fleet of hospital ships.

The torpedo comes of age

The deadly effectiveness of the submarine torpedo became apparent on 22 September with the loss of the obsolete armoured cruisers HMS *Aboukir*, *Hogue* and *Cressy*. While steaming in Indian file a couple of miles astern of each other upon a short choppy sea, an explosion rocked the leading warship *Aboukir*, which quickly listed to port. Within twenty minutes the cruiser turned turtle, and then plunged to the sea bed. Believing the lead vessel had struck a mine *Hogue* and *Cressy* approached with the intention of saving life. Two torpedoes exploded into *Hogue* just aft of the starboard bridge of the 12,000-ton warship; within five minutes the waters of the North Sea lapped over the quarter deck. Shortly after, an explosion from the bowels of the ship heralded her demise, minutes later she sank. The third of the four-funnelled Bacchante-class cruisers, *Cressy* reacted to a possibly imagined sighting of a periscope with an unsuccessful attempt to ram the submarine. The cruiser then halted to rescue survivors from her sister ships: now dead in the water *Cressy* was a sitting duck, then a lookout sighted the track of a torpedo heading in their direction. Before the warship could make headway, she reeled with the impact. A second torpedo raced ineffectually past her stern, but the third dealt the death blow rupturing the vessel's boilers. Survivors clinging to flotsam on the water reported 'a sudden explosion and a great column of smoke as black as ink which flew up as high as *Cressy*'s funnels'. The cruiser rolled over showing her wet keel glinting in the weak autumn sunlight, minutes later she disappeared below the surface.

Despite the submarine or torpedo being a modern invention, technological advances and resourcefulness culminating in this attack proved the submarine and her deadly armament had come of age. The submarine *U9* eluded avenging warships and safely returned to Wilhelmshaven. Her captain Otto Weddigen[3] received the Iron Cross, First Class; his twenty-eight man crew each received a Second Class Iron Cross. They were collectively feted as national heroes, for at the expense of six torpedoes they had destroyed 36,000 tons of warships and killed nearly sixty officers and 1,400 seamen. The losses in human terms would have been greater without the intervention of Dutch fishing trawlers who hauled the exhausted survivors aboard until they

Right: Otto Weddigen.

HMS *Aboukir.*

were relieved by Royal Navy destroyers.

Only 837 men survived the catastrophe, alerting the entire world to the effectiveness of this weapon and humbling the Royal Navy at so little expenditure. The face of naval warfare had altered dramatically, for David had slain not one but three Goliaths and slipped away undetected. The submarine menace eventually became a significant threat to Britain's dominance of the high seas. Across the mined and submarine-patrolled sea channels, the unarmed merchant and hospital ships plied their trade, gambling on making a safe passage across troubled waters.

On 18 October 1914 a particular maritime incident had repercussions throughout the Great War. In almost every justification for foul play German sources refer to the case of the *Ophelia.*

The capture of the German hospital ship *Ophelia*

The Kierstein Company were a German company, based in Hamburg. One of their steam ships the *Ophelia* operated on the London to Hamburg service, and on the eve of war, the passenger liner found herself berthed in London. On 4 August 1914, as Britain declared war on Germany, the *Ophelia* with 344 passengers including German reservists onboard, sailed from the Thames at noon.

The next day, a German *Kaiserliche Marine* torpedo boat directed her to Heligoland from there she entered the River Elbe, and shortly afterwards went to Hamburg. The Hamburg-America Steamship Company then commenced her conversion to a hospital ship. Three days later, she eased her way along the Elbe, passed through the Kaiser Wilhelm canal and emerged into the Baltic. She arrived at Kiel on 12 August where her fitting out continued. In compliance with the Geneva Convention, the enemy registered her as a hospital ship, duly receiving her certificate of accreditation on 11 September. The vessel now moored at Brunsbuttel Koog, cast off on 18 September, passed down the Elbe to Cuxhaven and the open sea where, for three weeks, she steamed up and down near Heligoland. During this time she performed no hospital work, apparently spending the sea time drilling her crew in boat and stretcher work.

On 6 October the British submarine *E9* sank the German torpedo boat *S116* in the mouth of the river Ems, and later that evening Captain Pfeiffer, Naval Staff Surgeon of *Ophelia* and therefore responsible, stated he received orders to steam to the Ems to search for survivors. At a position west of the Wesser, her log records 'Received counter orders, steamed back'. From this point the vessel's movements and communications are vague. Next morning, the captain stated he received orders from the Schellinghorn Signal Station to 'Proceed to the place of the incident'; these orders were not entered into the vessel's log. Curiously neither the captain nor the local pilot knew the chart position they were to head for. *Ophelia* arrived off the Ems at 8.20 pm and dropped anchor.

At 6.50 am on 8 October the log recorded 'Steamed under directions of the Pilot out of the Ems by land and sea marks on the search for a sunken torpedo boat'.

On 8 October, the British submarine *D4* [Commander Moncreiff] noted that the *Ophelia*, though painted white with a green horizontal band and a red cross on a funnel, did not fly a national flag. On discovering the approaching submarine, she hoisted the Red Cross flag, and fled to escape; in the process they hauled down the Red Cross flag. [The flag may not have been visible viewed from astern.] The submarine commander noted:

> *There was nobody in the neighbourhood, and nobody for a hospital ship to aid. With the exception of a German submarine, which I saw about twenty miles further west, at ten-thirty in the morning of the seventh. The German submarine dived as soon as she saw me; she appeared to be outward bound to sea. On the same day at about two forty-five in the afternoon I observed a Zeppelin, I saw nothing except the* Ophelia *on the 7th, 8th and 9th.*

The lieutenant commander of the British submarine, had no doubt that the *Ophelia* was scouting, a view supported by her powerful radio and signalling apparatus. The hospital ship then raced for the coast; the submarine may have eventually closed on her, but feared he would be lured into a trap near the enemy bases. Viewed on their own her movements could only be described as suspicious, and Moncreiff believed the vessel was not searching for shipwrecked mariners.

After evading the submarine, Pfeiffer received a signal to make for Hamburg, to clean the boilers; the vessel remained there for five days. The log omits any entry of boiler cleaning: the real intention of the visit appears to have been the lengthening of her masts, which would have extended the receiving capacity of her wireless. On 17 October a flotilla of German torpedo boats made a dash out of the Ems; they were pursed northwards, and sunk by a British squadron, near the position where *Ophelia* would again appear. The subsequent British Prize Court enquiry considered:

Ophelia.

> *Probably, this flotilla was on the 8 October looking to make the dash, and if the German naval authorities were unscrupulous enough it would have been very useful to them to use* Ophelia *in order to ascertain if they were still off the mouth of the Ems, rather than to have to send out one of the torpedo boats to scout when she might have met with the same fate as* S116.

Article Four of the Geneva Convention gives belligerents the right to detain vessels, but not to attack, or attempt to sink them in these terms: 'The belligerents shall have the right to control and search them... They can order them off, make them take a stated course, and put a commissioner on board and even detain them if the gravity of the circumstances requires it.' Thus on 18 October the destroyer HMS *Meteor* [Commander A F W Howard] stopped the *Ophelia* off the Goodwin Sands. Lieutenant Frederick Thornton Peters boarded the vessel and inspected the paperwork, prior to questioning the surgeon in command, [the captain acted as an interpreter] who advised that the ship had been ordered to proceed to position latitude fifty-two degrees North and longitude three degrees, fifty-one minutes East and to *look around.*

'I then questioned the Surgeon in command as to what he proposed to look for when he arrived at the named position. At first he replied that he did not know what in particular he had to look for: I suggested that he might have some idea of what he had to search for, and on my further pressing the question, he said that perhaps he would find some dead bodies. He also did not know how long he intended to remain in the area.' Given the vagueness of the orders, and the difficulty experienced in obtaining the scant information, Peters concluded the vessel was 'guilty of rendering an unneutral service', either by transmission of intelligence or improperly carrying war-like stores.

After searching the vessel devoid of any patients, nothing of a suspicious nature was discovered: the after hold did contain twenty to thirty feet of sand ballast which might possibly have concealed war-like stores, but this he thought unlikely. However he could find no trace in the ship's log ordering *Ophelia* to search within the co-ordinates stated. Following his report, the Admiralty ordered him to return to the enemy hospital ship, dismantle her wireless, and escort the *Ophelia* into Yarmouth.

The commanding officer of *Meteor* placed in command of *Ophelia* the Acting Gunner [Temporary] Mr C E Finch, for the passage from Yarmouth to Sheerness. Finch reported that all the crew wore Red Cross armlets, and most of the sailors' hats bore the names of destroyers. A press report falsely alleged that a large quantity of explosives was found on the vessel. The incident prompted a flurry of protests from Germany, protesting the vessel's innocence, likening the seizure to nothing more than piracy.

The Admiralty relocated the closely guarded *Ophelia* to the Nore, an isolated anchorage in the Thames estuary. On the afternoon of 5 November, the navy escorted the seized vessel to Gravesend, to disembark an almost fifty-strong complement of passengers and crew. A number of civilians, two other officers and about twenty sailors accompanied Captain Ritter, navigating officer of the *Ophelia,* into captivity. The men then went by rail to a prisoner-of-war camp.

The appeal case opened on 3 May 1915, and for the following three days both nations argued their corner at great length. On 21 May the appeal court President found that:

> Ophelia *was on the evidence lawful prize, having forfeited the protection of the Hague Convention by the fact she was not used for the special and sole purpose of affording aid and relief to the wounded, sick and shipwrecked. She made no real effort to render such service; that she was equipped as a signalling vessel, and had used her equipment for this purpose without satisfactory explanation.*

Germany had argued their case with particular reference to Article One of The Hague Convention, number ten:

> *Military hospital ships, that is to say, ships constructed or fitted out by States especially and solely with a view to assisting the wounded, sick and shipwrecked, the names of which shall have been communicated to the Belligerent Powers at the commencement or during the course of hostilities, and in any case before they are employed should be respected and cannot be captured while hostilities last.*

The affidavits for the Crown and the admission of witnesses, in particular a Commander Newman, who had a special interest in hospital ships, considered *Ophelia* not only unsuitable as a hospital ship, but that she was undoubtedly fitted and intended for signalling purposes. He came to this conclusion without knowing the vessel was suspected of being a signalling ship. Although not well adapted, primarily due to inadequate sanitary and other hospital arrangements, the key point of the Crown rested on whether she was *solely* adapted for hospital purposes.

In addition to the standard signalling equipment for receiving instructions on her duties, or for requesting assistance in the execution of them, *Ophelia* had an unusual amount of signal halliards working on brackets from the funnel. German defence witnesses claimed these were merely substitutes for another set of halliards, which interfered with the wireless apparatus. Yet the flags of the International Commercial Code were stowed away in the chart house, while an abnormal amount of special German code flags were stowed on hooks each side of the funnel. The earlier mentioned mast extension showed the great attention paid to the signalling capabilities of the ship. The practically conclusive proof that the vessel was especially equipped for signalling lay in the 600 green, 480 red and 140 Very signal flares she carried. Captain Newman advised a British vessel of the same class would carry about a dozen of each. Pfeiffer attested the green and red lights were intended to illuminate the sea at night, while searching for shipwrecked mariners or their corpses, as the vessel had no searchlight. The Court concluded the Very lights were used to acknowledge Morse signals received from a distance much greater than the Morse lamp they had on board could carry.

Presented with these facts the President of the Prize Court enquiry concluded that *Ophelia* was not adapted or equipped *solely* as a hospital ship, and thereby invalidated her protection under the Geneva Convention.[4] The case still remains a contentious issue among naval historians.

The wreck of the *Rohilla*

At the turn of the twentieth century, the British Empire spanned the globe and as British influence expanded throughout her colonies, overseas trade blossomed. Britain became the engineering workshop of the world, producing industrial machinery, locomotives, coal, hardware, cotton and fancy goods. It was also a boom time for the shipbuilding industry, whose order books reflected the shipping companies demands for the latest and most cost efficient vessels. British exports were unprecedented and every overseas consignment travelled by sea. With passenger air travel still in its embryonic stage, overseas travellers went by liner or passenger cargo steamers. Understandably, the shipping companies prospered, and wishing to retain their position in their highly lucrative trade, they continually reinvested in new vessels. Not only did a new ship cause a stir amongst prospective travellers, each new vessel embraced the latest advances in technology; significant factors as ever, were the running costs,

Rohilla.

or more accurately the fuel efficiency. Each vessel generally provided a quarter of a century of service to her masters, before making her final ignominious voyage to the breakers. Traditionally, shipping companies christen the subsequent replacement vessel with the name of the scrapped vessel, thereby retaining a sense of company history. The majority of vessels have an unremarkable career, while others, through a dire chain of events, attain everlasting infamy: the RMS *Titanic* being the prime example.

Although considerably smaller than the magnificent White Star trans-Atlantic liner *Titanic*, the British India Company steam ship *Rohilla* is also remembered for all the wrong reasons; infamy in shipping circles being directly linked to the mortality figures produced by a shipwreck. While under construction at the Belfast shipyard of Harland and Wolff, vessel number 381, gradually transformed from a series of frames and hull sections, to a vessel capable of carrying one hundred first-class passengers, and sixty-five second-class, entrusted to the care of a crew of 175. On the 6th September 1906, as the crowd's cheers drowned out the sound of the brass band, *Rohilla* trundled down the slipway. In deference to her destination, they named her after the people of Rohilkand, who populated the area east of Delhi. On completion, she would serve on the London to Calcutta service, with the similarly designed ship *Rewa* [torpedoed in 1918 while serving as a hospital ship]; throughout the winter season she would carry troops to offset operating costs. In 1908, she joined *Rewa* in the role of permanent troopships. Both vessels represented British India during the 1910 Spithead Review, staged for King George V. During the ceremony, *Rohilla* hosted the House of Lords and *Rewa* carried the House of Commons.

Two days after hostilities with Germany commenced, *Rohilla* was requisitioned as a naval hospital ship. She rapidly underwent conversion, and took up her new career equipped with a pair of operating theatres and X-ray equipment: her cabins became hospital wards. Ten days later, HMHS *Rohilla*, commanded by Captain David Landles Neilson, steamed from Southampton to the naval base at Scapa Flow to undergo training. While there, a nineteen-year-old midshipman from the battleship HMS *Collingwood* arrived. The patient was none other than Prince Albert, suffering with acute pain from a developing appendicitis. The *Rohilla* with her royal patient onboard was hastily despatched to Aberdeen where, on arrival, they were to collect the Royal Surgeon, who had travelled from London by express train. Amongst the ship's company were fifteen members of the Barnoldswick Ambulance Brigade, employed as Naval Sick Berth Reservists, who had been responsible for Albert's medical care; they supervised his transfer to hospital where two days later he was operated on. The prince survived to become King George VI; unfortunately twelve of the Barnoldswick men would perish on the final voyage of *Rohilla*.

HMHS *Rohilla* departed the Firth of Forth on Thursday 29 October 1914;

onboard she carried 229 persons on a mercy mission to Belgium to collect wounded. The following morning, the North Sea weather began to deteriorate, the heavy seas causing the vessel to roll considerably. As a preventative measure against hostile naval bombardments, the north-eastern coastline adhered to a night-time blackout. At sea, any illuminated buoys were extinguished, while those with warning bells were muffled. Deprived of these navigational aids master mariners then steered by dead reckoning, and sailor's intuition. Captain Neilson had taken his bearings as he passed the Tyne estuary, for he knew the Whitby lighthouse was unlit. He not only faced navigational hazards but the likelihood of a submarine attack.

Rohilla suddenly juddered under an impact: Neilson shouted 'Mine! my God' as he felt certain she had struck a mine. The vessel reverberated with a tortured grating sound. A ship passed on his starboard side and ten minutes later, it was reported someone was signalling the ship.

At twenty minutes to four in the morning, coastguard Albert James Jefferies sighted the hospital ship, bearing north-north-west and heading towards the Whitby rock. He used a Morse lamp to signal the ship, and when he thought she could hear, sounded the foghorn, but he received no reply. Captain Neilson ordered the Morse signal to be read; before the information could be acted upon, the disaster unfolded. Neilson thought heading his damaged vessel away from the coast would lead to a high loss of life, he ordered full speed ahead, [now reduced to twelve knots] and a mile along the coast deliberately drove *Rohilla* aground upon rocks near Saltwick Nab, one mile south of Whitby. The terrific impact impaled the hospital ship upon the outcrop, where she lay marooned five hundred yards from the shoreline, and surrounded by a gale whipped sea. The ship's lights went out almost immediately after she struck, owing to flooding in the engine room. Many of the engine room staff perished on impact, drowned by the inrush of water. Scores of life belts were washed away before they could be used, and only one of the ship's boats remained intact. *Rohilla* then broke in two across the well deck, the after section swinging violently around, tethered to the forward section by the propeller shaft. Upon the cliff top, the vigilant coastguard fired signal rockets summoning the rescue lifeboats; to this day it remains one of their most difficult rescue missions.

Under the captain's orders, they successfully launched the steamer's only sound lifeboat, prior to the arrival of the Whitby lifeboat. The boat, manned by six able bodied seamen, the bosun's mate and Mister Gwynne the second mate, attempted to take a line ashore. One survivor recounted:

> *We had spent a miserable night shivering on deck, for it was not until daylight we could do anything. Then the captain called for volunteers to take the only remaining boat and row ashore with a line. A lot of us volunteered and five of us were sent with the second mate. What a journey*

it was! We had hardly got afloat when one oar after another was smashed. It seems a miracle that we got ashore. We lost the line when a big wave came and nearly swamped us. It was a wonder that the boat righted herself, and when she did, she was half filled with water. Close in we were upset, and it was only with the assistance of the people on shore that we were able to scramble to safety through the water, which was breast high.

Throughout Friday night and Saturday, valiant efforts were made to reach the stranded ship. On Friday night, the Rocket Brigade fired rockets at the doomed ship but their efforts were defeated by the fierce wind, as the five rockets that landed on the ship were beyond the reach of the crew. The rocket rescue apparatus evolved specifically for maritime rescue: each rocket expelled a thin

Daily Mirror front page.

OUR MONSTER BIRTHDAY NUMBER.

The Daily Mirror

LATEST CERTIFIED CIRCULATION MORE THAN 1,000,000 COPIES PER DAY

No. 3,440. MONDAY, NOVEMBER 2, 1914 24 PAGES. One Halfpenny.

IMPRISONED ON WRECKED HOSPITAL SHIP: MEN JUMP INTO RAGING SEA AND SWIM FOR THEIR LIVES.

1903-1914 1903-1914

line, and once a connection between the vessel and shore existed, the original line acted as a feeder for a heavier rope. To the stronger line, they attached a bosun's chair: by using this primitive method, one by one the marooned seamen could be brought ashore. The gale force winds whipped up huge seas, breaking the vessel into three parts, the bridge now being the only place of refuge. James Langdale, coxswain of the Whitby lifeboat, first heard of the wreck on Friday; the wind and seas were so tremendous it would have been impossible to use the heavier boat. Gallantly they launched the smaller lifeboat, and although the tons of water pouring over *Rohilla* nearly washed them out of the lifeboat, they rescued seventeen people. Reaching the vessel a second time through worsening conditions, they recovered eighteen more.

Following an interview with a survivor, Doctor T C Littler Jones, surgeon of the RNR reported:

> *A few minutes before four on Friday morning there was a sudden crash and the lights went out. He proceeded on deck, but owing to the darkness, it was impossible to see where the ship was but she was fixed. He did not see the captain, but heard him giving directions perfectly calmly, and they were being carried out. A lifeboat went to them shortly after daybreak and four nurses and the stewardess were put in the lifeboat. The captain ordered the women to go first then the doctors, sick attendants, crew and officers, leaving him as the last to be rescued. He could not see them landed as the sea was very heavy and the wind very hard, and the spray went as high as the funnel. The second time about seventeen were rescued. He was the last to enter this lifeboat and helped to carry a doctor who was sick ashore.*

On Saturday morning, the Upgang lifeboat got within twenty yards of the wreck, but was driven off by heavy seas and the strong current. A trawler towed the lifeboat *Robert and Mary Ellis* close to the wreck, but could not approach close enough, and returned to Whitby. The Scarborough lifeboat also failed to reach *Rohilla*. The Whitby lifeboat launched from the beach, and rowed through the seas towards the wreck, but had to return owing to the severity of the sea. These brave, but futile efforts cast quite a gloom over the onlookers, many of whom had remained on duty on the cliffs throughout the night. That afternoon, the rocket brigade expended their last rocket; suddenly the plight of those onboard looked extremely grave. Faced with such a poor chance of survival, the survivors were signalled 'To risk it'. Captain Neilson suggested that the swimmers might try to make it to the shore. Many of the men took their chances in the raging sea; Neilson watched the currents, and directed the swimmers accordingly. About thirty men reached the shore thoroughly exhausted, but many failed. On Saturday night Chief Officer Band swam ashore; two other swimmers survived, however two more died in the attempt. The crowds on the shore made many gallant rescues by plunging into the surf and hauling the swimmers to safety. George Peart saved many lives this way. Fearing darkness would halt the rescue operation the Tyneside Territorial Engineers brought a searchlight by special train and assisted in the rescue work during Saturday night.

Subsequently Neilson received a signal from the shore, that a motor lifeboat was coming and signalled back 'Ship is breaking rapidly, look out for swimmers, low tide tonight: no time to lose'. He then called all hands together, told them that the ship could not last till daybreak, and advised them to make rafts. Some men improvised life rafts from pieces of timber, but were washed out to sea with the ebb tide or washed ashore dead. Those remaining onboard huddled together for warmth, for they had no food or heat and only a thimbleful of fresh water each.

Frank Dunkley. Junior Reserve Attendant. Royal Naval Auxiliary Sick Berth Reserve. Drowned.

The remaining fifty survivors were rescued at about seven on the Sunday morning. The weather had moderated and the Shields motor lifeboat *Henry Vernon*, after a nine-hour journey reached Whitby at one o'clock. After a brief respite, she went to the wreck, accompanied by Richard Eglon the second coxswain of the Whitby lifeboat. Gallons of oil poured on the sea helped calm the water, until the lifeboat was hit by a heavy sea. Those stranded on *Rohilla* had endured fifty hours of atrocious conditions, the Shields motor lifeboat despite sustaining damage on the rocks or wreck hove to. In a round trip lasting less than an hour the motorised lifeboat had rescued fifty souls. Press reports state the hospital ship carried 220 persons onboard, of these only 146 were saved.

The inquests into the deaths of the mariners confirmed they died of drowning, except one reputed to have succumbed to exhaustion. During the inquest, Captain Milburn, Lloyd's agent at Whitby stated:

He had gone to the harbour having seen the heavy seas he thought it was no use launching the lifeboat, so it was taken underneath the Spa ladder. The sea was very heavy and the wind was blowing from the east, with heavy rain squalls. The crew had great difficulty in getting off owing to the heavy sea and the strong northerly half flood. The boat reached the vessel and he saw the women taken off and landed, when the lifeboat returned. The lifeboat drifted about a half a mile before they managed to beach her. The same crew hauled her along the beach and launched her again. Despite rougher seas, she reached the vessel, which had settled down and commenced to break up. It was more difficult to reach her than before. This however was done, but he could not see if the lifeboat was damaged or not. The lifeboat was hauled up near the cliffs as the tide was rapidly rising. The coxswain said it was not prudent to try again and the witness agreed with him. They returned to Whitby and in consultation decided

> *that it was inadvisable to launch the heavier Whitby lifeboat, and they arranged that the Upgang lifeboat should be brought through the town by road and lowered onto the steep cliff to the south of the Nab. This was done but it could not be used owing to the high seas. He wired for a motor boat at Southgate and one started off but owing to the rough weather, she had to go back to Redcar in a damaged condition. On Saturday morning he went to Saltwick, and the Upgang lifeboat was launched between seven and eight o'clock, but owing to the wind, sea and current she was unable to reach the wreck.*
>
> *A motor lifeboat arrived from Tynemouth on Sunday morning in response to his telegram, and went to the wreck, the result being successful, and all those onboard were saved. A tug had been arranged to take the Whitby lifeboat, but she failed to reach the wreck on Saturday morning. Rockets were fired in an endeavour to establish communication with the wreck but for some reason or other all these failed. Plenty of lines were successfully fired over the wreck but they landed in places where those on the wreck could not get hold of them. A searchlight arrived from the town and was of great service on Saturday night. He did not think the Whitby boat could not have carried more survivors than she did. He expressed the opinion that a motorised boat using oil on the water could probably have rescued all on Friday night.*

Throughout the enquiry into the loss of the *Rohilla*, the principal witness Captain Neilson, remained adamant his ship had struck a mine. The fourth officer gave evidence stating how the first shock had made him think the ship had hit a mine, for he was knocked off his feet. This opinion was confirmed by other officers, who also agreed *Rohilla* had struck a mine, one stating he was knocked off his feet against a bulkhead. Another described the first shock, as being lifted up in a lift then being let down again. The coroner in summing up remarked that the war had deprived navigators of the benefit of lighthouses and other lights in the North Sea. The jury agreed the vessel struck something before grounding, and that the master navigated with seaman-like care in exceptional circumstances and was free from blame. They recommended the provision of rocket apparatus on passenger ships, and a motor lifeboat for Whitby. The reason why the vessel sailed so close to the coast appears to have been overlooked.

Some of the bereaved families reclaimed their relatives' bodies, while others recovered from the sea were placed in a trench-like grave at Whitby cemetery. The British India Steam Navigation Company later erected a memorial to the thirty-one officers and crew and a further sixty who drowned in the gale-lashed sea. Of the thirty-three bodies recovered from the wreck, only fourteen were identified.

As the loss of the vessel was due to striking an unknown object the *Rohilla* victims failed to meet the requirements for a war grave. Consequently, the Commonwealth War Graves Commission [CWGC] records only forty-one of the ninety-two Mercantile Marine deaths. The fifty-one missing names therefore are not commemorated on the Tower Hill memorial. Fourteen victims lie in Whitby, a further eight lie in various cemeteries. All the Royal Navy deaths and the solitary Royal Marine casualty are commemorated on Royal Navy memorials. In 1922 an alteration to the criteria required for a war grave ensured anyone who died as a direct result of contact with enemy forces merited a war grave. Errors in the spelling of the names upon the memorial also hinder research. For all the above reasons the reader should be aware that the details within one section of the roll of honour for *Rohilla* are incomplete.

The disaster had unfolded within five hundred yards of land, yet, despite the endeavours of the valiant rescuers, their rudimentary rescue rowing boats were no match when pitched against a tempest of such magnitude. The tragedy highlights the inadequacies of early twentieth-century maritime rescue, hampered by a lack of technological invention. Acts of rescue continued in a manner reminiscent of Grace Darling's exploits three quarters of a century earlier; subsequent successful rescues still owed more to the determination and gallantry of the volunteer lifeboat crews than the equipment. For their gallantry three gold and four silver medals were awarded to lifeboat crew men. The disaster led to a fundraising drive aided by the Royal Lifeboat Institute [sic] for a motorised lifeboat for Whitby. The new boat was launched in June 1919.

To generations of mariners, the perils of the sea were stoically accepted as an occupational hazard; however the introduction of submarine warfare severely increased the mortality rate of seafarers. If vessels like *Rohilla* could founder with such dire consequences within sight of land, the prospects for the unfortunates cast adrift in lifeboats mid-ocean were slim indeed. Generally the only hope of rescue for the often traumatised personnel lay in either the fortuitous appearance of a passing steamer or an outstanding feat of navigation resulting in a successful deliverance. Some 3,305 British Mercantile Marine [merchant navy] vessels amounting to 5,202,000 tons were sunk as a result of enemy action. Of these the Tower Hill Memorial, London, commemorates almost 1700 ships and more poignantly 12,000 Mercantile Marine casualties, male and female with no known grave other than the sea. The Hollybrook Memorial in Southampton Cemetery also commemorates almost 1,900 service personnel including many Mercantile Marine staff with no known grave. Countless more rest in British cemeteries, or that corner of a foreign field that is forever England.

Several months prior to the loss of *Rohilla* another hospital ship ran aground. The *Maine* was formerly an American steamer, but was acquired and used as a hospital ship during the South African war. On 19 June 1914, she was attached

An unidentified amputee soldier.

to a portion of the Home Fleet serving off the west of Scotland, when disaster struck. At two in the afternoon while sailing through thick fog, the hospital ship ran ashore about thirty miles south of Oban, at the eastern entrance of Loch Buy on the coast of Mull. Her distress signals were noted by the Cunard liner *Carmania* steaming in the Irish Sea, which then alerted Vice-Admiral Sir Charles Coke at Queenstown of the vessel's plight. Six destroyers at anchor in Bangor Bay were ordered to proceed with haste to rescue the sick and crew onboard *Maine*. Upon arriving on the scene, several destroyers and a cruiser assisted in transferring the wounded to the island of Mull, where they were placed under canvas to await transport to the mainland. Despite two powerful screw tugs being despatched from Greenock to pull *Maine* clear it appears she remained firmly grounded and was abandoned; the wreck was sold on 6 July 1914.

In 1920 the Admiralty purchased the *Panama,* a 484-bed military hospital ship which had served from 25 July 1915 to 23 November 1919. She latterly assisted in the repatriation of Allied and enemy personnel. *Panama III* [the third vessel to bear the name] was launched in March 1902 by Fairfield Shipbuilders for the Panama Steam Navigation Company. In 1920 the navy renamed the Glasgow-built 401 feet [122m] long twin-screw steamer *Maine*. She became a veteran of two world wars, the 1935 Abyssinian War, the 1937 Spanish Civil War and Greek Civil War. In 1939 in recognition of her being the oldest hospital ship afloat she proudly bore the international pennant number one. After an illustrious career, she

HMHS *Garth Castle was built* in 1910 for the Union Castle Mail SS Co. and became a hospital ship 4 November 1914. She was scrapped in 1939.

eventually arrived at the breakers in July 1948.

On 30 October, the day after the *Rohilla* disaster two Union Castle ships, the *Dover Castle* and *Garth Castle* arrived together at Southampton after disembarkation both vessels sailed to London laden with Government stores for Woolwich. Both ships were formally discharged on 31 October, but a dispute arose with the shipping company over their charter. It was eventually agreed *Dover Castle* should be considered as discharged on the thirty-first instant, and the *Garth Castle* would be on permanent Government charter as a hospital ship. In correspondence to the Union Castle Line, the Director of Transports advised the owners on the hire rates for the vessel. The contract paid sixteen shillings and sixpence [85p] per gross ton, per month for the first three months, and sixteen shillings afterwards; these rates were to be adjustable per gross ton over a whole period of employment, if it exceeded six months.

In effect the intermediate steamer *Garth Castle* acted as the replacement for the lost *Rohilla*; she joined the Naval Service on 4 November. After conversion, the steamer acted as a hospital ship for the Grand Fleet, pennant number YA2. She had a capacity for approximately 250 patients. During a Royal inspection of a Battle Squadron on 27 February 1915, the King paid an impromptu visit to

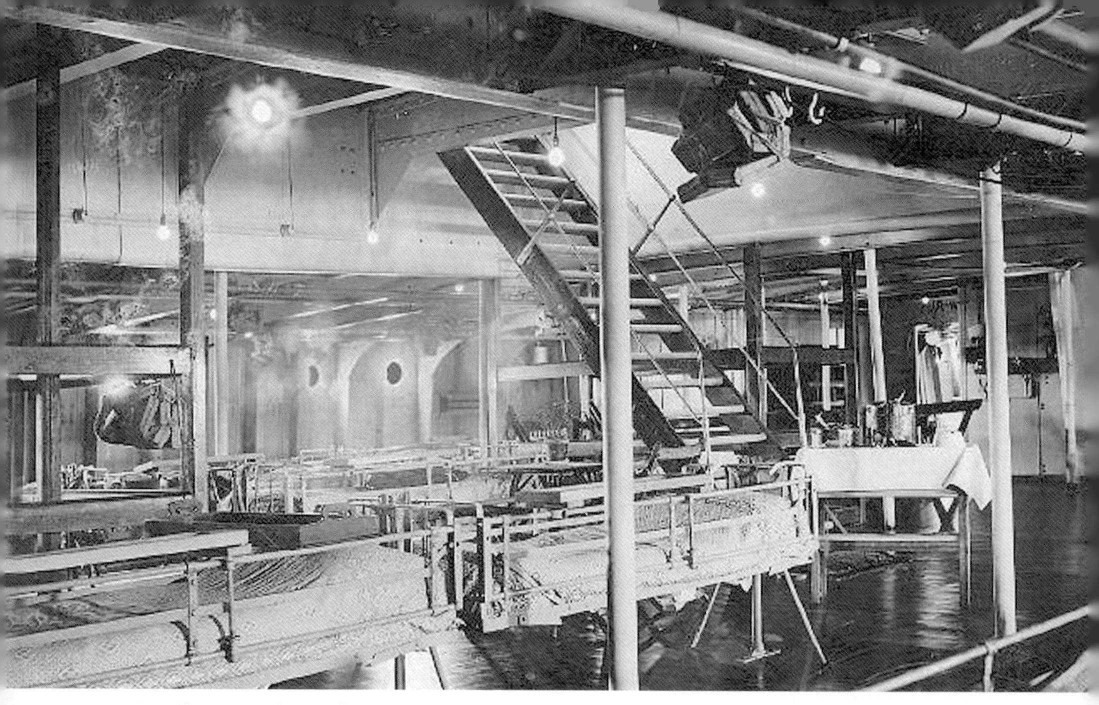

Ward on *Garth Castle*.

the vessel. During his half-hour tour, he expressed great satisfaction with everything he saw onboard, adding 'Although since the war began he had visited a large number of hospitals, he had not seen anything quite so nice'. The monarch renewed his acquaintance with the hospital ship on 24 June 1917 during another fleet inspection; this time the surgeons and nursing staff were introduced to the King. *Garth Castle* fulfilled her Admiralty role for the entire war barring a short period at Malta at the height of the Gallipoli campaign. She concluded her Great War military service during the 1918–19 Allied intervention against the Bolsheviks in North Russia.

Mine warfare and blockade

During the 1907 Hague Conference the regulating of the use of mines at sea was discussed at length. British proposals for the total prohibition of unanchored sea mines were refused by Germany and other states, who considered mines a legitimate method of defence, especially against a pursuing enemy. Britain also proposed the prohibition of the use of mines in establishing or maintaining a commercial blockade. This proposal was also fiercely opposed, however the Conference did agree on Convention Number Eight. Belligerents were prohibited from laying unanchored automatic mines which did not become harmless within one hour after they had been laid. Or from laying anchored contact mines which were not rendered inert, if they broke loose from their moorings. A third condition prohibited the laying of contact mines off the coasts and ports of an enemy with the sole purpose of intercepting commercial navigation. Great Britain and her Dominions signed and ratified the Convention. Germany had recognised the awesome potential of mines and had refused to sign the relevant section of the Hague Convention.

Soon after hostilities commenced Germany broke the Hague Convention, by laying contact mines in the international water off the Suffolk coast, and other sea routes. As the laying of mines in open water, beyond a belligerent's three-mile territorial waters violated the Second Hague Convention, the British reaction to the indiscriminate use of mines was swift. Britain accused Germany of a flagrant disregard for all the recognised usages of warfare. Previously nations employed maritime mines to defend harbours and coastlines, however, government sources claimed Germany now employed the mine in an offensive capacity. This new development infuriated the Admiralty, for while it was perfectly acceptable to destroy a vessel attempting to breach a security cordon it seemed abhorrent to the British sense of fair play to use it as a means of attack. They viewed the offensive mine 'not as a deliberate and controllable attack on an admitted foe, but as a haphazard and inhuman weapon against all who use the high seas'. The mine responsible for the sinking of HMS *Audacious* off the west coast of Ireland might just as easily have destroyed the nearby liner *Olympic*. In this and other incidents British sources claimed as the vessels of the Royal Navy had not witnessed enemy vessels discharging mines they drew only one conclusion. They asserted hostile merchant ships or trawlers were flying a neutral flag to elude suspicion while clandestinely laying mines. Infuriated by the indiscriminate laying of mines on one of the main trade routes to America, to the danger of not only British shipping but of neutral shipping, Britain took full advantage of this frightening development. Supporting her argument with incidents of further shipping losses to British and neutral vessels, Britain took a bold step to secure the protection of her maritime lifeline, while further restricting imports to German ports.

The Admiralty considered a wide and definite scheme of protection on their part not only necessary but imperative. Consequently from 5 November 1914, the Admiralty declared the North Sea a military area, and 'within this area merchant shipping of all kinds, traders of all countries, fishing craft and all other vessels will be exposed to the gravest dangers from mines which it has been necessary to lay, and from warships searching vigilantly by night and day for suspicious craft'. Britain had effectively declared a monopoly on the North Sea ostensibly to reduce the risk to non-combatant vessels. The Secretary of the Admiralty issued the following communication:

The German policy of mine-laying, combined with their submarine activities, makes it necessary on military grounds for the Admiralty to adopt counter measures. His Majesty's Government have therefore adopted a mine-laying policy in certain areas, and a system of mine fields has been established and developed upon a considerable scale.

In order to reduce risks to non-combatants, the Admiralty announce that it is dangerous henceforth for ships to cross the area between Latitude fifty-one degrees fifteen minutes north and fifty-one degrees forty minutes north. Longitude one degree thirty-five minutes east and three degrees east. ...Instructions have been issued to His Majesty's ships to warn east-going vessels of the presence of this new minefield.

The announcement incensed the neutral countries who interpreted the announcement as a Royal Navy attempt to sever their maritime trade with whichever country they chose to trade with. A British blockade of Germany severely restricted imports of food and assorted materials, including war materials; however neutral countries were receiving freight ultimately destined for Germany. The controversial British embargo on free-moving trade undoubtedly attempted to restrict German imports. Any neutral vessels suspected of carrying cargoes ultimately destined for Germany were turned away. These actions violated the recognised principle of the freedom of the seas and intensified the blockade against Germany, as all vessels entering the North Sea were now under British control. On 20 August 1914, after hearing the German Government were taking control of all foodstuffs, Britain ordered all foodstuffs destined for Germany were to be detained. Neutral vessels with contraband cargoes were directed to a British port, Britain purchased the cargo, and the neutral shipping company did not suffer a loss. They were not enforcing a total blockade as they did not close the North Sea to Scandinavian and Dutch vessels, who routinely trans-shipped cargoes to Germany. As developments in naval weaponry prevented the close blockade of enemy ports by a ring of warships, and the Declaration of Paris had not sought to abolish an 'effective' blockade, Britain reasoned her distant blockade was therefore effective and legal.

The opposing sides feared risking the wrath of the neutral United States of America as neither side wished the Americans to align with their opponent. For this reason Britain had not declared cotton, a fundamental requirement in the manufacture of explosives, as a contraband cargo [gun-cotton being produced by soaking the cotton in nitric and sulphuric acids, and then being allowed to dry]. American cotton exports to neutral European ports in the twelve months prior to June 1914 were valued at five million dollars. A year later sixty million dollars of American exports were delivered to European neutrals.

The above serves as a brief insight into an exceedingly complicated subject, of which some conception is required by the reader to comprehend the unfolding world crisis in maritime trade. Britain lost her first merchant ship to a submarine on 20 October. Approximately twelve miles off the coast of Norway, the 866 GRT ship (belonging to Salvesen of Leith) was intercepted by *U17*. The enemy boarded the coal-laden steamer and ordered the crew to take to the lifeboats. To spare a costly torpedo the boarding party scuttled *Glitra*, then, towed the lifeboats within sight of the coast. The first sinking without warning occurred six days later. While the politicians wangled and horse traded, a steady procession of merchant and warships of all nations failed to complete their final voyage or patrol. On 22 December 1914 an interview with the German Grand Admiral Alfred von Tirpitz appeared in the *New York Evening News*. Ominously the director in chief of German naval operations hinted at a new phase of naval warfare:

> *America did not raise her voice in protest, and has done nothing, or very little, against the closing by England of the North Sea against neutral shipping. What would America say now if Germany were to declare a submarine war against all hostile merchant shipping?*

This transpired to be not a private opinion but the first official announcement of a new policy – the submarine blockade of Great Britain.

The Hospital Ship

There is a green-lit hospital ship,
Green with a crimson cross,
Lazily swaying there in the bay,
Lazily bearing my friend away,
Leaving me dull-sensed lost.
Green-lit, red-lit hospital ship,
Numb is my heart, but you carelessly dip
There in the drift of the bay.

There is a green-lit hospital ship,
Dim as the distance grows,
Speedily steaming out of the bay,
Speedily bearing my friend away
Into the orange rose.
Green-lit, red-lit hospital ship,
Dim are my eyes, but you heedlessly slip
Out of their sight from the bay.

There was a green-lit hospital ship,
Green, with a blood-red cross,
Lazily swaying there in the bay,
But it went out with the light of day–
Out where the white seas toss.
Green-lit, red-lit hospital ship,
Cold are my hands and trembling my lip;
Did you make it home from the bay?

Grand Admiral Alfred von Tirpitz.

Notes

1. The Gross Registered Tonnage [GRT] is the total internal volume of a vessel, excluding areas like crew accommodation, measured in cubic feet. A hundred cubic feet equals approximately one ton.
2. The statistics are from *A popular history of the Great War.*
3. On 18 March while commanding *U29* he was rammed and sunk by HMS *Dreadnought*; all hands perished.
4. During the discussions for the revision of Hague Convention X and its substitution by the Second General Convention of 1949, the delegation sought to prohibit hospital ships from transmitting [but not receiving] secret code messages. The drafters of a revised Article 34 covering the modernisation of protective markings and signalling wished to prevent a repeat of the *Ophelia* incident.

HMHS *Vasna,* while still under construction in 1917, she was fitted out as a hospital ship by her builders Alex Stephen and Sons, Glasgow.

Chapter Two

1915. The Liner Requisitions Commence

As the winds of war spread, other nations aligned themselves with the belligerent powers, and as stalemate set in on the Western Front legions of men were pitched against fortified positions, at great loss in life and limb. When the Western Front fighting reached an impasse, other theatres of war offered a tantalising prospect of victory. So, more in desperation than hope, Britain and her allies waged war in distant climes. These new theatres of war were dismissed by various prominent leaders as nothing more than 'side shows' which drew away much-needed men and logistics from the Western Front. When Turkey became a Central Powers' ally, her navy – in contravention of International Law – closed the Dardanelles Straits, severing our Russian ally from French and British logistical supplies. The closure of the Dardanelles to shipping prompted the Royal Navy and French warships to attempt to force the Dardanelles, and hopefully regain access to the Black Sea. The naval operations launched from 19 February failed, along with others; instead on 25 April the Allied infantry landed on the shores of Gallipoli, and fought in vain to reach Constantinople. Despite initially being severely underrated as fighting material by the British, the Turkish stoutly resisted the invading forces, who ravaged by disease, severe weather and battle casualties evacuated the peninsula in late December. Far from the Western Front, troops clashed in German East Africa, the largest and richest of Germany's colonies. This is seldom recalled, yet who has not read or seen the movie *The African Queen*, inspired by the fighting for the supremacy of Lake Tanganyika? The media rarely refer to three significant theatres of war, namely Palestine, Mesopotamia [Iraq], and Salonika [Greece]. The conflict truly was a world war waged by nations great and small throughout the globe, not a conflict solely waged in or above the trenches of France and Belgium.

Inevitably, these and numerous other campaigns resulted in the deaths of thousands of Allied combatants and non-combatants; if their mortal remains were recovered they received a modest funeral. A junior officer usually wrote a letter to the deceased's next of kin: 'Your son was the life and soul of the battalion and will be greatly missed. You may gain comfort in the fact that he died instantly and would have felt no pain...' appears regularly in archive material. Eventually a modest pension would reach the family, and the military closed the file on the deceased person. Contrary to public opinion the front line officers' chances of survival were half those of a low-ranking soldier.

The wounded generally outnumbered the dead by a ratio of between two and four to one, depending on the intensity of the attack or repulse. Not all the

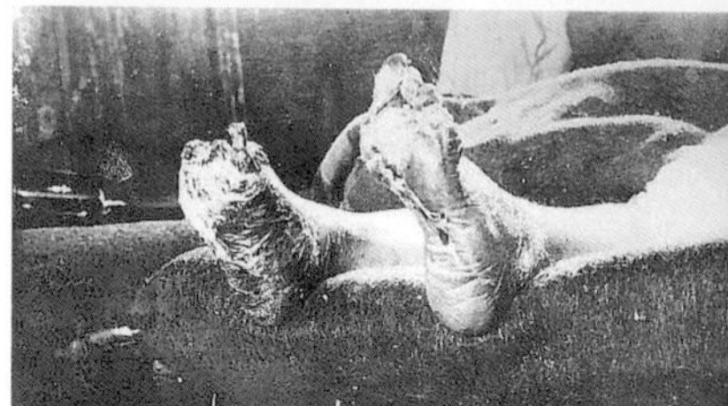

Trench conditions and the results.

incapacitated were wounded, for the dire living conditions in the trenches made the occupants susceptible to diseases. Apart from the more recognisable medical conditions we know today, Tommy Atkins suffered from conditions now unfamiliar to modern readers.

The first winter in the flooded Belgian low-lying trenches brought about a condition known as trench-foot. Long periods of exposure in water affected the soldiers' feet, which often broke out in a mass of chilblains and sometimes turned gangrenous. Soldier's Heart condemned the sufferer to long periods in hospital. The term neurasthenia encompassed a diverse range of nervous diseases and psychoses first scathingly referred to as shellshock. Another ailment originally baffled the medical profession; the first outbreaks of Trench Fever were originally diagnosed as a form of influenza or typhoid. Although contracting this disease was not fatal, patients were incapacitated for a lengthy duration. Thought to have been spread by the bite from a body louse, it was not until the final year of the war that it was proved the disease was transmitted by the excreta of the louse and not the bite. Another common insect, the mosquito, infected its victims with malaria then referred to as the ague. The problem was especially acute in Macedonia and Salonika; an early program of inoculation proved ineffective, however quinine produced satisfactory results. The demand for quinine salts in 1916 led to the RAMC issuing to the army 66,000,000 five-grain doses equivalent to twenty-one tons of quinine. During the Salonika campaign malaria claimed more casualties than the enemy. Flies were also airborne spreaders of disease, none more so than at Gallipoli where dysentery became endemic; a soldier could go into battle with a rifle in one hand and his trouser waistband in the other. The use of poisonous chlorine gas in the early stages of the war produced the first instances of troops with tortured lungs leading to instantaneous death or an extremely protracted illness supervened by death. Man's inhumanity knew no bounds as different strains of poison gas were invented to counter the development of the gas mask and kill more efficiently. These and many other medical cases added to the wounded requiring evacuation or treatment in vast military base hospitals. The Government was evidently pleased with improvements in medicinal care for, in early February 1915, the Prime Minister Herbert Asquith stated in the House of Commons that about sixty per cent of our wounded recovered and became fit for service, a record far above any previous war.

In 1915, forty-three additional hospital ships including carriers were added to the fleet. While it is beyond the remit of this work to document the participation of all the shipping companies involved, a brief insight into a sample of vessels involved may be beneficial to the reader. While the major shipping companies made a significant contribution to the war effort, several successful entrepreneurs made their own personal contribution to the war effort by placing their luxury yacht at the disposal of the Admiralty. Their contribution is generally overshadowed by the larger and better known passenger cargo liners from the world-renowned shipping companies.

The *Liberty,* a seven-year-old private yacht of Lord Tredegar of the Royal Yacht Squadron, appears on a contemporary postcard captioned 'The first hospital ship to receive wounded'. However, this is at odds with the documented service period of 1915 to January 1919. The yacht used as a naval hospital ship was present at Gallipoli. Following the 23 April 1918 raid on the port of Zeebrugge, the victors returned to port. The first batch of wounded were immediately transferred to the 886 ton *Liberty*, where the wife of the raid planner Vice-Admiral Roger Keyes, in recognition of St George's Day presented each wounded man with a red rose, prior to their departure by rail to military hospitals. After paying heavy duties in 1915 Lord Tredegar's finances went into decline, in 1920 he sold *Liberty* and the lease of his town house, possibly in order to retain his stately mansion.

The tea magnate Sir Thomas Lipton also made his yacht available, and on one voyage transported overseas a field hospital. During 1916 the private yacht

Liberty, was built in 1908, pictured here in hospital ship livery. She was the largest privately owned yacht in Britain and property of Lord Tredegar, who finanaced her conversion.

Grianaig was hired by the navy, until July 1918 when the army used her. Another small vessel, the hospital steamer *Queen Alexandria* belonging to the Council of the Royal National Missions to Deep Sea Fishermen, was placed at the nation's disposal by the chairman William F A Archibald. The steamer, captained by Sir Charles E H Chadwyck-Healey Bart RNR, was run and maintained at his expense for the majority of the war. Her crew comprised most of her original North Sea crew and Shipp, her old skipper, carried the rank of a RNVR sub lieutenant, the society's Home Superintendent served on board as Surgeon Lieutenant F W Willway RNVR.

Lord Brassey, a member of the Royal Yacht Squadron and the first editor of *Brassey's Naval Review* owned and raced the impressive steam yacht *Sunbeam*. On the outbreak of hostilities he made his yacht available to the British Red Cross. In early 1915 *Sunbeam* commanded by Brassey conveyed medical supplies to Rouen, returning home laden with wounded soldiers. In the summer Brassey appointed J R Carter, a former master of the royal family's *Britannia*, as master. The yacht then spent a year in the Mediterranean, terminating when Brassey agreed to loan his yacht to the Royal Indian Navy where she served as a hospital ship for the duration of the conflict.

The Canadian Pacific Railway Company operated steamships including the stately-looking 5,905-

Saint Margaret of Scotland.

GRT *Empress of India*. Built in 1890, the clipper bow twin-funnelled craft had three masts which looked capable of accepting sails. Almost a quarter of a century later the company sold the obsolete looking steamer in 1914 to the Maharajah of Gwalior for conversion to a 325-bed hospital ship. Later that year the renamed *Loyalty* entered service from 2 October until three weeks after the 11 November 1918 armistice.

The Royal Mail Steam Packet Company supplied eight of their buff-coloured funnel vessels *Agadir*, *Araguaya*, *Asturias*, *Balantia* and her sister ship *Berbice;* also *Drina*, *Essequibo*, *Tagus* for hospital ship use. The twin screw *Araguaya* made twenty voyages for the Royal Canadian Medical Service. Commissioned from May 1917 mainly on the Liverpool to Halifax service she returned over 15,000 wounded to Canada. The Harland and Wolff-built *Balantia* worked as an inter-West Indies island steamer. After a recall to Britain she served under a different name from 1916. In 1915, the Scottish Branch of the British Red Cross Society raised 20,000 pounds from flag days and public subscription towards the conversion of a hospital ship. Not satisfied with financing the conversion of the re-named *Saint Margaret of Scotland*, the Scots used surplus funds to provide a dozen ambulance motor launches for service in the Eastern theatres. The hospital ship manned mainly by Scots remained under the management of the Royal Mail Lines.

The Cunard line needs no introduction for they have a long and illustrious pedigree in sea travel. At the time of the 1854 Crimean War the company provided the 1,440-ton *Andes* for use as a hospital ship. During the First World War the majority of the fleet were employed in civilian or government work as merchant cruisers or troopships. Two Cunard liners, the RMS *Mauretania* and *Aquitania,* temporarily acted as hospital ships to alleviate the situation concerning the unprecedented amount of sick and wounded from Gallipoli.

The 45,647-ton *Aquitania* had a varied military career, which must have confused the enemy no end. The liner briefly became an armed merchant cruiser but the paint had hardly dried on her modifications when she was ordered back to port. A period as a troopship followed, during which she conveyed 25,000 men to the beaches of Gallipoli. She became a hospital ship on 4 September 1915, her wards held 4,182 beds, an amount unequalled by any other British hospital ship. At the height of the Gallipoli campaign she returned to Southampton carrying nearly 5,000 patients twenty ambulance trains were required to disperse her patients throughout the country. The *Aquitania* was fitted with an apparatus capable of using electrolysis to extract hypochlorite from sea water. The weak, unstable greenish acid that occurs in solution or salts is used in bleach or disinfectants. The product dispensed with the need for carbolic acid: after one voyage the equipment had recovered the financial outlay and no secondary cases of infection developed. She ceased to be a hospital ship on 27 December 1917, and by the spring of 1918 she was refitted as a

Aquitania, formerly of the Cunard Line, served as a troop transport during 1915 and took 30,000 to the Dardanelles. She served in the Mediterranean as a hospital ship during 1916. She could accommodate 4,182 bed cases.

troopship. In response to disastrous developments on the Western Front *Aquitania* reverted to a troop transport and made nine trips across the Atlantic bringing across 60,000 American troops to reinforce Allied defences.

In 1897 Cunard lost the coveted record for the fastest North Atlantic crossing to the German liner *Kaiser Wilhelm der Grosse.* In 1902 the British Government began negotiations with Cunard to develop two super fast passenger liners capable of regaining the prestigious Blue Riband to Britain. The Government agreed to grant Cunard 2,600,000 pounds towards their cost; on the proviso that both of the 31,900-GRT liners were capable of being armed and available for war service. As a result the keels of *Lusitania* and her five-foot longer sister ship *Mauretania* were laid down on the slipways of Swan, Hunter and Whigham Richardson at Wallsend on Tyne. The four-stack liners would have an impressive service speed of approximately twenty-five knots. The

Mauretania, sister ship to the *Lusitania,* formerlya transatlantic passenger liner for the Cunard Linc. She alternated as a troop and hospital ship.

Mauretania made her maiden voyage in mid-November 1907. Two years later *Mauretania,* the fastest of the pair, had recaptured the Blue Riband for both the fastest Atlantic west bound and east bound crossings, records she would retain for two decades.

In June 1915 *Mauretania,* affectionately known as the Maurie, served as a troopship. While transporting troops to Gallipoli she survived a torpedo attack; the liner's high turn of speed allowed her to take evasive action. At the height of the Gallipoli campaign larger vessels were drafted in to alleviate pressure on the medical services. As a result at the end of August *Mauretania* returned to Liverpool for adaptation to a hospital ship. She departed on 22 October outward bound for Gallipoli, where she joined the great liners *Aquitania* and *Britannic*. The total staff onboard the three liners reached 400 medical officers, 900 nurses, and about 3,500 rank and file of the RAMC. The *Mauretania* had accommodation for nearly 2,000 patients; during her four months as a hospital ship she made three voyages from Gallipoli. In November 1915, after German allegations of improper use, a neutral delegation inspected *Mauretania* at Naples. The United States, Swiss and Danish consuls were satisfied by the inspection and denounced the allegations. Following the Allied withdrawal from the Turkish peninsula the demand for her services waned; the following March she reverted back to a troopship.

The Union Castle line of 1914 operated forty-one sea-going vessels, nineteen of which went into Government service. The company supplied the backbone of the British fleet of hospital ships; by 1915, thirteen of their ships were employed as hospital ships: although a few vessels sailed only briefly under the International Red Cross flag. The *Kildonan Castle* for example operated as a 600-bed hospital carrier from 6 October 1915; five months later she became an armoured merchant cruiser with the Glasgow-based 10 Cruiser Squadron. Another short term hospital ship the 15,007-GRT *Dunvegan Castle* operated in 1914 as a cross Channel troopship, before returning the following year to the South African mail service. Her use on the mail run was interrupted for over six months following her commission on 6 October 1915 as a 400-bed hospital ship. The Union Castle hospital ships comprised: *Braemar Castle*, *Carisbrook Castle*, *Dover Castle*, *Dunluce Castle*, *Dunvegan Castle*, *Galeka*, *Garth Castle*, *Gascon*, *Glenart Castle*, *Glengorm Castle*, *Gloucester Castle*, *Guildford Castle*, *Goorkha*, *Grantully Castle*, *Kildonan Castle*, *Llandovery Castle* and *Salta*. The company also manned the 305-bed *Western Australia*. The history of Union Castle and the War 1914–19 records that in the course of the war their ships brought a total of 354,000 British wounded and over 9,000 enemy wounded to Southampton.

The Peninsular and Oriental Navigation Company [P&O] merged with the British India line in 1914. When war broke out the Government requisitioned more than half of their 200-strong fleet; up to the armistice eighty-one of these were lost due to enemy action. Company vessels requisitioned as hospital ships included the *Assaye*, *China*, *Dongola*, *Egypt*, *Kalyan*, *Morea*, *Plassy*, *Sicilia*, *Somalia*, *Syria* and *Soudan*; the latter also acted as the Royal Navy Sick quarters at Yokohama.

The 450-feet long and 7,396-GRT *Assaye* was built by Harland and Wolff in 1899. She operated as a peacetime troopship between Southampton and colonial India she continued as a troopship until May 1915 when she became a 488-bed hospital ship in operation until March 1920.

Built by Harland and Wolff and completed in 1896 the *China* was designed to operate on the Australian service. She was one of five sister ships built for the company; the 7,912-GRT vessel served as a hospital ship until a year after the armistice.

In peacetime during winter months the passenger trade slackened off; companies offset the loss in revenue with contracts for shuttling troops back and forth to the colonies. During the world crisis this activity naturally increased. The ten-year-old, twin-screw *Dongola* served as a troopship until she commenced four years' service as a hospital ship commencing from 25 May 1915. Capable of carrying 506 bed-bound patients, *Dongola* served at Gallipoli, and spent the final year of the war between the Persian Gulf and India.

The two-funnelled *Egypt* was built at Greenock in 1897. Her steam triple-expansion engine drove a single screw producing a service speed of sixteen knots. After conversion at Durban she served as a hospital ship during the Boer

Grantully Castle was built by Barclay, Curle & Co, Glasgow in 1910. Temporarily served as a troopship in 1915 for the Gallipoli campaign.

The *Morea* was built by Barclay, Curle & Co. Ltd, Glasgow and spent five months as a hospital ship. She was converted to an armed transport and served throughout the war.

War, a role she returned to on 2 August 1915. After conversion she emerged from the dockyard resplendent in the paint scheme of a hospital ship, destined for the Mediterranean war zone. The 461-bed mercy ship bearing the pennant number fifty-two remained within this inland sea for the majority of her service, until her decommission in 1919.

After a refit she returned to civilian service in 1921; in May of the following year she collided in dense fog with the French steamer *Seine*. The *Egypt* sank within twenty minutes; eighty-six lives were lost and a cargo including gold specie valued at approximately 1,054,000 pounds sterling.

At the turn of the century P&O ordered five 'S'-class ships from Clydeside shipbuilders. Launched as *Sardinia*, *Sicilia*, *Syria*, *Soudan* and *Somalia*, excluding *Sardinia* four of the sisters served as wartime hospital ships. The *Soudan* and *Somalia* joined the Grand Fleet as hospital ships mainly based in fleet anchorages: however at the peak of the Gallipoli conflict both ships departed to the Aegean waters, where they and others stood offshore acting as base hospitals. The wounded were nursed onboard pending their transfer to the larger homeward-bound hospital ships.

Despite the war losses, the company, like so many others, prospered during the war years. Lord Inchcape became chairman in 1915 [a position he held until 1932] and orchestrated an expansion of the company, by the absorption of several other prominent shipping lines. The company continued to flourish until

Nevassa served as a troop transport before conversion to a 600-bed hospital ship. She was to serve in the Second World War during the Normandy landings.

the early 1920s' depression, when it became increasingly difficult to find sufficient trade for their 500 ships. In the intervening ninety years the company has prospered, the brand name being synonymous with luxury cruise ships or the humble cross-Channel ferries.

Despite the takeover the British India Steam Navigating Company retained its identity. The following steamers were among those requisitioned, some only temporarily, as hospital ships: *Devanha*, *Erinpura*, *Tanda*, the *Neuralia*, at the time the largest ship in the fleet and her sister ship, *Nevassa*. Among others were *Rewa* and the *Rohilla,* a very early loss. The *Varela* was constructed for the mail service between Bombay and the Persian Gulf; she had the distinction of being the first of the fleet to be requisitioned as a hospital ship. Requisitioned on 2 August 1914, the 450-bed ship operated in the Persian Gulf providing medical services during the Mesopotamia Campaign. Her three sister ships similarly served in the Gulf. During 1917, the Government requisitioned *Vasna* while still under construction; the last vessel of the four-ship class left the builders' yard as a 613-bed hospital ship. Lord Inchcape also placed the new Karachi offices of the British India line at the service of the Government of India for use as a military hospital.

The role of Indian troops during the Great War rarely receives a mention today, despite contributing 1.3 million combatants for the defence of the Empire. The Indian Divisions waged war on the Western Front, East Africa,

Gallipoli, Mesopotamia [Iraq] and other Middle East theatres. In 1914 the almost new *Tanda* was made available to the city of Madras as a hospital ship. The shipping company offset her running cost by donating 20,000 rupees a month towards her upkeep. After conversion to approximately a 450-bed hospital ship for the Madras War Fund, the 6,956-GRT vessel entered service on 2 October 1914. In deference to her financiers they renamed her *Madras*: under this guise she served continually until November 1919. On completion of her war service she returned to her owners and adopted her original name.

The 5,128-GRT *Erinpura* launched by Denny Shipbuilders in October 1911 was one of seven sister ships. She had the distinction of being the first British India ship on the Eastern Service to be fitted with a wireless radio. Named after a town in Jodhpur in Rajasthan she operated on the highly successful Bengal to Singapore Straits service in peacetime. After two years' wartime trooping in the Middle East she became a 475-bed hospital ship for the Indian Expeditionary Force on 1 May 1916. From late 1917 she operated for some eighteen months as a defensively equipped ambulance transport, terminating her service on 13 June 1919. Two days later, while homeward bound from Bombay to Marseilles, she entered the Red Sea heading for the Suez Canal. While off the Yemen coast she foundered on the Mushejara Reef, ninety-six miles north-west of Aden. Firmly wedged bow-first she resisted the efforts of the Royal Navy cruiser, HMS *Topaze,* and a Perim Salvage tug to tow her free. Attempts by passing British India vessels all failed, the bow remaining resolutely gripped by the reef. The company decided to remove the bow section forward of the bridge front, then tow the stern section to Aden. The company ordered a new bow section from the original builders to be married up with *Erinpura* at the company's Mazagon Dockyard in Bombay. By this time she was reputedly referred to as the 'longest ship in the world, having a bow in Dumbarton and a stern in Bombay'. It was 1923 before she returned to service. In 1941, while in convoy to Malta, she was attacked and sunk by German bombers.

The German submarine blockade

German naval sources calculated over two hundred submarines were needed to operate an effective blockade of the British Isles. The warship construction programme of Imperial Germany had concentrated on producing sufficient capital ships to rival the might of the Grand Fleet; in February 1915 she had at her disposal only twenty-eight U-boats. A score of these craft were capable of long range patrols, the remainder were almost obsolete and suitable only for defensive coastal work; maintenance work and crew rest periods ashore reduced this number further. The Great War submarines fell into three categories, U-boats were large submersibles generally used in the Atlantic approaches. UB-boats were smaller in size and usually operated in the channel. The UC-boats converted from mercantile submarines were small in number. Usually only a handful of submarines were on patrol; a few confined their activities to the Western Approaches where all the Atlantic shipping converged bound for the Mersey, Bristol Channel and Channel ports. The Thames Estuary always merited a vigilant submarine, as did the waters off Tyneside and Hull. Due to their insufficient numbers the marauders' kills were few and losses were initially sustainable. When the British ship *Tokomaru* belonging to the Shaw Saville and Albion Company and also the Leyland ship *Ikaria* were torpedoed off Havre by *U20*, the *Tokomaru* sank but a damaged *Ikaria* made port with assistance. An incensed French Minister of Marine protested:

> *Up to the present, by a sort of self respect, German seamen have generally not sunk Allied merchant-ships ships until they have taken off the crews or authorised them to escape. Almost the only departure from this rule which they have had to reproach themselves has been the criminal attack, off Boulogne, upon the French liner* Amiral Ganteaume, *full of Belgian women and children. Today the German navy has decided to violate International Law systematically and deliberately. The officers have received orders to respect nothing in future, and to place themselves outside the pale of inhumanity. Thus on 30 January, a German submarine [U20] torpedoed without previous notice, two British merchant-ships in the vicinity of Havre. The whole world will rise in horror at such an act of war, which is unworthy of a civilised nation.*

Asturias in Royal Mail Steam Packet Company livery. During her role as the largest cross-Channel hospital ship livery she was attacked by a U-boat.

Asturias torpedo attack

Two days after this incident the first recorded act of aggression directed towards a British hospital ship arose on the first of February 1915, when a hostile submarine launched a torpedo at the hospital ship *Asturias*. The Government requisitioned the Royal Mail steamship *Asturias* as a hospital ship in August 1914, much to the annoyance of her regular passengers. Formerly employed on the South America service, the steamer became extremely popular with the fashionable people, who appreciated her luxury and remarkable steadiness, even in the roughest seas. After a spell in the dockyard, the vessel emerged in a fresh white livery, her hull having the wide green painted stripe interrupted by two red crosses alerting the world to her humanitarian role. Amidships a huge red cross, illuminated at night by floodlights, reached from the taff rail, to the upper edge of the standard five feet [1.5 metre] wide green band. The height of the internationally recognised Red Cross emblem extended over the height of two decks, leaving no doubts as to the role of the vessel. In addition to the national flag all hospital ships also prominently flew the flag of the International Red Cross. Due to her internal modifications she now contained swinging cot beds for 1,200 patients, but generally carried about a thousand. On one trip she carried 2,700 patients! Her operating theatre performed countless life-saving operations; however the improvement in medical arrangements no longer demanded the emergency use of her theatre during the short Channel crossing.

On 1 February the vessel carrying a staff of doctors and nurses was outward-bound to Havre to embark wounded soldiers. The French Ministry of Marine made the following announcement on 2 February 1915:

> *Yesterday at 5 pm fifteen miles north-north-east of the Havre lightship a German submarine discharged a torpedo, which however did not hit the mark, at the British hospital ship* Asturias, *thus violating the explicit condtions of the Hague Convention of 18 October, 1907, relative to the absolute respect due to hospital vessels. By the Tenth Convention regulating naval war signed at The Hague in 1907 by Germany in common with other naval powers, hospital ships are sacred. Article One of the Convention states- Military hospital ships- that is to say ships constructed or adapted by states specially and solely with the view of aiding the wounded, sick and shipwrecked, the names of which have been communicated to the belligerent powers at the commencement or during the course of hostilities, shall be respected and cannot be captured while hostilities continue.*

This unprecedented act of aggression in the war to end all wars was seized upon by the media who reported in their words the 'conclusive story of German barbarity'. Within a fortnight of the attack the Secretary of the Admiralty issued the following statements of the master and officers to the press.

Havre, 2 February. At 4.15 pm on 1 February with the Principal Medical Officer [PMO] I inspected ship finishing at 5 pm. Going towards the bridge from the main saloon Mr Fletcher, cadet, reported to me, a torpedo just fired at us passing astern. I at once went to the bridge and upon the second officer confirming the statement that he observed the wash of a submarine two points on the starboard beam I then starboarded three and a half points, sending to the engine room instructions to give the ship all steam possible. After that until passing the lightship I made a zigzag course.

Seeing a French destroyer on my port bow I sent a wireless message that a torpedo had been fired at me and missed. There was also a fishing boat in the vicinity of the French destroyer on my port quarter. Apart from the testimony of my officers a number of people on board not only saw the course of the torpedo but also observed the submarine following in our wake. It was a very light and clear evening and at 5.15 broad daylight and by no possibility could the character of the ship be mistaken.

Charles Law, Master.

At 5 pm on 1 February whilst in charge of the bridge the ship being north-north-west fifteen miles from Havre lightship, I observed a smooth in the water about two points abaft the starboard beam 500 yards away. About 150 feet from the smooth I distinctly observed the track of a torpedo which passed us close under our stern...

A N Thomson, Second Officer.

Hearing that a torpedo had been fired at us, I ran on deck, and saw the periscope of a submarine on the starboard quarter. I then went aft, and could distinctly see the wash of a periscope in our own wake, slightly on the starboard quarter. At 5.25 I lost sight of it. We were increasing our distance all the time; I had no glasses with me.

Basil A H Yoolten, Cadet.

Almost five weeks after the attack on *Asturias*, the German Embassy in Washington issued the following statement, which contained no reference to hospital ship lights or the Red Cross markings: 'The Government are sorry to admit that the British hospital ship *Asturias* was attacked by a German submarine. The ship was mistaken as a transport. She was at the time carrying the lights prescribed by regulations for ordinary merchant ships. Fortunately the torpedo did not explode, and the moment the ship was recognised as a hospital ship the attack was abandoned.'

War zones and contraband.

The *Asturias* attack may have been an accident but the apology arrived when the Admiralty were dealing with a fresh development in the war at sea. The 4

The *Asturias,* with distinctive paint scheme and fully illuminated, became the first hospital ship targetted.

February edition of the *Reichsanzeiger,* the official gazette, announced to the world:

1. The waters around Great Britain and Ireland, including the entire English Channel, are herewith declared to be a military area. From 18 February every hostile merchant ship met with in this War Zone will be destroyed, nor will it always be possible to avoid the dangers which therewith threaten the crews and passengers.
2. Neutral ships will also incur danger in the military area, because, in view of the misuse of neutral flags ordered by the British Government on 31 January[1], and the accidents of naval warfare, it cannot always be avoided that attacks may involve neutral ships.
3. Traffic northwards around the Shetland Islands in the west part of the North Sea, and a strip of at least thirty sea miles in breadth along the coast of Holland is not endangered.

All too aware of the shortage of craft to enforce this proposed blockade, some German commanders knew they faced an uphill struggle. Submarines were under construction for the steadily expanding fleet, and would eventually come close to isolating Britain; in the meantime they had insufficient tools to effectively complete the task in hand. Germany anticipated as a result of the ominous threat, British ship owners would not risk their ships at sea, and the civilian officers and crews would refuse to jeopardise lives; in this respect the initiative failed. Reacting to the two weeks' notice of a submarine blockade, the Prime Minister summed up the threat as 'a campaign of piracy and pillage', a gross violation of international law.

The inauguration of the blockade produced no discernible reduction in the movement of British mercantile shipping. A few instances of success in sinking British merchant ships were not enough to paralyse trade. Between 23 February and 3 March 805 vessels of over 300 tons entered British ports and 699 cleared the harbours. On 19 February the campaign against neutral shipping commenced with the torpedoing of the Norwegian ship *Belridge*. Fortune favoured the New Orleans to Amsterdam-bound ship; she failed to sink and the oil-laden ship was towed to the Thames Estuary. Mercifully the lack of U-boats prevented a severe onslaught upon the unarmed merchant men; old fashioned courtesies still existed but very much dependent on the nature of the commander. Others adhered to orders and put the safety of the boat first by remaining submerged and firing without warning.

During mid February the Foreign Secretary responded to American and international concerns over Britain's interception of German-bound non contraband goods. He reminded the world 'That we have maintained the principle that a belligerent should abstain from interference with foodstuffs intended for the civilian population. Despite being intended for civilian consumption, in times of emergency the military could requisition the food especially now the German Government have taken control of all foodstuffs in the country. The new conditions [the submarine blockade] themselves contrary to international law have compelled an abandonment of the treaty'[2]. He concluded his despatch with the following words:

The announcement by the German Government of their intention to sink merchant vessels and their cargoes without verification of their nationality or character and without making any provision for the safety of non combatant crews or giving them a chance of saving their lives has made it necessary for his Majestys' Government to consider what measures they should adopt to protect their interests. It is impossible for one belligerent to depart from rules and precedents and for the other to remain bound by them.

Britain waited until 1 March before announcing any retaliation against the German blockade aimed at preventing commodities of all kinds, including food

for the civilian population from reaching or leaving the British Isles or France. Anglo-French forces now aimed to prevent commodities of any kind from reaching or leaving the German Empire. The measures enforced by the British and French Governments were without risk to neutral ships or non-combatant lives. Both Governments agreed to detain and take into port ships carrying goods of presumed enemy destination, ownership or origin. This amounted to a blockade of German ports, which many considered should have been taken much earlier in the war. The British blockade caused serious problems with neutrals particularly America, but the friction would reduce considerably after a maritime disaster.

On 22 April Germany preceded an attack north of the Ypres sector with the release of chlorine gas. Described as the latest example of 'German frightfulness' it seemed Germany would employ whatever means necessary to attain victory; but a fortnight later Germany did the unthinkable. Despite the threat of submarine attack the Cunard liner Lusitania *continued to run between Liverpool and New York. Her passengers were assured the 'greyhound of the seas' could outrun any U-boat; besides Germany would gain nothing from the destruction of a vessel carrying neutral American passengers.*

While berthed in New York preparing for her 1 May departure a series of disturbing notices issued by the Imperial German Embassy, Washington, appeared in some of the American newspapers. Travellers were reminded that the waters adjacent to Great Britain were a war zone and vessels flying the flag of Britain or her allies were liable to destruction in those waters. Travellers sailing in the war zone do so at their own risk. Most of the prominent first-class passengers also received a telegram warning, 'Have it on definite authority *Lusitania* is to be torpedoed'. Hardly anyone was deterred by the threats: considered to be nothing more than bluster, the liner departed on schedule. After

Lusitania, 'Greyhound of the Seas' shortly after her arrival in New York.

crossing the Atlantic on a bright and sunny 7 May the Cunarder steamed along the south coast of Ireland. The vessel reduced speed to about eighteen knots so that she might arrive at Liverpool to coincide with the tide.

Captain Turner anxiously paced the bridge, for he knew submarines were reported in the area. Suddenly from the other end of the bridge came the cry 'There's a torpedo': Turner raced across to the starboard side in time to see the torpedo explosion. The torpedo struck just after 2.15 pm, fifteen minutes later the great liner sank in 310 feet of water. First-hand accounts claim a second torpedo exploded; it now seems accepted that this was due to the ignition of small-arms ammunition and detonators in the ship's cargo hold. There had been nearly 2,000 people onboard *Lusitania*, a number of Americans were among the 1,195 drowned. The sheer brutality and wanton disregard for life stunned the world and antagonised America. Despite this it would take two years before she abandoned her policy of neutrality.

The Dardanelles debacle

As an afterthought to the inept planning for the 25 April landings on the shores of Gallipoli, the casualty figures for the Battle of Mons were used to calculate the level of casualties expected in the early stages of the amphibious landings. The first major clash of the war resulted in 7.5 per cent of the 20,000 men involved being killed, wounded or missing presumed dead. In deference to expected difficulties facing them the expected casualties of the 75,000 French, British and Australian New Zealand Army Corps [ANZAC] of the Mediterranean Expeditionary Force [MEF] were calculated at the higher ratio of ten per cent. Two hospital ships, who between them had a capacity of only 700 patients, were assigned to evacuating the wounded to hospitals in Alexandria, Cairo or Malta. Events proved the arrangements to be woefully inadequate after the first three days fighting 2,500 of the MEF lay dead, a further 6,000 men were wounded. Two day's after the landing, while men suffered awaiting medical treatment the well-equipped hospital ship *Hindoo* rode at anchor off Cape Helles awaiting orders, blissfully unaware of the heavy casualties. Meanwhile the troops ashore packed boats with wounded, then rowed amongst the transport ships imploring them to take onboard the wounded. Some of the transports were designed to act on the return journey as hospital carriers, but when they had less than half of their quota of wounded on board were ordered to sail for Egypt. As they sailed over the horizon other vessels crammed with seriously wounded were denied permission to sail. Another transport laden with 1,600 patients including 300 severe cases departed for Alexandria; during the voyage four doctors worked ceaselessly to treat the multitude of patients.

Faced with the imminent collapse of the casualty evacuation system the Admiralty hastily despatched more hospital ships or carriers to the Aegean waters. Due to the shoal waters surrounding the barren peninsula, deep draught vessels had to lie off the coast. Their cargoes were discharged into lighters capable of operating in the shallows. After unloading their freight shore-side the lighters returned with the wounded laid out in rows upon their decks. The ill and wounded were either transferred to the transports or taken to a waiting hospital ship. The seriously debilitated were placed in shallow wooden trays, then hauled aboard by sheaths and rope onto the deck of the mercy ship. Off the beaches small hospital ships such as *Galeka* or *Sicilia* acted as medical reception centres for the soldiers and seamen. Once full they departed, allowing another hospital ship to take up station. Sixty miles from the peninsula lay the island of Lemnos which had a fine natural anchorage at Mudros. Around the fringe of the bay tented hospital units received lightly wounded casualties, while off shore rode the hospital ship *Oxfordshire*. The Bibby line ship remained for the duration of the campaign and stood off during the ANZAC withdrawal. As the casualties continued to escalate the locally established facilities proved inadequate. Within a couple of hours' steaming off the Dardanelles the hospital reached their maximum capacity and casualties were evacuated further afield. Larger vessels were drafted in to relieve the strain and by the end of June the total naval and military casualties arising from the Dardanelles campaign were 1,933 officers and 40,501 men.

In 1915, the hospital fleet absorbed a further forty-two vessels. The most likely explanation for the expansion would be the Dardanelles campaign and the late October commencement of the Salonika campaign. Due to the forbidding terrain and the determined Turkish defence of their homeland the Allied force made little headway in the Dardanelles. As a result space on the beachhead was at a premium and sufficiently close to the enemy front to be within artillery range. Due to the danger tented army hospital units were established on the fringes of neighbouring islands, requiring the constant ferrying to and fro of the sick and wounded. To alleviate the overworked smaller hospital ships the Admiralty requisitioned as hospital ships the ocean giants *Aquitania*, *Britannic* and *Mauretania*, between them the trio could carry over 9,500 casualties. The *Franconia* briefly served as an ambulance carrier ferrying over 1,600 Gallipoli casualties to Alexandria, Egypt. Merchant vessels desperately needed for imports were now assigned for aid at the Dardanelles where they acted as hospital ships often before they were painted white. Devoid of the standard white colour scheme these ships were generally referred to as 'black' ships as opposed to the 'white' ship label used throughout this particular campaign for a hospital ship.

The Aegean island of Imbros lay fifteen miles from the Anzac beachhead and a further two miles from Suvla Bay, the scene of a bungled and catastrophic August offensive. Between 9 and 11 August vessels including the *Clan MacGillivrah* drafted in as a hospital transport provided sterling service rescuing the Suvla Bay wounded. From the fly infested, shrapnel strewn battle zones a procession of white ships ferried the casualties to Imbros, effectively a halfway house where, after treatment, the casualties were graded on the severity of their injuries. Any patients deemed capable of recovery within four weeks were transferred to Lemnos approximately fifty miles away. Severe cases were evacuated by black ship from Lemnos to Egypt some 650 miles away or alternatively to Malta.

After the intial medical examination a nurse or orderly attached a card label to the button of the patient's pyjama jacket. Prominent on each label were the initials BL for boat-lying [cot cases] or BS for boat-sitting, effectively splitting patients into two primary categories. A broad red stripe alerted medics to look for dangerous symptoms, while red labels indicated the patient required careful observation during the voyage and required immediate attention on arrival.

Vessels such as *Simla* [II] and *Seang Choon* had their five minutes of fame here during these operations, their past glories being recalled on a faded hospital ship postcard; a typical 'white' ship being the *Seang Choon* purchased from her original owners the Bibby Line in 1910. Previously named the *Cheshire* she served in the South African war as a troopship. She was requisitioned from her new owners in 1915 as a British troopship taking troops to Gallipoli. After disembarking her troops she was converted to a hospital ship or carrier assigned to Anzac Cove. Approximately two dozen hospital ships and twenty assorted troopships and transports were involved in the Dardanelles theatre.

While anchored off the peninsula taking on casualties all the stationary liners were extremely vulnerable to attack: however, the enemy submarines despite being active in the region honoured the immunity of the hospital ships. About this time the enemy began to protest about Britain's misuse of her hospital ships, claiming they were being used to transport troops and munitions.

At Gallipoli several nations provided expeditionary forces including Australia and New Zealand, and any concerns over the fighting capabilities of ANZAC troops from the two fledgling commonwealth nations were soon dispelled. Apart from the military muscle provided by the ANZACs they provided hospital ships for the return of their wounded. The Australian hospital ships and carriers included *Grantala,* the first requisitioned Australian hospital ship, *Karanowna*, *Karoola*, *Wandilla* and the *Kyarra,* specially drafted in as a transport at Gallipoli. New Zealand provided the 5,282-ton *Maheno* and the 6,437-ton, twin-screw steamer *Marama*.

Britain condemned Germany for abandonment of the rules of cruiser warfare, yet brought about the abolition by the introduction of fresh orders guaranteed to fuel the fight between submariners and merchant men. Winston Churchill issued orders for all British merchant ships to paint out their names and port of registry, and to fly a neutral flag, preferably American, while operating in British waters. Ships' crew were ordered to treat captured submariners as criminals and

The *Maheno,* built by William Denny & Bros of Dumbarton. Served as a New Zealand hospital ship from May 1915 to June 1919.

deny them any rights usually accorded to prisoners of war. Mercantile captains were ordered to immediately engage the enemy either with their own armament or to ram any surfaced submarine. Any civilian captain not engaging the enemy or who chose to surrender his vessel would be prosecuted. The captains were now stuck between a rock and a hard place: they either risked capture by the enemy (who would try them as a *franc tireur*) or the British Government charge of cowardice in the face of the enemy. Unfortunately, in February a copy of the order was seized when the enemy boarded a steamer.

Men like Captain Charles Algernon Fryatt needed no further encouragement: his Tilbury ferry twice had encounters with U Boats. His vessel SS *Brussels* outran the first submarine and when challenged weeks later by a larger and more powerful U-boat, Fryatt attempted to ram it. It was forced to make an emergency crash-dive and when the submarine surfaced some distance away, it had a pronounced list. After returning safely to Tilbury the Admiralty recognised the bravery of Fryatt with the presentation of an engraved gold watch, and a congratulatory announcement in the House of Commons; the German Navy viewed matters differently.

Captain Charles Algernon Fryatt.

The following year on 22 June a flotilla of torpedo boats and destroyers captured the *Brussels* and crew. Fryatt was brought before a German military court where he stood accused as the *franc tireur* who attempted to ram *U33*. After a brief hearing he was found guilty; the sea captain was executed by firing squad. Master mariners now knew a similar fate awaited them if they engaged the enemy. Germany thought the execution would deter masters from putting out to sea, but they underestimated the courage and tenacity of the men and women of Britain's Mercantile Marine.

The *Baralong* incident

As the tally of Mercantile Marine vessels lost to submarines steadily rose, grave concerns were raised over Britain's capacity to defend herself, nevertheless take the war to the enemy. With sickening regularity vessels with their precious cargoes were sent to the bottom of the sea by enemy torpedoes, or mines. The more nimble merchant vessels did have a slender chance of escape by outrunning their surfaced attacker; unfortunately this option did not apply to the ponderously slow oil tanker. The nation began to arm her merchant ships and by July, some 250 steamers were armed or fitted to receive a gun. To preserve their non-belligerent status the weapons were fitted aft where they were of use only for defence, against an attacking or pursuing enemy. The arming of merchant vessels was not illegal, for until the end of the Napoleonic War merchant ships carried guns; the practice ceased after the 1856 Declaration of Paris abolishing privateering. Due to the sinking of inbound tankers and faced with an impending fuel crisis, the Admiralty imposed a speed restriction upon their modern oil-burning warships, except in an emergency. Ideally the Mercantile Marine should have received anti-submarine protection from British destroyers, yet the Admiralty had insufficient for their own fleet duties. To compensate for the shortfall in 1915, the navy procured an assortment of mercantile vessels for special duties. The mystery ships ranged from sailing ships to passenger cargo liners and add an interesting chapter to the war at sea.

These innocent looking civilian ships were manned by Royal Navy personnel charged with the task of luring enemy submarines within range of the vessels' concealed armament. These decoy or 'Q ships' as they were better known masqueraded as helpless merchant ships and those onboard were encouraged to take on the appearance of merchant navy sailors. Scruffy attire and unkempt hairstyles were encouraged the wearing of uniform and the saluting of officers no longer applied, to prevent alerting an observing belligerent submariner from guessing the craft's true role. A variety of other ruses all added to the deceptive appearances of both the ship and her highly trained naval crew. Initially the vessels were equipped with concealed four-inch guns, depth charges and under water torpedo ships were also added; yet outwardly the appearance of the vessel remained as innocuous as any of its peers.

The Q ships plied the seas, and in particular the slaughter zones of the Western Approaches, acting as live bait in an attempt to make contact with an enemy submarine, and lure the vessel to the surface. At this point in the conflict the U-boat generally surfaced alongside its victim whose commandant hailed the belligerent master announcing his intention; whereupon the ship's crew were granted time to evacuate the vessel prior to the enemy boarding their prize. Once onboard time-delayed explosive charges were placed in the bowels of the ship, rather than expend a precious torpedo. Submarines are at their most vulnerable upon the surface, but were not endangered by a defenceless merchantman, whose crew were generally more preoccupied with abandoning ship than futile resistance. Once a mystery ship lured a submarine alongside, the crew replicated the frequently panicky abandon ship procedure of their merchant navy counterparts. Throughout this ruse the hidden captain stealthily surveyed the submarine's position, as the gunners with their concealed armament tensely awaited the order to fire. Upon receiving the order, hinged bulwarks or large dummy cargo crates instantly dropped to the decks revealing the Q ship's firepower. When the guns roared into life the submarine received a broadside at point blank range, from which few survived. Inevitably a submarine survived to tell the tale of this *ruse de guerre*, thereby confirming German submarine losses were due to such clandestine ships and not mines as previously thought. The enemy now exercised extreme caution when approaching merchantmen, for they never knew if their target was a wolf dressed in sheep's clothing. With the safety of their own craft paramount, some enemy commanders understandably elected to remain submerged and sink their prey by torpedo without warning.

The Q ship tactic operated with intermittent success, destroying a dozen submarines, before the tactic of inviting attack proved to be too costly, both in lost tonnage and gallant seamen. Nonetheless, men like Commander Gordon Campbell added further illustrious chapters to the Royal Navy: Campbell being one of several 'mystery ship' recipients of Britain's premier gallantry award. Campbell received the Victoria Cross for the North Atlantic action of 21 April 1917, during which he deliberately turned his ship *Dunraven* [Q5] into the path of a torpedo; the disabled ship pumped forty-five shells into *UC71* before she took her final plunge, add to the great traditions of the Royal Navy. In direct contrast, the shameful '*Baralong* Incident' blemished the Admiralty reputation for fair play and provided the *Kaiserliche Marine* with an explanation for their lack of humanity at sea.

The controversial incident occurred on 19 August 1915, approximately one hundred miles south of Queenstown [Cobh] Southern Ireland and involved a 1901-built steamer, which originally belonged to the Ellerman and Bucknall Steam Ship Company. In 1914, she briefly served as a naval supply ship, the following year she underwent conversion to a mystery ship. The decoy ships continually changed their names and appearance; now known as the Q ship *Baralong* she masqueraded as the neutral *Ulysses S Grant*. While purporting to be an American tramp steamer, with the Stars and Stripes fluttering from her mast, she encountered the stationary 6,300-ton *Nicosian* with a surfaced enemy submarine astern.

The Leyland line cargo boat on the final leg of her voyage from New Orleans with a cargo of American munitions, fodder and 800 mules destined for the Western Front, had received orders from *U27* to halt. Doctor Charles B Banks of Memphis, Tennessee, a graduate of Harvard Veterinary School, described his experience on the cargo vessel:

> *The* Nicosian *left New Orleans on 28 July and all went well until 19 August when the ship was nearing the Irish Coast and all hands including the 800 mules were looking forward to landing within the next forty-eight hours.*

> *We were within a five hour run of the* Arabic *when she was sunk and we heard her wireless call for assistance, the call reaching us at 9-15 am, just one hour and five minutes after we had picked up the SOS call from the steamship* Dunsley. *At 11-15 am we had a similar call from the British steam ship* Baron Erskine [outward bound from New Orleans for Avonmouth carrying 900 mules. Sunk by shells from a U-boat] *At 2-30 pm we sighted a submarine about one mile ahead of us and almost immediately heard a shot, evidently a blank, calling us to stop. We started a wireless call for help, and then the submarine turned loose on us with shrapnel, the second shot tearing away our wireless apparatus. By this time the submarine was within sixty yards of us, and she gave our Captain twenty minutes to get the crew into the boats. The last boat, in which I took refuge with the Captain, was hardly clear of the ship when the submarine opened on the steamer with two guns, fully twenty shells striking the* Nicosian. *Fortunately only two found a mark below the water line...*

After granting the crew an opportunity to abandon ship by lifeboat, *Kapitanleutnant* Bernhard Wegener[3] onboard *U27* prepared to torpedo the *Nicosian.* Some accounts refer to a signal from the approaching bogus neutral steamer, requesting permission 'to save life only'; after affirming the signal the submariners expected the men in the lifeboats to be rescued.

The Q ship *Baralong* commanded by Lieutenant Godfrey Herbert, now within a short distance of *U27,* dropped the bulwark camouflage; seconds later almost three dozen shells pierced the submarine which rapidly sank. Eleven

A German postcard commemorating victims of the the British Q-ship *Baralong*.

submariners including the captain dived into the water, and struck out for the abandoned freighter, through a hail of small-arms fire. Five men survived the onslaught, and reached the deck of *Nicosian* which *Baralong* now came alongside. Herbert ordered a dozen Royal Marines led by Sergeant Collins to 'Get them all, take no prisoners'. The marines joined by crew members clambered aboard and commenced the manhunt with murderous intent. The unarmed submariners, already traumatised by the chain of events, attempted to conceal themselves or dived overboard. The helpless swimmers became target practice, and the sea became tinged with blood. Sporadic bursts of gunfire onboard the mule ship announced the discovery of another escapee. None of the Germans escaped the murderous mob who justified their orgy of death as a form of retribution for the sinking of merchant shipping. The entire incident was simply murder on the high seas.

The Daily Chronicle published the following, very carefully worded, account from an undisclosed gunner from the *Baralong:*

> *As soon as we appeared around the bows of the* Nicosian *the submarine fired one shot at us, which went wide. The marines then opened fire with a well aimed volley which swept the decks of the submarine and seemed to demoralise the crew, for they immediately left their guns and rushed for the conning tower, several going overboard, but whether they were shot by rifle fire or whether they dived over from panic I cannot say.*
>
> *We then opened fire with our port and stern guns, but the first shot hit short* [sic]. *However, I should say it hit the submarine below the water line. The next shot hit the conning tower, which appeared to be split in half, sending two men flying into the air. The next and successive shots all hit the submarine which gradually sank, every one of her crew being either drowned or shot, and only a few parts of bodies and a large quantity of oil remained on the surface.*
>
> *The action lasted four and a half minutes during which time we fired thirty-seven rounds between the two guns. We then took on board the crew of the* Nicosian *who numbered 107, not one of them was killed or wounded. Our casualties were nil.*

The cargo of logs in the holds of *Nicosian* possibly prevented her sinking. The Q ship took her in tow and at 2.30 the next morning she was relieved by tugs sent out from Queenstown.

After the Admiralty received Herbert's report, they immediately ordered suppression of the shameful affair. [The Admiralty prohibited public access to the '*Baralong* File' for fifty years. It became accessible only after the death of Herbert.] Commander Herbert claimed he issued the order to fire on the escapers, as he feared they may attempt to scuttle the vessel. The explosive charges may already have been in place prior to the arrival of *Baralong*, perhaps the enemy were caught in the act of scuttling but we can only speculate. Extremely dark deeds were committed inside the steamer, and disturbing rumours still circulate. The Admiralty threatened the officers and crew of the vessels involved with dire consequences if they discussed the affair with non-participants. However, after returning to America the appalled mule drivers, who had witnessed the incident from their lifeboats, informed the American press of the British flagrant misuse of the American flag, while murdering unarmed German sailors.

Germany formally complained through American diplomatic channels, and demanded the captain of the Q ship be tried for murder. Britain dismissed the charges, alleged to have been committed on a highly charged day when eight British steamers were sunk in the Western Approaches. In addition, they defended the act as an 'operational necessity', absurdly claiming the Germans may have armed themselves, and escaped on the *Nicosian*. Accounts do refer to a quantity of rifles stored on the ships bridge, but if the escapers had armed themselves with the weapons, how could they escape? Had the vessel begun to make headway the auxiliary cruiser would have blown the unarmed *Nicosian* out of the water. Instead they suggested the incident should be investigated by impartial American naval officers, who could also arbitrate on three similar incidents involving German naval vessels, all occurring within a forty-eight-hour period of the '*Baralong* Affair'.

Due to the American protests over the sinking of the *Lusitania* Germany suspended unrestricted submarine warfare on 1 September, having already sunk some 750,000 tons of Allied and neutral shipping. Two days later the crew of the Q ship had heard the distress calls from the 15,801 gross tonnage White Star passenger liner *Arabic*. Her voyage from New York to Liverpool terminated off the Old Head of Kinsale, when the torpedo from *U24* impacted. Forty-four lives were lost in the sinking, including two neutral American civilians. On the same day, the British submarine *E13* stranded on a Baltic sandbank was remorselessly shelled by two German destroyers who failed to offer the crew an opportunity to surrender or escape. The shelling continued, until Danish torpedo boats positioned themselves in the line of fire; but not before fifteen sailors died. The third incident referred to occurred two days later, when the German submarine *U38* captured and sank by gunfire, the Turnbull Brothers' collier-transport *Ruel*. Once her crew abandoned ship, the submersible's crew machine-gunned the crowded lifeboats, killing the captain and seriously wounding seven others.

Germany refused the British proposals, replying that all three cases were competently investigated by German authorities. The naval forces intended only to destroy hostile ships, and in no way slay helpless persons who were attempting to save their lives. The assertions to the contrary of the British Government must be repudiated with all decisiveness as untrue. Some time later a series of reprisal Zeppelin raids were launched against London and the east coast due to the *Baralong* murders: Germany announced 'no consideration would be given to the deaths of innocent civilians'.

On 24 September 1915, the *Baralong*, now under a different commander but still sailing under the Stars and Stripes, lured the submarine *U41* within range of her weaponry. A broadside of shells disabled the submarine, whose crew rapidly abandoned the sinking vessel. Two wounded survivors reached a lifeboat belonging to *Urbino,* a vessel they sank earlier, and managed to haul themselves aboard. After a while a ship approached, unfortunately for the survivors it was the *Baralong* which steered directly towards the lifeboat. As the bows loomed above the lifeboat both men flung themselves overboard and were sucked under the surface by the vessel's wash. The bow wave had tossed the lifeboat clear of the steamer hull and both seriously weakened men returned to her dubious safety, only to see their attacker returning. This time *Baralong* hove to, both men were hauled onboard and detained in a sheep pen which was open to the elements. There was little sympathy for the prisoners whose vessel, within the previous forty-eight hours, had claimed four merchant ships. As neither of the men failed to succumb to their wounds Sergeant Collins was ordered to shoot them if they were still alive by midnight. He refused the order and both men were transferred to a trawler and taken ashore to be interrogated.

The Admiralty now faced with a second *Baralong* incident, stalled all attempts to have the wounded men repatriated to Germany; nonetheless one of the prisoners informed the German section of the American Embassy of the latest abuse of the American flag. Britain had adopted the moral high ground in her war against the so-called 'pirates' of the German submarines but recent events showed her to be as ruthless as her opponent. The American newspapers now published first-hand accounts provided by the *Nicosian* mule drivers, [who included a millionaire's son, and the sons of a banker and a clergyman in pursuit of adventure] which were eagerly read, especially by her eight million German America citizens. Germany found herself presented with a rare gift of sensational propaganda and played her ace for all it was worth. The story broke at a time of heightened diplomatic protests by America to Germany, providing another reason for the anti-war lobby to avert a national call to arms. Had American with her vast resources joined the fray in 1915, the Great War would have been considerably shorter perhaps the *Baralong* atrocity helped condemn the world to three more years of bloodshed.

The loss of HMT *Marquette*

The advance contingent of the British Salonika Force arrived in Greece in early October 1915; the now almost forgotten campaign lasted for three dismal years. During the interim numerous hospital ships traversed to and fro recovering the sick and wounded. The hospital ships became regular visitors to Salonika, for the non-battle casualties of the British Force ultimately amounted to 481,262;

of this number some 162,517 service personnel succumbed to malaria.[4]

At the port of Alexandria, Egypt, the 552-bed hospital ship *Grantully Castle* prepared to sail for Salonika, [now Thessaloniki], being scheduled to leave on the same day as the transport ship *Marquette*. The latter ship belonged to the Atlantic Transport Company, but the 7,057 gross registered tonnage vessel was requisitioned as a troopship the previous year. On 19 October, HMT *Marquette* cleared Alexandria laden with a vaguely described Government cargo of stores and ammunition.

In reality the cargo consisted of approximately two dozen officers and over 500 other ranks of the British 29th Division Ammunition Column, plus their ammunition wagons, horses and also hundreds of army mules. The staff of the Number One New Zealand Stationary Hospital were also onboard, comprising eight officers, nine non-commissioned officers and seventy-seven other ranks [inclusive of thirty-six nurses]. When the crew are included she is reputed to have carried some 740 souls onboard.

The troop ship left Alexandria escorted by the four funnelled French destroyer *Tirailleur*, across the Mediterranean into the Aegean Sea. On the fourth day of the voyage, once darkness descended, the destroyer left the troopship. The next morning as *Marquette* neared Platanona Point, some thirty miles south of Salonika, she steamed into periscope view of *U35* commanded by *Kapitanleutnant* Waldemar Kophamel. The submariner crew sprang into well-rehearsed activity, and within seconds a torpedo surged from the submarine towards the troopship. The torpedo exploded at 9.15 am, within a few minutes she developed a list to port and the Aegean Sea soon lapped over the bows of *Marquette*: in less than fifteen minutes she would plunge to the sea bed. Onboard the angle of her tilting decks severely hampered the lowering of the lifeboats, as the davits jammed the descending lifeboat occupants were precipitated into the sea. Those who did not drown remained in the water for roughly eight hours, during which many succumbed to hyperthermia due to the winter temperature of the sea. The survivors were rescued by the destroyers HMS *Lynn* and the French destroyers *Mortier* and *Tirailleur*. The death toll of the West Hartlepool registered ship comprised some 167 nurses, officers and men from New Zealand and Britain nine of the nurses onboard died. A Royal Naval minesweeper discovered a tenth victim in a drifting lifeboat. The deceased, Staff Nurse Margaret Rogers, was identified by her name engraved upon her watch, a practice common with nurses. She received a military funeral and lies in Mikra British Cemetery near Salonika.

Despite the tragic loss of the troopship, the hospital ship *Grantully Castle* reached Salonika safely. Had the New Zealand medical staff and their equipment travelled on the hospital ship they would have reached Salonika without mishap. Perhaps the sinking highlighted the unwarranted risk of sending non-combatants abroad in vessels which were *bona fide* targets, while outward-bound hospital ship accommodation lay vacant. It is possible due to the sinking of the *Marquette*, that the Admiralty decided to ship outward-bound medical stores and personnel via hospital ship to the theatres of war. The decision stretched the legal definitions of the Geneva Convention admittedly the hospital ships were still being used to alleviate the suffering of the sick, but the decision gave Germany viable grounds for protest over the misuse of hospital ships.

The rise and fall in demand for hospital ships reflected the military strategies or more accurately the butcher's bill arising from each fresh assault or campaign. When an unexpected casualty rate arose additional vessels were requisitioned to augment the existing fleet of hospital ships. Unfortunately the conversion of a suitable commercial vessel to a fully equipped hospital ship took a minimum of five weeks, depending on the work content and the limited availability of the specialist hospital equipment. Added to equipment shortages the graving docks and shipyards were already under considerable pressure to increase productivity in warship production and replacement mercantile vessels. In addition the maintenance and dry-docking requirements of the 8,000 British vessels operating to and fro on the high seas further restricted the availability of the skilled labour and dock facilities. It therefore became imperative to minimise the amount of ships requiring dockyard services to alleviate the pressure on the overburdened facilities.

As a shortfall measure to emergent demands troop transports were used on their return voyages to evacuate the wounded. Known as hospital carriers, they were modified to make the most of the existing fittings and were generally adapted in around nine days, significantly less time than a hospital ship.

As an example in the difference of the two classes of vessel, consider the *Kildonan Castle* which entered service as a hospital carrier on 6 October 1915 until 20 May the following year. During her conversion her saloons were cleared of tables and all unnecessary furniture and replaced with double tier beds. Any

The *Neuralia* later became an armed ambulance transport.

vacant spaces were fitted with beds or cots, boosting her capacity to some 600 patients; all the remaining cabins were left in situ for the use of the less seriously wounded or sick. On a hospital ship all the cabins, bar those used by the staff, would have been removed to allow partition into suitable hospital wards. Preparation and operating theatres were fitted, as were laundries and where possible cot lifts were fitted. Apart from the wards she and other carriers differed from a hospital ship as they usually lacked proper pantries fitted with hot presses, sterilisers and a full range of equipment.

The majority of the hospital ships diligently served their country without making sensational headlines. The 9,182 gross registered tonnage British India Steamship *Neuralia* served as a 630-patient hospital ship, from 12 June 1915 until the final day of August 1919; her five minutes of fame occurred in 1915. It was a fine day as the British transport *Southland* made passage through the Mediterranean, laden with Australian reinforcements for the Dardanelles. When the trooper was within sight of Strati Island, approximately forty miles from Mudros, she was torpedoed abaft of the main mast, killing some of those onboard. Two of her forward compartments merged into one with a thirty foot [9 metre] gaping hole in her side, her chances of survival initially appeared slender, yet despite the crisis all onboard remained calm. The lifeboats were swung out in an orderly and methodical fashion, and the shipwrecked men embarked. Meanwhile her wireless distress calls were picked up by HMHS *Neuralia* who quickly arrived on the scene. She had a Lascar crew of seamen and firemen, and such was their eagerness, they almost came to blows in their anxiety to save life from what appeared to be a sinking ship. The hospital ship lowered her boats and rowed across to the troopship now surrounded by her own lifeboats. As the empty boats approached, the *Southland* boats parted to allow them swift access to the stricken vessel. Approximately 470 men were transferred to the boats of *Neuralia*; unfortunately the incident claimed twenty-two lives. Three men were killed immediately by the explosion, the remainder died when one of the life rafts capsized. The *Southland* did reach Mudros, where on completion of temporary repairs, she headed back to Britain.

The 1912-built *Neuralia* survived the war; during the Second World War the vintage liner again served her country, acting as a troopship. A survivor of the Utah and Omaha beach landings, her luck finally expired off Southern Italy, when she struck a mine and sank on 1 May 1945.

HMHS *Anglia* and the lesser-known *Lusitania*

At the dawn of the twentieth century, W Denny, the Dumbarton shipbuilders completed their latest vessel, yard number six hundred and nineteen. Her owners, the London and North Western Railway Company, named the 1,862-ton vessel *Anglia*. The vessel, some 329 feet long, had a beam [width] of thirty-nine feet, driven by a 424-horsepower, triple expansion engine. Her twin screws

Anglia in fleet livery when serving on the Irish Sea run.

propelled *Anglia* along at a decent speed of twenty-one knots. The popular passenger vessel travelled between Holyhead and North Wall, Dublin. Within days of the declaration of war, the Admiralty commissioned *Anglia* as an armed boarding steamer, now equipped with three guns of six-pounder calibre. She fulfilled this role until late April 1915, then underwent transformation to a hospital ship. Internally the vessel's accommodation would have received a rudimentary makeover, however her outward appearance altered significantly. The hospital ship hulls were painted white from stem to stern; just below the deck level ran a wide green band, only interrupted at intervals by huge painted red crosses. The hospital ship livery also required the upper works to be white. Instantly recognisable as a non-combatant hospital ship, each vessel sailed under the protective shield of the Geneva Convention.

During November 1915, King George V had an accident during a visit to the Western Front; *Anglia* had the honour of bringing home the King. She briefly rose to prominence due to her royal passenger; the monarch was fortunate for later that month a disaster befell the hospital ship.

The vessel, commanded by Captain Lionel John Manning with a crew predominately from Anglesey, departed from Boulogne on a mercy mission with about 400 wounded officers and men onboard; many of whom were cot cases. On 17 November 1915, as the vessel steamed towards Dover at 1230 hours, she hit a mine laid by the submarine *UC5* one mile east of Folkestone Gate. The

Series of photographs of the sinking of HMHS *Anglia*.

detonation ruptured the hull on the starboard side forward. A crew member of *Lusitania,* a passing London collier, outward-bound for Cadiz noted:

> *After the explosion the bows of the hospital ship seemed to melt away until the sea lapped her rails and splashed the decks. Mortally wounded as she was, the* Anglia *surged forward in a vain attempt to reach the shore before she sank. Her siren roused every vessel near, and from every quarter came boats to the rescue. Those watching from the decks of the* Lusitania *saw soldiers coming up from below and assemble on the deck, calmly waiting for the order to pass into the boats. Every moment their footing became more precarious as gradually the* Anglia *settled by the bows.*

Rifleman W Kenyon, 5th King's Liverpool. Resided in Seacombe, Cheshire, he enlisted on the day war was declared. He went to France in February 1915, became ill in March and was away from his regiment until 20 May, returning just after the charge at Festubert. He participated in the charge at Loos, on 25 September. After falling ill on 16 October, he was invalided home on 17 November on board HMHS *Anglia*, where he had a narrow escape from death.

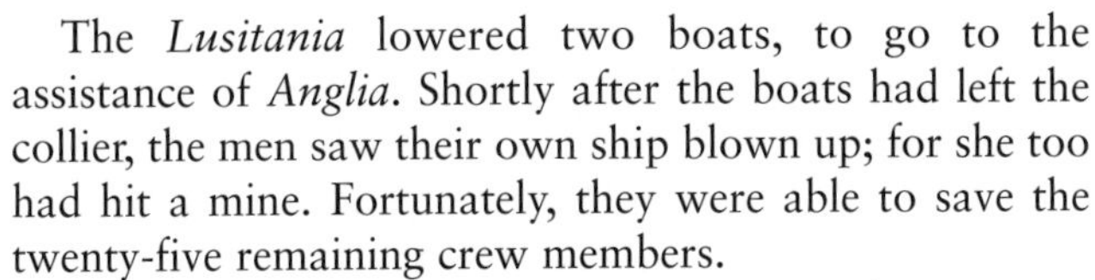

The *Lusitania* lowered two boats, to go to the assistance of *Anglia.* Shortly after the boats had left the collier, the men saw their own ship blown up; for she too had hit a mine. Fortunately, they were able to save the twenty-five remaining crew members.

Rescuers raced to HMHS *Anglia* whose stern continued to raise; as it rose, the vessel heeled over to starboard, as if about to turn turtle. Due to the ingress of the sea, the engine room had to be abandoned. Her twin screws continued to rotate, the port propeller drove her forward, albeit in a circle due to the list; this added considerably to the difficulties of the rescuers. Meanwhile the starboard propeller, now clear of the water, raced high in the air. A rescue boat passed beneath this flailing propeller, and rescued forty men, but of these two died before reaching the shore. Some of the wounded, unable to retain their footing, slipped into the sea, from which they were snatched by sailors who jumped overboard to help in the rescue. The crew worked selflessly supported by the nurses who worked with great devotion to transfer the wounded to safety. When the nurses were asked to go to the boats they refused, instead they suggested 'Fighting men first'. One nurse remained below bandaging the stretcher cases. She would not leave the ship but sat with the wounded. There were about eighty stretcher cases that had arms or legs off, and could not help themselves; they perished with the steamer. One of the survivors, Rifleman William Kenyon of the 5th King's Liverpool Regiment, stated during an interview that four nurses and a matron were onboard; only the matron and two nurses were saved.

The majority of the survivors were rescued by the four-funnelled British destroyer *Ure*, who due to her twelve-foot draft, at one point sailed over the submerged bows to rescue survivors. The River-class destroyer then transferred the survivors to the Submarine Depot ship HMS *Hazard*[5], whose size prevented her coming too close. It was a timely rescue, for *Anglia* sank within fifteen minutes of striking the mine. The end came with dramatic suddenness. With wounded soldiers, nurses, doctors, and sailors clinging to the stern, the *Anglia* seemed for one brief moment to stand on her bows, and then she disappeared. Contemporary accounts vary on the death toll of the 350 men onboard; the initial figure of eighty-five dead rose to 124 lost. When the dead bodies of some of the wounded soldiers, wrapped in the Union Flag, were landed from a small boat, they caused a great deal of distress and sorrow. Also visible from the shore were two masts of the *Anglia*, with the hospital flag still flying six feet above the surface. The war grave classified wreck of *Anglia* still lies in eighty feet of water. A member of the Church Lads Brigade gave the following graphic account of his experience:

> *I was aboard the hospital ship* Anglia. *We left Boulogne at 11 a.m., and all went well until we sighted the cliffs of Dover. It was then 12.40 p.m. About a minute later a very loud explosion occurred. We knew what that meant. Everybody did what they ought not to have done: run about and do all sorts of things. Meanwhile the ship took a very nasty tilt as the front part was already under water. Everybody rushed for the boats, but alas! They did not know how to manipulate one until two of the seamen went up, and lowered one full. There was a bad swell on at the time, so half of them were tipped out into the water. As far as I remember, only one boat lowered. Coming towards us at full speed was a gunboat. She ran right alongside of us, and some of the lucky ones managed to jump on to her as she went by. She came back, and floated about twenty or thirty yards away, and anybody who could swim, struck out to it. Of course, many of us could not swim, so we stuck to the ship, and watched those who could. The ship gave another nasty tilt, and she now had her stern high in the air. Well, I managed to get a lifebelt, and slipped this on. I thought if I could not swim, I would float. It was a terrible sight to see the wounded men crawling up the gangway on to the deck, lying there to go down with the ship, some with legs off, and others with arms off. We could not help them. As luck would have it, I saw many lifebelts in a cabin, so I started giving these out to them. Meanwhile, another boat had come quite close, and started picking some up. She managed to save quite a lot, when, just as she was breaking all records, up she went. In my opinion, we were both torpedoed.*
>
> *Well, I stuck to the old ship, and she gradually started to go down, foot*

HMHS *Anglia*.

> *by foot. Up came a great big wave, and this polished her off – also me for the time being. What a sensation, all my breath was squeezed out of my body, and I gave myself up. Down, down, down – what a depth, and how I did struggle! It seemed years! At last, I came up, caught half a breath, and clung to a floating box. I was then dashed against an upturned boat, and almost let go of my box. I had lost my lifebelt. Wave upon wave came, and absolutely drowned me. Well, I kept hold as long as I could, but my strength was gradually giving way. I was almost giving way when something banged my head, and I was grasped by the hair and lifted up, and then someone else collared hold of me, and between them they got me into the boat, and I don't remember anything until we landed back at the gunboat. I managed to struggle up the gangway, and they carried me down into the mess-room. I very soon got into a blanket after being rubbed down, and am now very much at home in hospital.*

The ship's master Captain Manning, who resided at 4, Lemand Street, Hoylake, Cheshire gave evidence during the inquest into the death of Richard Roberts, the chief steward of HMHS *Anglia*. He stated in his evidence that there were nearly 500 on board, including 160 cot cases and 200 walking wounded. The explosion took forward of the bridge on the port side. He was on the bridge, which was blown to smithereens, and he was thrown onto the lower deck. He ran to the wireless room to send out an SOS signal but met with the operator with his face all covered in blood. He indicated to the witness that the machinery had been destroyed. He then assisted to get a boat clear full of people. The vessel had a nasty list, and was down by the head in a sinking

Nurses helping the wounded to abandon ship.

condition. He was picked up from the sea unconscious. He thought the ship went down in twenty minutes and was of the opinion she had struck a mine. The cot cases included men without arms, legs and feet, and many of them must have perished. They received every assistance from all vessels in the vicinity, whom he wanted to thank.

The captain had received a severe bruise on the right thigh, and his left ankle and his wrist were sprained. The jury expressed their deep sympathy with those onboard. They returned a verdict of 'Death from drowning due to the sinking of the ship following an explosion'.

Prior to military service Rowland Darlington served in the Garston section of the Liverpool Police Force. A keen member of the Garston swimming club, he could never have foreseen how invaluable his aquatic exercise would be. While serving at the front with 6th Siege Battery Royal Garrison Artillery he received wounds serious enough to merit hospitalisation in England.

> *I am now doing well. I was wounded on the 10th instant, the wound in my right thigh being so serious that I had to undergo two operations on the 12th and 13th. On the 16th I was a cot patient on the ill fated hospital ship* Anglia. *I was as helpless as a kitten, having a couple of pounds of meat out my thigh, and being very weak through loss of blood. I was nearly done for. I crawled up the gangway and climbed over the rail, and then fell into the water and swam for a torpedo boat of which there were many about. Needless to say the gallant tars did their utmost for all of us. If it had not been for the gallant navy none of us would have survived.*

Some members of the crew of HMHS *Anglia* arrived at Holyhead on Friday 19 November. With the exception of two Liverpool survivors, those listed below resided on the island of Anglesey.

LJ Manning, Valley, captain.

RH Horner, 20 Maesbyfryd Road, chief officer.

Geo. N Thomas, Plashyfryd Terrace, second officer.

Owen Price, 1 Armenia Street, third officer.

Geo. Bagnall, 4 Foundry Street, boatswain.
William Williams, 13 Mill Bank, quartermaster.
H Pierce, Maeshytryd Road, second engineer.
H Williams, Valley, Holyhead, fourth engineer.
Owen Roberts, Bartville, Holyhead, leading stoker.
TH Meakin, 28, Porthyfelin, electrician.
Douglas T Rockey, 22 Holborn Road, wireless operator.
R Jones, 43 Station Street, seaman.
R Roberts, 10 Well Street, seaman.
John Roberts, 16 Harp Street, seaman.
Robert Evans, 19 Gilbert Street, seaman.
John Higgins, London Road, seaman.
Hugh McKevitt, 5 Galton Street, Liverpool, seaman.
John Williams, seaman.
Edw. Williams, Holborn Road, fireman.
Roland Griffiths, Benthwfa, fireman.
RJ Jones, Field Street, fireman.
W Smithson, 44 Rokeby Street, Liverpool, fireman.
J Jones, Ty Du, fireman.
W Williams, Church Lane, trimmer.
M Fennelly, Cross Street, steward.
John T Hughes, Maeshyfryd Road, steward.
Rich. Thomas, Station Street, steward.
Hugh Thomas, 10 Leonard Street, steward.
W. Bagnall, 4 Foundry Street, cook.
W Hughes, 28 Henry Street, carpenter.

In the aftermath of the sinking, the First Lord of the Admiralty received from Lord Stamfordham the following telegram:

> *The King is shocked to hear that the hospital ship* Anglia, *which so recently conveyed his Majesty across the Channel has been sunk by a mine. His Majesty is aggrieved at the loss incurred, and trusts that the survivors have not unduly suffered from the terrible exposure to which they must have been subjected. Please express the King's heartfelt sympathy with the families of those who have perished.*

After the demise of the hospital ship the *Daily Mail* advised readers that the mine may have been laid by one of the German submarines or by some suborned neutral vessel. It was no doubt to prepare the world for such an episode that last Friday the German wireless published a report that British hospital ships were being used for the conveyance of troops and munitions of war. The tale was entirely false, but the circulation of such falsehoods indicates a German intention to attempt a new variety of foul play. It would not be the first time that such an outrage has been committed. So far back as February a German submarine deliberately fired a torpedo at the British hospital ship *Asturias*.

Considering the magnitude of the tragedy it seems crassly insensitive to capitalise on such an event, but that is precisely what a leading hot drinks purveyor did. A pen and ink drawing in a newspaper advert depicted the stricken vessel and traumatised survivors above a statement from an alleged survivor:

> *We were just wondering how long it would be before we reached 'Blighty', someone said 'Oh about half an ...'. The sentence was never finished. There was a sound of iron, wood, china and glass being wrenched and crushed like a frail toy in the hands of a giant. We all climbed as best we could to the parts of the ship highest out of the water.*
>
> *The* Anglia *was going down quickly. I could see the side of the ship disappearing inch by inch. I was fixing on a lifebelt in the middle of the deck when I heard a shout. I walked to the side and saw two or three ships close to hand; they seemed to have risen out of the water.*
>
> *When we got onboard we were given dry clothes in exchange for our wet ones, also a cup of hot Bovril. The Bovril was a Godsend. It went right through me like the warmth from a fire. Personally I am sure most of us would have suffered severely from the cold and exposure if it hadn't been for a timely cup of Bovril.*

Some time later, the villainous *UC5* ran aground on a sandbank off Harwich; she betrayed her position by issuing a series of distress calls. The following day the destroyer *Firedrake* captured the submarine, which was subsequently towed to the Thames[6].

Precisely four months after the disaster the *London Gazette* reported the King graciously conferred the decoration of the Red Cross on the undermentioned ladies in recognition of their valuable services and devotion to duty on the loss of the hospital ship *Anglia* on 17 November 1915.

> Royal Red Cross 1st Class. Queen Alexandra's Imperial Military Nursing Service [Retired List] Mrs M S Mitchell, Acting Matron.
>
> Royal Red Cross 2nd Class. Miss A Meldrum [Sister]. Miss E A Walton [Staff Nurse].

The total British casualties on all fronts up to 9 December were announced as 528,227. As the year drew to a close preparations commenced for the

The German *UC5* minelayer, a fairly new submarine. It is believed she made twenty trips across the North Sea, and laid about 240 mines.

Not the best of omens for the troops queuing to board a transport moored alongside the hospital ship *Aquitania*.

withdrawal of all Allied troops from the Gallipoli peninsula. Government statistics for the Dardanelles campaign up to 11 December were 11,921 casualties. A gradual reduction in troop numbers now began, and during what transpired to be the only well-managed operation of the entire campaign, on the nights of 19 and 20 December the remaining troops were spirited away under the cover of darkness. In the ten days preceding the evacuation almost 84,000 patients from the Suvla and ANZAC beachheads were taken by ship to the isles

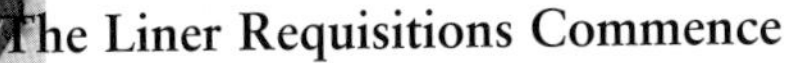

of Imbros and Lemnos. The Cape Helles contingent on the extreme tip of the peninsula departed on 8 to 9 January. The Government announced on 23 December the total Dardanelles casualties up to 11 December were 11,921.

The United States Government had protested during November on Britain's policy of directing friendly vessels into port to facilitate the search for suspected contraband cargoes. The practice involved a considerable delay for shipping as a standard search of a large liner carrying 500 passengers and cargo, by a trained unit of ten officers and twenty men, could take up to eighteen hours. The American objection caused hostility in Britain, amid concerns of American attempts to prevent our naval blockade. In response Britain explained for vessels to remain stationary for the long period required for an intensive search, while in water patrolled by enemy submarines, invited an attack. For this reason the vessels were directed to port. The Foreign Secretary Sir Edward Grey replied:

> *...I am convinced the real question is not of legal niceties of contraband and other things, but whether we are to do what we are doing or nothing at all. The contentions of your Government would restrict our operations in such a way that Germany would evade them wholesale, and they would be mere paper rights, quite useless in practice. ...As it is, it looks as if the United States might now strike the weapon of sea power out of our hands, and thereby ensure a German victory.*

There were also growing concerns over a rumoured American proposal guaranteed to upset Britain.

Notes

1. On 31 January the Admiralty advised shipping companies that the raising of a neutral flag was a recognised *ruse de guerre* previously adopted in distant conflicts, and not contrary to any international law, providing no act of aggression was committed under cover of the flag.
2. The 1909 Declaration of London which the Government announced on the outbreak of war as the basis of maritime practice. Their release was aided by Germany's action.
3. During his ten patrols Wegener sank twenty-nine ships totalling 29,402 tons.
4. These figures are according to: The History of the Great War Medical Services: Casualties and Medical Statistics of the Great War [HMSO, London, 1931].
5. In 1918 HMS *Hazard* sank due to a collision, four crew died.
6. The minelayer German submarine *UC5* was captured on the east coast in April 1916; she had just laid two mines when a British destroyer captured her. To prevent damage by the two mines a torpedo lieutenant attired in a diver's suit made the mines safe by removing the detonators. She became a great attraction; the Admiralty used her for propaganda purposes within this country and America.

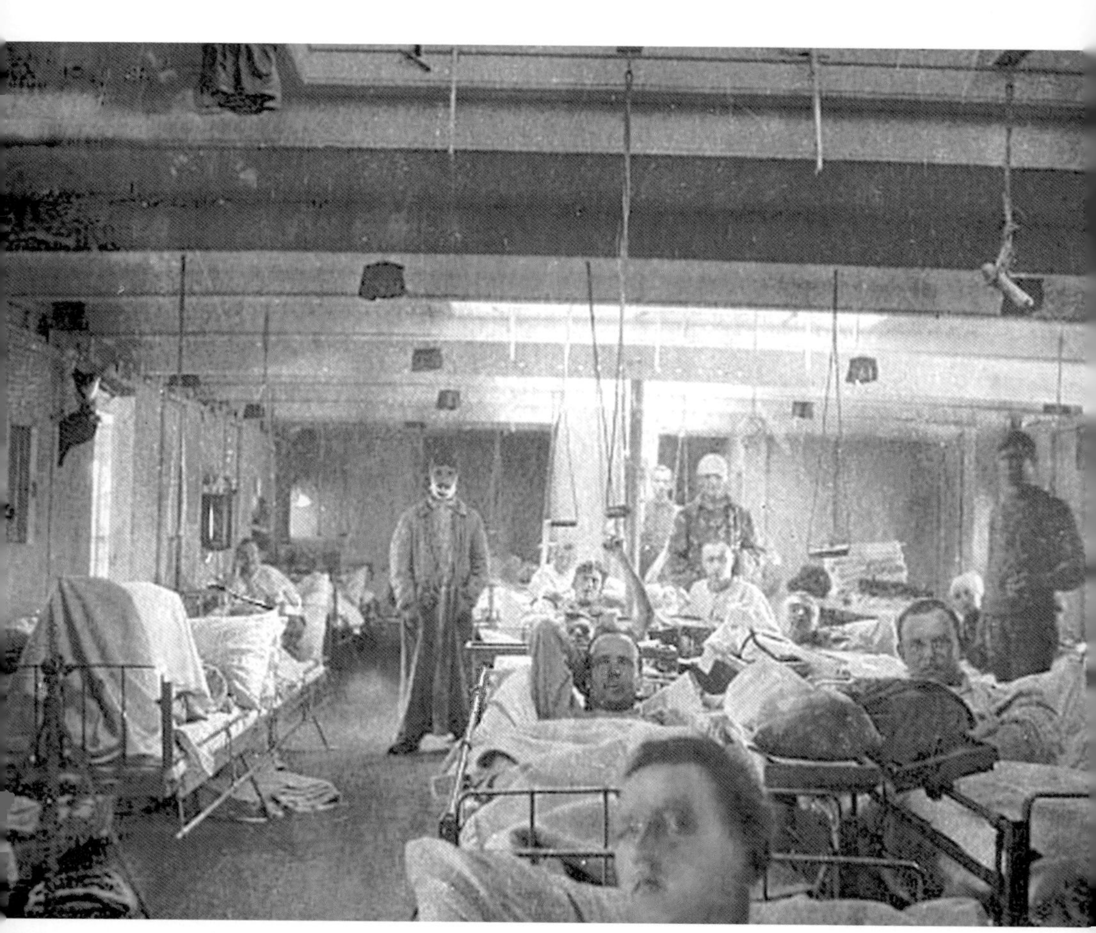

Wounded Tommies in a British hospital ship.

Chapter Three
1916. High profits and Substantial Losses

The Hospital Ship

Wonderful and white, she steameth up the river,
Radiant and silent, amid those of murky grey,
Bearing her freight of men – transformed forever,
White Ship – symbolic of a breaking day.

Snatched from grim death, she brings the brave who battled,
Helpless and maimed, but never vanquished quite!
Out of red storms, that roared and hissed and rattled,
Homeward in peace – from the torment and the fight!

Fearlessly she faces all the foes that threaten,
Proudly gleams her light, athwart the haunted sea,
For she carries that which never can be beaten.
The spirit- reborn – of great things yet to be.

Signed with the cross. In our own midst uplifted.
That crucified afresh the new soul shall arise,
Welding all peoples, ignorant and gifted,
Indissolubly one, in a world sacrifice.

Another ship there is – an unknown ocean,
On which our brave so fearlessly embark,
Symbolic ship of death and grand devotion,
The one 'white thing' – amid the dreadful dark!

Our living ship we greet – with no word spoken.
God's ship of death is passed – out of our sight.
But glory floods the heart that grief has broken.
Hailing our ship – so wonderful and white!

Winifred A Cook, March 1918.

President Woodrow Wilson.

In mid-January President Woodrow Wilson issued a note proposing the Allies should disarm their merchant ships if Germany agreed to adhere to the recognised practice of 'cruiser' warfare against all merchant shipping. This required a submarine to surface, and halt the vessel which should not be sunk until those onboard had escaped to the relative safety of lifeboats. The President hoped Germany would revert to the fundamental principles of maritime law and humanity. The Allies were expected to surrender their maritime right of defence. America hinted if the Entente Powers failed to embrace the proposal they would treat armed merchant steamers arriving in American ports as auxiliary cruisers subject to detention. As a safeguard Britain ensured their armed merchant ships avoided American ports until the autumn. Nonetheless, it became a game of bluff and counter-bluff for the Allies doubted America would implement the threat, for they needed the services of British ships to maintain their healthy cross-Atlantic trade. Both the German military and naval authorities interpreted the Wilson despatch as an indication of retaliatory measures against the British blockade. Buoyed by mistaken support from the United States, the Imperial German Navy announced on 8 February a resumption of 'intensive' submarine warfare; passenger traffic was to sail unmolested, but armed merchant ships were to be sunk on sight. Furthermore through diplomatic circles American passengers were to be discouraged from travelling on armed merchant steamers.

The total British tonnage lost in the preceding year was 997,992 tons, and our shipbuilding output in the same year was only 650,000 tons, as against an output of 1,360,000 tons in 1914. The British loss of ships of more than 500 tons each was increased by submarines, mines and other enemy devices to 317 vessels. In addition to the German submarine campaign in home waters and the Mediterranean, there were many fires and explosions in vessels bound from

HMHS *Soudan seen here in the Grand Harbour, Malta.*

North and South Africa to Europe. During the war 321 British vessels and 212 foreign vessels were sunk by German agency, but there were heavy losses from incendiary fires, which accounted for much of the grand annual loss of 726 vessels of 500 tons gross register and upwards (of the value of nearly thirty million pounds). To summarise, the losses of British and neutral shipping in 1915 exceeded 1,800,000 tons, while the heaviest loss in any year before the war was 500,000 tons. And as our shipbuilding industry was diverted by war conditions to the making of munitions and the construction of warships, the losses which would have been made good in normal times became very serious.[1]

A shortage of labour, caused by the wholesale enlistment of men for Kitchener's Army, considerably delayed the unloading of ships in United Kingdom ports. A steamer which in peacetime took an average of three days to unload might now take up to three weeks. The delays reduced the Mercantile Marine cargo-carrying capacity by almost one third. The 2,000 steamers in Naval and Army employment added to the shortage of vessels available for trade use. As the submarine campaign began to bite neutral shipping owners were reluctant to risk their vessels in British coastal waters, and inevitably British freight charges began to rise. In 1914 the cost of transporting rice from Burma to Britain was in the region of 21s 9d a ton; by the end of 1915 this had increased to 150 shillings a ton. The rate for carrying Argentine wheat, previously 18s a ton, rose to 150s, and the freight charge for exporting Welsh coal rose by 800 per cent. On some key trade routes when carrying export goods before returning laden with imports, the freight charges after deducting the ship owners' extra expenses amounted to as much as thirty-nine times as much as the pre-war profit. The 1913 net profits for the shipping industry were calculated at 20,000,000 pounds compared with 250,000,000 pounds for 1915. Allowing for the deduction of a fifty per cent tax on all war profits, there was an estimated increase in profit of over 540 per cent. Had the Government commandeered the merchant navy it would have resulted in the abolition of the extortionate freight charges on imported food and war materials and lowered the freight charges on exported coal, cotton goods and other manufactured items which collectively helped to partly finance the war. Instead the increased profit combined with the enemy U-boat campaign had a serious economic effect upon our finances, industrial activities and supply of

foodstuffs. The cost of living soared, spawning industrial unrest among workers striving to maintain their already austere standard of life. As a result our sea-borne exports were almost as severely taxed by ever-increasing freights as German exports and imports were by the actions of the Royal Navy. The German naval staff aimed to increase the cost of our Mercantile Marine traffic until it equalled the price of German freight delivered to neutral ports. These unexpected factors contributed to the growing success of the submarine policy and ensured the enemy maintained the pressure upon Allied shipping.

With their coffers swollen by unprecedented profits the more successful shipping companies swallowed up their smaller opposition. The onset of war led to a dramatic decline in Australian emigration, prompting the shipping company of G D Tyser to merge with the Commonwealth and Dominion line of London. Due to the merger all the existing vessels were scheduled in 1916 to be renamed. The new names were all preceded with a Port prefix. One of the fleet the 6,443-GRT *Marere,* departed Fremantle with a general cargo bound for Mudros [now Moudhros] and Gibraltar. On 18 January, at a position thirty-six miles east of Malta the German submarine *U35* captured and sunk *Marere* by gunfire. She became the company's first war loss; her untimely loss occurred prior to the proposed name changes. The merchant ship crews had taken to their lifeboats and were rescued by the hospital ship *Neuralia.*

Less fortunate were the crew of the Zeppelin *L19* which on 2 February 1916 crashed into the North Sea in the vicinity of Grimsby. The twenty-two-man crew climbed onto the gas envelope and hailed a distant British trawler. The *King Stephen* stood off while her skipper, Bill Martin, listened as *Kapitanleutnant* Odo Loewe requested rescue. Due to their bombing raids on the East Coast the airship crews were dubbed 'The Baby Killers' – possibly the tough fishermen had no compassion for men who waged war on non-combatants. The *King Stephen* abandoned the airmen to the mercy of the North Sea, claiming, had the twenty-two men been taken aboard they could have overpowered the nine man crew. It was another example of the cruelty and lack of humanity in an increasingly bitter war waged on the high seas.

Britain maintained she had a legal right to defensively arm her merchant ships and refused to comply with America's proposal. All too aware of the need of British shipping so essential for his nation's continued prosperity, and possibly annoyed by Germany's adoption of a fresh submarine strategy, Woodrow Wilson decided to let sleeping dogs lie. Instead on 15 February, he released an account advising merchant ships had a legal right to protect themselves from attack. The United States would consider any submarine attack against a defensively armed merchant ship, leading to the loss of American lives, as a transgression of 'international law' and the formal assurances guaranteed by the German Government.

In the final week of February the port of New York welcomed her namesake, the ocean liner *New York* among her passengers was Doctor C J Edgar from North Halifax, Quebec who was returning home on sick leave. Edgar had served for several months as a surgeon with the British Medical Corps on the hospital ship *Carisbrook Castle* and the Anchor Line vessel *Massilia*, a 375-bed hospital ship. The doctor reported how the previous March[2] the Mediterranean based *Massilia* was twice pursued by German submarines for more than twenty miles, despite being painted as a hospital ship. He speculated that it was only the superior speed of *Massilia* that saved her from being torpedoed.

Hospital ships of other nations also encountered difficulties as they plied across the shipping channels. While this work focuses predominately on British hospital ships our Allies also lost vessels due to belligerent actions. Our Italian ally had interned the German *Konig Alberta* belonging to the Norddeuster Lloyd line. After conversion to a hospital ship the renamed *Ferinando Palasciano* sailed under the Red Cross flag. On 18 January a suspicious German submarine *U11* ordered the hospital ship to Cattaro for inspection. After thirty-six hours they released the ship to proceed on her way.

The four-year-old 175 feet long *Marechiaro* was built in Ancona in 1912 for her Naples owners. Three days after the boarding of the previously mentioned vessel, the *Marechiaro* now employed as a small hospital ship, sank after striking a mine laid by the German *UC12* near San Giovanni di Medua, Albania. The mine claimed the lives of twenty-five crew members but the British trawlers *Selina* and *Hastings Castle* rescued 112 injured.

The Austro-Hungarian Red Cross number one hospital ship, the *Elektra,* bound from the North Adriatic to Southern Dalmatia, was torpedoed off Cape Plalanka by the French submarine *Ampere* on 18 March. One sailor drowned and two Red Cross nurses were seriously injured. The captain beached his damaged vessel in Borovica Bay, to await repair. The role of *Elektra* was known to the Allies and she bore the prescribed visible markings the French admitted the ship was attacked in error. A repaired *Elektra* returned to service in early September.

The loss of the Russian hospital ship *Portugal*

Prior to her role as a Red Cross hospital ship the *Portugal* belonged to the *Messageries Maritimes* of Marseilles. The 5,533-ton vessel happened to be in the Black Sea at the beginning of the war. The ship's owners placed the vessel at the disposition of the Russian Government who converted the steamer into a hospital ship. At Odessa the Russians registered the vessel as a Red Cross ship attached to the army of Caucasia. Her French officers and crew continued to serve alongside the Red Cross personnel. The steamship was painted white with a red band around her hull, the funnels were also white with large red crosses, and a Red Cross flag fluttered at the mast. With her transformation completed, the Russian Government duly reported the steamer's humanitarian role to the

Bulgarian and Turkish Governments and obtained from them recognition of the vessel's immunity. The Russian hospital ship *Portugal* left Batumi to collect sick and wounded, in her wake trailed a string of flat-bottomed craft, which would convey the wounded from shore to the hospital ship. On 17 March 1916, one of these boats had become waterlogged *Portugal* hove to off Rizeh on the Turkish coast of the Black Sea, to allow an opportunity to pump out the semi submerged craft. Given the fine weather and the ship's exemption from attack the Captain assumed the delay would not endanger his command. Accordingly when a lookout man cried out 'periscope approaching' no anxiety arose.

The submarine *U33* commanded by *Kapitanleutnant* Gansser[3] slowly approached the stationary *Portugal* and discharged a torpedo which missed. A second torpedo launched from the opposite direction, at a range of thirty or forty feet, struck *Portugal* amidships in the engine room. A huge explosion severed the hull in two halves and most of those onboard were pitched into the whirlpool between the fore and aft sections. The initial explosion paled into insignificance compared to the detonation when the steamer's boilers blew up; the two halves of *Portugal* went down simultaneously.

Nikolai Nikolaevitch Sabaev, secretary to the Russian Red Cross Society's Third Ambulance Detachment with the Army of the Caucasus, recorded a graphic account of the sinking:

> *At about eight in the morning, somebody onboard shouted out 'submarine boat'. At first, this news did not produce any panic; on the contrary, everybody rushed on deck to be first to see the submarine. It never entered anybody's head to suppose that a submarine would attack a hospital ship sailing under the flag of the Red Cross. I went on to the upper deck, and*

Russian hospital ship *Portugal,* with broken back, plunges to the bottom of the Black Sea after being torpedoed by *U33*.

noticed the periscope of a submarine, moving parallel with the steamer at a distance of about 170 or 200 feet. Having reached a point opposite to the middle of the Portugal, *the periscope disappeared for a short time, then reappeared and the submarine discharged a torpedo. I descended from the upper deck, and ran to the stern, with the intention of jumping into the sea. When, however, I noticed that most of the people on deck had lifebelts, I ran into saloon number five, seized a lifebelt, and put it on, but then I fell down, as the* Portugal *was sinking at the place where she was broken in two, while her stem and stern were going up all the time. All around me unfortunate sisters of mercy were screaming for help. They fell down, like myself, and some of them fainted. The deck became more down-sloping every minute, and I rolled off into the water between the two halves of the sinking steamer.*

I was drawn down deep into the whirlpool, and began to be whirled around and thrown about in every direction. While under the water, I heard a dull rumbling noise, which was evidently the bursting of the boilers, for it threw me out of the vortex about a sazhen, *or seven feet away from the engulfment of the wreck. The stem and stern of the steamer had gone up until they were almost at right angles with the water, and the divided steamer was settling down. At this moment I was again sucked under, but I exerted myself afresh, and once more rose to the surface. I then saw both portions of the* Portugal *go down rapidly and disappear beneath the flood. A terrible commotion of the water ensued, and I was dragged under, together with the* Portugal. *I felt that I was going down deep, and for the first time realised I was drowning. With the swiftness of lightning, all my past life flitted before my brain. I remembered my relatives, and it seemed as if I could see their grief and tears at the news of my death. My strength failed me, but I kept my mouth firmly shut, and tried not to take in water. I knew that the moment of death through heart failure was near. It so happened however, that the disturbance of water somewhat abated, and I succeeded in swimming up again.*

I glanced around. The Portugal *was no more. Nothing but broken pieces of wreck, boxes which contained our medicaments, materials for dressing wounds, and provisions were floating about. Everywhere I could see the heads and arms of people battling with the waves, and their shrieks for help were frightful. It is impossible to describe the horrors of that scene, and the remembrance of it will remain with me for the rest of my life. About eight or nine* sazhens [fifty-six or sixty-three feet] *away from where I was, I saw a life-saving raft, and I swam towards it. Although my sodden clothes greatly impeded my movements, I nevertheless reached the raft, and was taken onto it.*

About twenty persons were on it already, exclusively men. Amongst

> *them was the French mate, who assisted the captain of the* Portugal, *and he and I at once set about making a rudder out of two oars which were on the raft, and we placed an oarsman on each side of it. We had been going about eight minutes when we saw the body of a woman floating motionless, and dressed in the garb of a sister of mercy. I ordered the oarsmen to row towards her but they said it was a corpse, and we should do better to save some of the people who were still keeping themselves alive on the surface of the water. I seized hold of an oar, and as the woman floated nearer, I caught her with it and dragged her towards us. I pulled her out of the water as far as her waist, and listened to her heart, which I found was still beating, though very slowly. We then raised her onto the raft. She was unconscious, quite blue, and with only feeble signs of life. We began to rub her, and bring her to her senses. She at last opened her eyes and enquired where she was. I told her that she was saved. Soon however, she turned pale, said she was dying, and gave me the address of her relatives, to inform them of her death. She began to spit blood and was quite delirious, but gradually a better feeling returned, and she was soon out of danger.*
>
> *We went on rowing towards the shore for a considerable time, as we did not wish to accept offers to go onboard the motor launch and trawler, and we asked the men in those two craft to hurry up to the scene of the wreck, and save those who perhaps were still surviving. As a matter of fact the motor boat saved several other persons. At last a launch, towing a boat full of the rescued took us in tow, and we reached the shore in safety.*

In the preamble to the above article the 1917 publication cites eighty-five souls perished in the atrocity; they comprised forty-five of the Red Cross staff, twenty-one from the Russian crew, and nineteen of the French crew. *The New York Times* dated 23 November 1916 records there were no wounded onboard, but among the 115 who perished were several members of the Russian Medical Corps and fifteen ladies of the Red Cross. The Turkish Government accepted the blame for the sinking, claiming in the uncertain morning light the *Portugal* was mistaken for a transport.

A replacement hospital ship the *Vperiod* suffered a similar fate. After leaving Batumi to collect wounded the unescorted hospital ship was torpedoed and lost. An official Petrograd report advised 'on 9 July 1916, the vessel which carried all the distinguishing signs was sunk without warning by an enemy submarine. Seven men lost their lives, the others were saved'. As a consequence in December 1916, Russia refused to recognise the hospital ship *Bulgaria,* the explanation being the Turkish fleet had torpedoed two of their hospital ships.

During an early March meeting attended by Kaiser Wilhelm, the German chancellor Theobald von Bethmann Hollweg and General von Falkenhayn presented their case for the resumption of unrestricted submarine warfare. Wilhelm was undecided and postponed making a decision; he never gave an answer. On 13 March the military and Bethmann Hollweg agreed vessels entering the designated war zone whether they be unarmed or armed merchant men were to be destroyed without warning.

Following the loss of *Lusitania*, and Teutonic concerns over an American entry into the war, Germany pledged no further passenger ships would be attacked. But on 24 March the sinking of a French cross-Channel passenger steamer drew severe condemnation and the wrath of President Wilson. The ferry *Sussex* carried 325 passengers and fifty-three crew and steamed between Folkestone and Dieppe, a route not used by the troopships ferrying troops from England to France. Pustkuchen, the commander of *UB29* watching through his periscope claimed he mistook the passengers on deck for troops, making the vessel a legitimate target. At a position thirteen miles south of Dungeness, the captain and first mate who were on the *Sussex* bridge, saw (150 metres distant) a rapidly approaching torpedo; *Sussex* took evasive action by swinging away to starboard, but it was too late. The torpedo exploded a short distance forward of the bridge, shearing off the bow and taking to the seabed the diners and stewards ensconsed in the first class saloon. Several wounded American citizens and members of the American Field Ambulance were among the eighty casualties in the confusion some of the Americans were reported as killed.

The severely damaged *Sussex* was beached prior to a tow into a Boulogne dry

The beached Channel steamer *Sussex*. She was towed into Boulogne and repaired.

dock for repairs. As a submarine had not been sighted an enquiry sought to ascertain whether the damage was due to a mine or torpedo. Due to the presence of neutral Americans on board the *Sussex*, the German Ambassador in Washington, in an attempt to ease diplomatic tension, claimed the ferry had not been attacked by a submarine, but had struck a mine. While in the graving dock during a search amongst the waterlogged detritus in the damaged section, investigators discovered fifteen suspicious fragments of metal. The fragments were compared with plans and mines in possession of the French and British naval authorities. They were confirmed as not belonging to a mine. Two of the distorted fragments were screw bolts – one stamped on the head with K56 and the other K58. Captured torpedoes examined in France and England contained the same screw bolts, securing the war head [*kopf*] to the air chamber; the remaining fragments were all identified as German torpedo components.

On hearing of the reneging of another assurance President Wilson threatened to break diplomatic relations with Germany. On 18 April Wilson informed Congress of an ultimatum sent the previous day to the German Government. The note condemned the German policy of unrestricted submarine warfare, warning the United States would not tolerate the continuation of such a policy and demanded it be revoked by the German Government. Alarmed by the American reaction Germany ceded to the American demands, but only after failing to make the agreement conditional on the removal of the Allied blockade. Contrary to the wishes of his naval chiefs Wilhelm II ordered the directive of 13 March to be cancelled. He preferred a resumption of 'cruiser' rules warfare requiring a submarine to surface before attacking a vessel. The decision infuriated the naval minister Alfred Von Tirpitz, who later attributed Germany's wartime defeat to its weakness at this time in the face of American opposition. On 4 May Germany met American demands and agreed to return to the rules of international law. However, Germany reserved the right to return to unrestricted submarine warfare if American pressure failed to dissuade Britain from continuing her ever-tightening blockade of Germany.

Jutland, the clash of Titans

The Grand Fleet of the Royal Navy played an essential if exceedingly boring task of maintaining the blockade, a factor which may have contributed as much to victory as the land campaigns. Locating enemy patrols was like looking for a needle in the proverbial haystack, for the North Sea covered 140,000 square nautical miles: in comparison the area of vision for a light cruiser squadron was less than five square miles. The navy days of intense boredom were sporadically interrupted by chance relatively small naval engagements; all were eclipsed by the 31 May colossal clash of naval firepower waged sixty miles off the Jutland peninsula of Denmark.

The German High Seas Fleet had been commanded by a passive Admiral von

Pohl until this year; his successor the aggressive Admiral Reinhardt Von Scheer recommenced naval hit and run raids on the English coast. The German High Seas Fleet under Admiral Scheer entered the North Sea from the Baltic intending to lure and trap a squadron or two of British cruisers off the Jutland coast. Scheer was unaware British Intelligence had alerted the Grand Fleet of their intrusion. The British fleet at Scapa Flow weighed anchor and Admiral John Jellicoe sailed with his force of twenty-eight Dreadnought battleships to intercept the enemy. Admiral Beatty in command of a Rosyth based force of four battleships and six scouting battle- cruisers also headed for Denmark.

The German naval hierarchy in 1916.

Beatty's force encountered a similar advance patrol which fled, enticing the British towards the High Seas Fleet. Beatty fell for the trap; at 4.00pm a long range duel began: two British battle-cruisers were sunk when fire or a shell penetrated the magazine. On *Indefatigable* the resulting explosion claimed over 1,000 lives, thirty minutes later and the *Queen Mary* sank; within a few minutes 1,266 souls perished. Now Beatty beat a hasty retreat northwards towards Jellicoe's main battle fleet. Around six in the evening the main battle commenced during which another battle-cruiser was lost. As the losses rose Admiral Beatty famously remarked 'there seems to be something wrong with our bloody ships today'. The British outnumbered Scheer's force which emitted a covering smokescreen and headed for home, only to be intercepted by part of the British fleet. Scheer ordered his battle-cruisers and destroyers to engage the British and cover their retreat. Fearful of torpedo attack in the diminishing light the over cautious Jellicoe turned away, bringing the curtain down on one of the most controversial naval episodes in Royal Navy history. As the main vanguard of the German fleet had abandoned the action the Royal Navy claimed a strategic victory. However, the Germans claimed a tactical victory based on the number of ships sunk in what they refer to as the Battle of the Skagerrak, but sustained sufficient damage never to challenge the Royal Navy's dominance again.

The British Grand Fleet lost three battle-cruisers, three armoured cruisers and eight destroyers; over 6,000 officers and crew died. The enemy lost some 2,500 men, a battleship, one battle-cruiser, four light cruisers and five destroyers. The lack of a decisive victory undermined British confidence in the Royal Navy; the German High Seas Fleet returned to base never to venture out again *en masse* except to capitulate. The Battle of Jutland was a turning point in the war at sea. After Jutland Germany realised the only foreseeable chance of defeating British dominance at sea lay in the deployment of adequate numbers of submersibles. The submarine and not the capital ship developed into the dominant naval vessel of the Great War; their only hope of reversing their fortunes lay in the resumption of unrestricted naval warfare.

The killing fields

Two further factors dominated the middle year of the war, the siege of Verdun and the Battle of the Somme. Internal wrangling within the German High Command continued over the merits of unrestricted submarine warfare. General von Falkenhayn, the Chief of Germany's General Staff, now looked to his naval peers for a return to unrestricted warfare in support of his planned Western Front offensive against the French.

Falkenhayn decided to launch an offensive against the French fortress of Verdun sited approximately 175 miles east of Paris. Here he anticipated the French would fight to the last man rather than yield further ground to the invading force; sadly posterity proved him right for both sides lost over 325,000 men in the process. The offensive intended to bleed the French army dry, destroy French morale and leave Britain's major ally in such a weakened state she might be favourable for a peace treaty on German terms. Without French support the enemy calculated Britain would be defeated by the end of the year. On 21 February the German bombardment commenced along a fifteen mile front announcing the opening phase of a titanic struggle which finally drew its last gasps in the middle of that December. During the intervening desperate months strategic positions fell and were recaptured, and the French looked to their British ally for an offensive to ease the pressure on Verdun.

At the end of 1915 Sir Douglas Haig took over command of the BEF from Sir John French. The new commander began to explore the viability of a major British offensive on the Western Front capable of producing a decisive breakthrough and rolling the enemy back to the coast. Originally scheduled for August the demands on Verdun required the attack to be brought forward to late June. The 'Big Push' would be launched over the rolling Somme countryside where unusually inclement weather for that time of year delayed the infantry attack. The infamous, opening day of the Somme offensive on 1 July 1916 produced an unprecedented amount of casualties, irrevocably proving human flesh was no match for machine-gun bullets. More than 1,000 officers and 20,000 other ranks predominately from Kitchener's New Army were killed, fatally wounded or posted as missing; over 1,300 officers and 34,000 other ranks were wounded. Of the 21,000 killed on that fateful sunny morning, almost thirty per cent died as a result of wounds, from which they would have recovered if they had received prompt medical attention. Unable to recover the wounded due to the remorseless shelling and small-arms fire, many of the wounded took shelter in shell-holes, covered themselves with their ground sheets and waited for their lives to ebb away. The Germans to their credit offered several unofficial truces, so the British could remove their wounded from certain sectors of the Somme front line. But, despite this philanthropic gesture, it took several days to recover those who had not succumbed to their wounds. Under the intense fire power the initial attack melted away; the catastrophic advance produced a gain of approximately a mile in depth along a three and a half mile front.

The Western Front base hospitals were inundated with wounded men broken in body or mind, thousands of whom required evacuating back to the United Kingdom. Due to the insistence of Queen Victoria, in 1855 the Government built the Royal Victoria Military Hospital, Netley, situated on the shores of Southampton Water for the treatment of men wounded in the Crimean War. The hospital originally had its own pier but in later years wounded military personnel were transferred by rail from Southampton docks. During the Great War a large hutted Red Cross hospital was built to the rear of the hospital, increasing the patient capacity to 2,000. Its proximity to the battlefields of France and Flanders proved extremely useful for the influx of Western Front evacuees despatched from the ports of Rouen and Le Havre.

An Advanced Dressing Station on the Somme.

At the start of the Somme offensive the strain on the system is evident after considering the war diary of the hospital ship *Lanfranc*. Inevitably, tidal factors and a lack of vacant berths extended the crossing times but even so a real sense of urgency is apparent on seeing the rapid turn around of the vessel. Chartered as a hospital ship from 6 October the previous year she could officially accommodate 403 persons, but evidently carried far more in times of crisis.

> *2nd July.* Lanfranc *departed Netley and proceeded to Cowes Roads. Anchored in Cowes Roads until 8.10 am when ship hove anchor and sailed for Havre. Arrived and made fast at 9.40 pm. Commenced embarking patients at 10.30 pm and continued throughout the night.*
>
> *3rd July. Finished embarking the patients at 4.15 am. The patients onboard were officers fifty-six, other ranks 673, total 729* [cot cases 225, noncot 504]. *Cast off at 4.30 am and sailed for Southampton. Arrived and anchored off Netley hospital at 1.00 pm. Hove anchor 5.00 pm and proceeded alongside the quay. Made fast 6.30 pm and commenced disembarking at once. We finished at 9.00 pm, cast off at midnight then proceeded to Havre.*
>
> *4th July. Arrived Havre and anchored in outer harbour at 10.00 am. Hove anchor and proceeded alongside quay at 11.40 am. Made fast at 12.50 pm. Commenced embarking at 3.00 pm and finished at 10.00 pm. Patients embarked thirty-nine officers, 878 other ranks* [cot 414, noncot 503]. *Cast off and sailed for Southampton at 11.00 pm.*
>
> *5th July. Arrived and anchored off Netley at 10.00 am. Hove anchor and proceeded alongside quay at 2.30 pm, made fast at 3.45 pm. Commenced disembarking at 7.00 pm. 1215 Private P Willoughby 1st Lancashire Fusiliers died on board at 10.30 pm due to a gunshot wound in the pelvis and haemorrhage. He was transferred ashore at 10.40 pm for burial at Netley. Finished disembarking patients at 11.30 pm. Cast off and proceeded to Cowes Roads at midnight.*
>
> *6th July. Anchored Cowes Roads at 12.20 am. Hove anchor at 2 am and sailed for Havre. Arrived and made fast 12.30 pm. Commenced embarking patients at 1.25 pm, finished after various stops at 10.25 pm. Patients embarked officers sixteen, other ranks 989, German prisoners seventy-eight* [cot 301, noncot 782] *total 1,083. Cast off and sailed for Southampton at 10.50pm*[4].

She arrived and anchored off Netley at 9.30 the following morning and began disembarking patients some time after 1.30. Officially *Lanfranc* had accommodation for 403 patients but had on board 680 more than her capacity. By seven in the evening all the patients were transferred ashore, forty-five minutes later *Lanfranc* cast off for France. This hectic schedule was replicated by all the cross-Channel hospital fleet, whose periods of maximum activity

Barges operated on France's internal waterway system carrying wounded deemed too seriously injured to risk moving by road.

coincided with major attacks or counter-offensives.

Due to the Somme offensive the Germans at Verdun received no further fresh divisions and their advance diminished in intensity, allowing the French to successfully counter-attack. Meanwhile the Somme offensive continued until late autumn when the weather halted the offensive. Throughout the offensive ambulance trains evacuated some 745,000 sick and wounded. Ambulance barges sedately moving at three miles an hour operated on the French internal waterways. They rarely travelled after dusk, and each trip lasted between one or two days. Approximately a half dozen strong flotilla of ambulance barges plied the La Bassee, Lys and Somme canals, each unit consisted of six wide barges towed singly or in tandem. The barges carried the more seriously wounded, deemed too weak to make the arduous journey over deeply rutted roads or by rail. In the first seventy-two hours of the 'Big Push' some 550 wounded were transported by barge. During 1916 17,000 casualties travelled by barge, requiring over 560 barge trips. Their contribution is significantly under valued throughout the war the ambulance barges operating in France and Flanders extricated over 53,000 sick and wounded.

The mining of *Galeka*

Two rival shipping companies once vied for the trade between the United Kingdom and South Africa, namely the Castle Packet Company and the Union Line. Both companies merged and on 8 March 1900 the new company registered the name of the Union Castle Line. The merged fleets with their lavender grey hulls and vermillion painted funnels operated on a clockwork timetable between the two nations. The company provided an efficient mail service, carried fare-paying passengers and general cargo. In April 1912, the Royal Mail Line took control of Union Castle though the latter continued to manage the fleet.

A souvenir of halcyon days, a *Galeka* Mercantile Marine badge.

Prior to hostilities over-capacity in mercantile shipping led to large scale lay-ups of vessels, a surplus which would prove to be very fortuitous once the impending submarine campaign gathered momentum. As the storm clouds gathered redundant vessels languishing at lay-up berths were granted a new lease of life. Amongst the mothballed Union Castle fleet the *Norman*, *Dunvegan Castle* and *Carisbrooke Castle* were brought into service; the latter steamer served as a hospital ship. Within a year thirteen Union Castle vessels were operating as hospital ships, supplemented by the *Western Australia*, a vessel staffed by the

The *Galeka* was built for the Union Castle Steamship Co. in 1899 by Harland & Wolff, Belfast. She became a hospital ship in June 1915 and was lost after hitting a mine in the English Channel the following year.

company for the Admiralty. According to the book 'The Union Castle and the War 1914–19' Union Castle hospital ships brought home 354,400 wounded officers and men from France, the Persian Gulf, the Mediterranean and elsewhere. The company steamers based at Southampton [now a closed port known as Number One Military Port] engaged in the overseas and cross-Channel services brought in a total of 331,404 wounded British officers and men and 8,279 enemy wounded.

The 6,772-ton *Galeka* only made one voyage under the Union Steamship flag before the amalgamation. In 1914, *Galeka* [sister ship to *German* and *Galician*] served as a troopship and during the Gallipoli campaign she landed Australian troops at Suvla Bay [C beach]. In June of the following year she was requisitioned as a hospital ship. An article within the British Journal of Nursing dated 24 July 1915 informed readers:

> *The* Galeka, *the ship on which English nurses have brought sick and wounded from Mudros to Alexandria has recently been in harbour, being fitted up as a first-class hospital ship and will soon be in use. She is painted green and white with red crosses, and at night has green lights along the deck and crosses in red lights, very picturesque on the sparkling water. The staff of eight sisters is quite imperial: one regular, one reserve, two Australian, and four of the part requisitioned by the Dowager Countess of Caernarfon, and for the time being taken over by the War Office. The sisters greatly enjoy this hospital ship service, and now that the* Galeka *is properly fitted they will be able to make the patients much more comfortable.*

During the autumn of this year the Germany navy introduced the *UCII* class of submarine minelayers. Each submersible carried eighteen mines, and seven torpedoes, an eighty-eight millimetre gun and three torpedo tubes completed her armament. One of these vessels, the *UC26* of the Flanders Flotilla, cleared her port on 24 October and during the two consecutive days laid a series of small minefields. Due to deteriorating weather her search for targets for her seven torpedoes became impractical; the submarine commander Mathias Graf von Schmettow aborted the patrol and headed for the shelter of her Zeebrugge base.

On 28 October 1916 the severe gale had whipped up a heavy sea through which *Galeka* pitched and rolled as she steamed towards Le Havre to collect the wounded. Onboard were sixty-one officers and other ranks of the RAMC, also fifty-six Union Castle crew. On arriving at the defensive boom across the Channel into the harbour at Le Havre, she was ordered to wait until receiving a signal to enter harbour. The *Galeka* drifted offshore awaiting the anticipated signal. At 6.15 am while approximately five miles north-west of Cape Hague she struck one of the mines laid by *UC26*. Fortunately no patients were onboard; however, the explosion claimed the lives of nineteen RAMC

HMHS *Galeka* firmly aground.

personnel. Despite the severe weather conditions the ship's master Captain J Wilford managed to beach his ship at Cape Hague. She remained firmly grounded and despite salvage attempts over the next twelve weeks the vessel was written off as a total loss.

The loss of the former White Star liner *Britannic*

During the heyday of the transatlantic passenger trade, two renowned steamship companies vied with each other for passengers. This inter-company rivalry coupled with the latest developments in marine engineering led to the Cunard company's 1907 introduction of their express liners *Lusitania* and *Mauretania* of 31,550 tons and 31,940 tons respectively. The liners' steam turbines generated sufficient power to allow a top speed of just over twenty-five knots. The reply of the rival White Star Line was to order a trio of four-funnelled 'Olympic' class liners. The vessels of awesome dimensions displaced about half as much tonnage again as the Cunard vessels but travelled at a more sedate speed than the Cunarders. This was not an engineering oversight, for what the Olympic class lacked in pace they more than compensated for in their first-class opulent surroundings and five star hotel style amenities. These new vessels dubbed the 'Big Three' were the *Olympic*, *Titanic* and *Britannic*, the latter vessel being provisionally named the *Gigantic*, when in November 1911 Harland and Wolff commenced her construction.

The construction of the third Olympic ship abruptly halted due to the 1912 loss of her now infamous sister ship *Titanic* and the ensuing maritime enquiry. Several contributory factors attributing to the great loss of life on *Titanic* were highlighted during the enquiry. Consequently, the required improvements to the hull design were incorporated into the skeletal framework of *Gigantic,* the last of the 'Big Three'. The experiment of an inner skin adopted in *Olympic* was adopted in *Britannic*; this consisted of heavy plating extending for more than half the length of the vessel. The inner skin extended from the watertight bulkhead in front of the forward boiler room to the after end of the turbine room. Theoretically *Britannic* would be able to float with any six compartments flooded; her strengthened hull also offered extra protection from serious damage. She was fitted with the latest type of electrically driven lifeboat-lowering equipment by which a large number of lifeboats could be put over the side far quicker than by the old davit system. Her length overall was 903 feet, and her gross tonnage 48,156 tons – yards longer than her sister ships. She justifiably claimed to be the finest and largest British merchant ship. At about this time the company began referring to her as *Britannic*; a century later debate continues over whether the vessel changed name after the *Titanic* tragedy or changed to a more patriotic name in the face of an impending conflagration.

The Belfast yard launched *Britannic* on 26 February 1914, she then weighed over 23,000 tons. The weight on the launch trigger was 560 tons, and the time occupied in the launch from the moment the trigger was released to the time when her bows dipped in the water was exactly eighty-one seconds. The fitting out of the vessel suffered further delays due to a shortage of materials that became increasingly prioritised six months later when Britain took up arms. *Olympic* became a troop transport in September 1915; three months later as *Britannic* neared completion the Admiralty requisitioned her as a hospital ship with a capacity for 3,300 patients. The elaborate fittings and furniture intended for the great liner remained in the warehouses; sadly *Britannic* was destined never to carry a fare paying passenger. Her various decks housed twenty-three wards interconnected by ten lifts staffed by seventeen Boy Scouts. Of these ten came from Liverpool, [forty-six Liverpool scouts served within the company as Bridge Boys during hostilities], six from Southampton, and one hailed from Gravesend. She must also have been the only vessel to have a chartered accountant working as a stoker. The unnamed South African had travelled to Britain to enlist, but had been rejected; instead, he satisfied his patriotic urges by serving on the *Britannic.*

The White Star liner had an operating speed of twenty knots [just over twenty-three miles an hour] and one day covered 508 miles. The electrical generators onboard *Britannic* produced sufficient electricity to power a large town; her generators had the capacity to light over 150,000 lamps. During her

HMHS *Britannic* receiving patients or stores from HMHS *Galeka*, during the Gallipoli campaign.

role as a hospital ship, some 2,000 sidelights illuminated the vessel; consequently by night she was brilliantly lit from stem to stern. On the hull side, a gigantic red cross had no fewer than 300 high power lights on each arm of the cross to advertise the humanitarian role of the vessel. On her first voyage she brought back from Mudros 3,300 sick and wounded to Southampton. She made five mercy voyages including the final evacuation of the Gallipoli peninsula when *Britannic*, *Mauretania* and *Olympic* rescued thousands of wounded.

On her sixth and final voyage she left Southampton on 20 October for Mudros on the isle of Lemnos [now Limnos] in the Aegean Sea for the recovery of sick and wounded from the Salonika campaign.

A week prior to her departure the War Office [5] requested the Director of Transports' office to 'arrange conveyance in her for 115 Officers and 386 other ranks [RAMC], 161 Nurses, and 311 tons of medical stores. Pending a decision on the general question as to whether medical personnel should be conveyed on hospital ships'.

Three days later came the reply: Director of Transport asks that the case for next Friday be allowed to proceed as being arranged prior to the decision. The prohibition now imposed by the board is on the grounds of expediency rather than illegality. Whether this case should be allowed seems entirely a matter for naval decision.

Finally HF Oliver on 16 October confirmed the request: propose to agree as a special case. In future cases it might be well to allow the women to go in hospital ships and bar the men. It would add to the safety of the women nurses and no question is likely to arise about the legality of conveying them.

On 23 October 1916, a War Office telegram to the I G C Egypt confirmed: *16326 Q M G 2a Hospital ship* Britannic *left Southampton for Mudros on 20 October. Has on board transhipping at Mudros, the following:*

For Egypt.
Officers 15
Chaplains 16
Other ranks 2
Medical stores 1,865 packages.

For Malta.
Officers 5
Chaplains 1
Lady Doctors 10
Nurse 1
British Red Cross members 2
Other ranks 1
Medical stores 96 packages.

For Salonika.
Number 33 Stationary Hospital comprising:
Officers 10
Other ranks 181
Stores 165 tons.

Also:
Nurses 156
British Red Cross members 2
Medical stores 795 packages.

For India.
Officers 17
Nurses 52
Assistant Surgeons 4
Dental Mechanics 8
Other ranks 1

For Mesopotamia.
Medical stores 15 packages.

As the 115 officers and 386 other ranks RAMC personnel were non-combatants they could be carried on the vessel, but the presence of the khaki-clad troops fuelled German rumours of the misuse of British hospital ships. The transportation of medics and medical stores became a routine procedure.

The White Star appointed Captain Charles A Bartlett, a company man for twenty-one years' to command the great white liner. His ship now entered the Zea channel, a waterway running between the mainland of Greece and the Cyclades archipelago, whose islands are now popular holiday destinations. The early morning sun reflected off the still waters as the great ship glided through the channel; her passengers heading for their breakfast briefly lined the rails captivated by the beauty of the Greek villages scattered across the hillsides. In the ship's wheelhouse the officers completed the formalities of the eight o'clock watch changeover, unaware of the vessel's imminent demise. Perhaps they were complacent about danger, for less than twenty-four hours earlier minesweepers declared the passage at the island of Kea to be clear of mines. This was at odds with the local opinion, for early on that fateful morning the villagers had witnessed what transpired to be a German mine-laying submarine operating in the channel.

An unidentified RAMC soldier. Only the absence of a rifle and the Red Cross insignia differentiated the non-combatant medics from the regular infantrymen.

At precisely 0800 hours on Tuesday 21 November 1916, the breakfast gong summoned those off duty to the dining room. No sooner had the off-duty personnel settled for breakfast when an ominous crash and simultaneous reverberation throughout the length of the vessel heralded disaster. Eyewitness accounts erroneously claimed they saw a torpedo miss the stern while a second detonated at the bow. The ships officers' also stated the explosion was due to a torpedo, for they mistakenly believed it was then technically impossible to anchor a mine in the one hundred fathoms [600 feet] deep channel. The culprit the German mine-laying submarine *U73*, is reputed to have been one of several transported by rail in four sections to Constantinople. Once assembled they became the scourge of the Mediterranean vessels; several hours before the hospital ship's arrival the Greek villagers witnessed this submersible plant a series of mines in the Zea channel.

The impact from the explosion blasted a great hole in the port bow of

Britannic. Moments later a second explosion occurred when the coal bunkers ignited. One account states: 'The hatches of number two hold were blown fifty feet into the air and the decks were covered in splinters from the hatch boards.' With all the post-*Titanic* modifications incorporated into her hull *Britannic* should have survived this damage but her system of watertight doors failed to close. Despite having six of her forward compartments flooded she should have remained afloat. Unfortunately the nurses had opened countless portholes to air the vessel in readiness for the patients' arrival. As the ship settled lower in the water, the sea poured through the opened ports. Captain Bartlett drove the ship forward in a hopeless attempt to beach the rapidly sinking vessel on Kea Island. Meanwhile the majority of the 1,130 to 1,500 personnel on board, in compliance with orders, attempted to abandon ship. The vessel's forward momentum severely hampered the launch and boarding of the lifeboats, and the rotating screws were responsible for numerous casualties. Captain C A Bartlett remained on the bridge of his doomed vessel barking out orders to his officers as the ship was sinking beneath his feet. He remained onboard until the waters lapped at his feet, then leapt into the water and struck out to a stray collapsible lifeboat from where he watched his vessel disappear beneath the waves.

The White Star Line *Britannic* was destined never to carry a fare-paying passenger. She was sunk in 1916 while seving as a hospital ship.

Numerous press reports acknowledge the resoluteness of certain individuals. We can only marvel at the young Boy Scout, who, after the explosion, approached the purser and asked if he could be of service. The boy stood gamely at his post for ten minutes while the boat was sinking. When the purser gave him his orders, he went off with the remark 'It has been a big explosion sir, but I don't think it will do us much harm'. Miss E A Dowse the matron routinely wore her campaign medals upon her uniform, testimony to her surviving the siege of Ladysmith. On board the hospital ship she managed seventy-six nursing sisters, mostly belonging to the Queen Alexandra nursing staff, together with

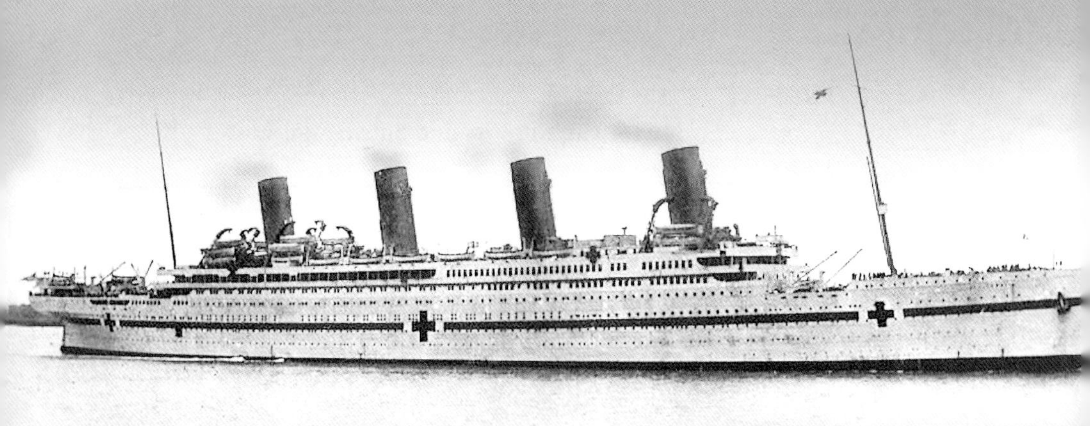

HMHS *Britannic,* sister ship to the ill-fated *Titanic*, was fitted out with 3,110 beds.

four stewardesses. On this leg of the voyage, they had no patients onboard, except a few of the staff who were down with slight indispositions. When evacuating the ship the matron acting with much composure lined her nurses up on deck in military fashion, where they calmly waited their turn to board the boats.

Nurse Ada Garland who occupied the first boat lowered on the port side later recalled:

> *At 8.15, we heard a loud report, which seemed as if something ran against the side of the ship. We all stood up, some rushed from the dining hall. There was a loud clatter of falling plates and glasses, the stewards were ready to dash out of the room then suddenly came to their senses and told us to sit down and have our breakfast as we had only run into a barge. I sat down and resumed breakfast when the order rang out 'Ladies go to your cabins, put on your life belts and go up to the boat deck'. We all walked out very quietly and quickly down to C deck to our cabins. I did not run until I got to the top of the corridor, then I ran down to my room took off my coat from the peg, also my hat, and picked up my rug off the bed... I then ran up the emergency staircase passing Matron on the way who remarked 'Hurry up children'. Coming up on the boat deck, I put on my coat, tied my lifebelt very tight and was ready – for what? I thought everybody looked rather frightened, but they all kept perfectly quiet. In a few minutes the order came 'All sisters go forward port side' and we all calmly walked forward. We received orders to get into number seventeen boat as quickly as possible, and we all started scrambling over into a boat which was hanging over the side ready to be lowered. I remember scrambling up, when the barber said 'Put your foot on my knee sister', which I did and got in much easier. We were about thirty ladies in our boat, when the order was given for eight men and the boatmen to get in. They all took their oars and the order came to lower. We were gradually lowered over the side to the water; I noticed it was not such a great distance. That shows our beautiful boat was sinking sure and fast. We*

bumped against the side of the boat a good deal when we reached the water and it seemed several minutes before we could get away from the structure. At last the men, after pulling hard managed to get a few feet away from her.

The Reverend John A Fleming, a Presbyterian minister [he died in 1953], gave his account of the disaster in a book entitled *The Last Voyage of the* Britannic a portion of which is reproduced here 'Courtesy of the National Museums Liverpool [Merseyside Maritime Museum]'.

I had just reached the boat deck again when I caught sight of those ill-fated lifeboats unaccountably drawn in, and smashed to matchwood by the huge propellers. Eight of our orderlies, one of our medical officers, and over twenty ship's crew lost their lives, and as many again were broken and bruised.

One was proud of the men of the RAMC that day. I spent most of the time side by side with them, while the vessel was sinking below our feet... The word was soon passed from the boats to draft the men forward in fifties, and we took them up thus from the promenade to the boat deck. When each fifty was counted out we bade those remaining wait, not a man endeavoured to rush, but quietly waited his turn. Soon all the men were to their stations, and off on the boats.

They were off none too soon, for the ship suddenly gave a great list, and we knew she could not tarry too long afloat. There was nothing left for us to do but grasp chairs, and cast them overboard to support those who might take to the water. I cannot remember what happened then. I think I must have gone below again. In any case, I found myself emerging from the main stairway just behind the bridge, at the other end of the vessel. As I came alongside I could see the placid waters dotted everywhere with our boats, and here and there someone I knew swimming contentedly in the buoyant waters, supported by a trusty lifebelt. The decks seemed quite deserted, but as I came along I found a crowded boat just about to be lowered. Major Priestly, the hero of Wittenberg, who had taken charge of the orderlies, was alone with me on that part of the deck, but for a young ship's officer who saw every boat there into the water, and the gallant men who worked the ropes. Those in

Rev Fleming.

the boat called me in with them, and tried to prevail on the Major to come also; but with the spirit which marked his work in Wittenberg, he went to have a last look around, lest any should be left. A few minutes later he escaped in the next boat which proved to be the last to leave the ship.

After narrowly escaping a serious mishap just as we touched the water, our first concern was to get clear of the fast-sinking ship. Unhappily we had no one with us who knew anything of boats, and our boat was very overcrowded. The men pulled with a might to be clear, and yet to tarry near enough to the ship to pick up any who had plunged into the sea. And then we waited with heavy hearts to see the ship go down. We had not more than a few minutes to wait. We could see the waves already splashing well over the bows and playing with it, as waves play with the sand dreadnoughts of the children on the beach. Gradually the waters licked up and up the decks while the furnaces belching forth fierce volumes of smoke as if the great engines were in their last death agony. One by one the monster funnels melted away as wax before a flame and crashed upon the decks till the waters rushed down, and report after report rang over the sea, and told of the explosion of the boilers. The waters moved over the deck still, the bows dipping deeper and deeper into the sea, until the rudders stood straight up from the surface of the water, and tarrying thus for a few moments, dived perpendicularly into the depths, leaving hardly a ripple behind.

Not so long before, one could see nothing but the Britannic, *the hills on the adjacent island seemed very small. Now all that was left of Britain's greatest ship, that took more than two years to build and represented some two million pound sterling, was a score of crowded boats, and a little wreckage on the wave. And it only took fifty minutes to go down.*

Lance Corporal E Cyril Gregory of the RAMC wrote to his mother from his hospital bed in Malta, where he lay recovering from his injuries to his leg.

...On the 21 November at about 8.15 am we were close to Zea Island, I was having a break when a torpedo hit the bow of the ship. We received orders to parade on H deck with our lifebelts and then waited for orders to proceed to the boats. While the boats were getting launched, the ship was making for the shore. At this time she had a big list to starboard. The boat I was in had about sixty men in and we were getting sucked into the propellers. I with a great many more, jumped into the water for the purpose of swimming to some wreckage. No sooner had we done this than the suction from the propellers took me underneath and then I went beneath the waves.

The next thing I remember was getting to the surface a little away from the propellers and my leg and arm was hit by something. All around men

Lance Corporal E C Gregory RAMC from New Brighton, Cheshire. He survived his lifeboat being sucked into the propellers, but received injuries to his leg.

were shouting for help and clinging to wreckage. One of our patrol launches picked me up after being in a very exhausted condition. As soon as I was pulled into the boat I vomited for all I was worth. In the boat were men laying with arms and legs off. Seated next to me was an officer who had a flask of brandy and he gave us a drop each. As we were making for the shore the boilers on Britannic *exploded, and a little later the funnels dropped off one by one.*

She was then sinking very fast, and in a few minutes she was nowhere to be seen. We were still picking up men, also Captain Bartlett. After sailing for about half an hour we came alongside the quay. The inhabitants who were Greeks were very kind to all of us. They carried me ashore and in an old fashioned house were a couple of old women who got me into bed, as I was very cold and my teeth were chattering. They brought me some brandy and before long they were crying. Of course the house was full of wounded. We had Greek doctors visit us; they put my right leg in a splint, and gave me some ether and water to drink. We left Port .... on a destroyer where we lay on the deck with flags, blankets and sacks to keep us warm. The sailors were very kind to us and brought us hot cocoa and tea, for which we were very thankful. We arrived at a place called Piraeus, Greece at 7pm, and then in motor cars to a Russian and Greek hospital, where we got our wounds dressed. The first night none of us could sleep, but soon got settled down. We had milk and water for breakfast, macaroni and minced meat for dinner, and milk and water for tea.

The inhabitants did not care much for us and we were glad when we heard that the hospital ship was coming to take us away. We left on the 26 November, and on the ship all the RAMC and sisters met. They were dressed up in French and English sailor's clothes and looked very comical. The next day they received new clothes. We arrived in Malta on 30 November 1916, and left ship for the Bavire hospital, which is situated on a hill and overlooks the sea. This was my experience. Up to now I am glad to say, my leg is getting on alright, and I am able to walk about. Hope to be out of hospital as soon as they like.

Sorry to hear that G King of Magazine Lane, New Brighton is missing. No one saw him from the time she got torpedoed and it is feared he was lost, along with a few more of our staff.

Private George W King RAMC. The twenty-four year old was posted as missing after the disaster. The missing soldier was wounded in France at the latter end of July, while serving as a stretcher bearer. On returning to duty he served as an orderly on the great liner.

Private George King a fellow RAMC resident of New Brighton, Wallasey was wounded at the latter end of July while serving as a stretcher-bearer in France. On recovery the twenty-four year old received a posting as an orderly on the hospital ship. Private Gregory's concerns were justified for George King perished on *Britannic*.

Twenty-nine-year-old stewardess Violet Constance Jessop had a remarkable claim to fame, for she had survived three major incidents while working on the 'Big Three'. The serious collision between *Olympic* and HMS *Hawke* paled into insignificance compared to her escape from the wreck of *Titanic*. The five foot two inches tall woman again found herself in peril, this time in a lifeboat being sucked into the rotating propellers of *Britannic*. Despite being unable to swim, Violet leapt overboard but was sucked under the boat's keel, which struck her head. After struggling to the surface of the vortex her auburn hair caught the attention of her rescuers. Upon being hauled to safety she watched the death throes of the *Britannic*: the great liner dipped her head a little, then a little lower and then lower still. All the deck machinery fell into the sea like a child's toys. Then she took a fearful plunge, her stern rearing hundreds of feet into the air until, with a final roar, she disappeared into the depths, the noise of her going resounding through the water with undreamt of violence.

Some years later Violet Jessop visited her doctor complaining of headaches: he discovered she had once sustained a fractured skull, no doubt a result of her blow against the hull of *Britannic*.

On 30 December 1916, the *New York Times* published further details of the loss of *Britannic* as recounted by Henry Pope, a fifteen-year-old cabin boy from the liner *Lapland*. The youngster from London was previously a sea scout assigned to Purser Lancaster on the vessel's final voyage.

Alice May Swaffield Milward, a nurse with the Voluntary Aid Detachment [VAD]. She served as a nursing sister in a military hospital at Etaples, where one day sixty patients died in her ward. According to family legend the nurse survived the sinking of *Britannic*.

The reporter described Pope as an intelligent boy, small for his years, who told his story with a flourish:

> *The officers and crew of* Britannic *believed that she had been torpedoed because the explosion, while it shook the 50,000 ton ship fore and aft made little noise, as if a torpedo had passed through the hull forward and exploded in the centre of the ship, where the inrush of water had deadened the sound. If it had been a mine, the officers said it would have exploded against the side of the ship with terrific violence.*

After describing the role of the scouts onboard he continued…

> *The officers told us the explosion was forward of number one hold, which was blown away with the 'glory holes' where the stewards live, the cook's cabin and sea scout quarters. So far as we could find out, in the short time before* Britannic *was abandoned, only one man was killed by the explosion, the night watchman who was asleep in his bunk. Thirty men were killed by the smashing of the lifeboats, which became entangled with the big propellers, and others died afterwards in the hospital at Athens. Three sick bay attendants were drowned through one of the boats being dropped by the stern, while the boat was held up in the davit. Five scouts were in that boat, but they hung on to the standing part of the boat falls and were not lost.*

The wireless operator's frantic distress calls alerted the British cruiser HMS *Heroic* which made full speed to the disaster zone now marked by dozens of lifeboats a local fishing boat ably assisted in the rescue operation. The British G-class destroyers, *Scourge* and *Greyhound,* also rendered valuable assistance. Some of the survivors struggling in the waves were rescued by the islanders of Kea, whose women ripped their clothes up to bandage the wounded. Groups of survivors from the rescue vessels were landed at Phaleron, four miles away from Athens, approximately one hundred injured arrived at Keratsini Bay and Piraeus and two died shortly after landfall due to their injuries.

The wounded were taken to a Russian hospital where they were visited by the British Minister at Athens, Sir Francis Elliot, who also visited the survivors at Phaleron. After a few days' leave the uninjured departed on a Malta-bound ship; from there they were re-assigned.

A press article reported:

> *The loss of life is not great as at first feared, the dead numbering four and the missing 26, a total of 30. Thirty-one of the ship's company were posted as dead or missing.*

Four of the victims were buried at the St Denis Cemetery, Piraeus. The British Naval Attaché attended and all the other Entente Legations were represented and sent wreaths. Detachments of British and French sailors followed the coffins to the burial place.

In the aftermath of the disaster the by now customary claims and counter-claims commenced. Britain cited the sinking of *Britannic* by a German submarine as an act in conflict with international law, and one of atrocious barbarism. However, the German Admiralty denied the involvement of a German submarine, claiming the perpetrator was a Turkish submarine recently sold by Germany to the Turkish fleet. Furthermore, Berlin questioned the validity of the voyage of the *Britannic* by claiming she was transporting fresh troops to the theatre of war.

Kapitanleutnant Kaleu Siess, the commander of *U73*, whose log confirmed he had solely lain mines.

> *According to reports so far to hand the ship was on its way from England to Salonika. For a journey in this direction the large number of persons onboard is extraordinarily striking, which justifies the forcible suspicion of the use of the hospital ship for purposes of transport. In as much as the ship carried the distinguishing marks of a hospital ship in accordance with regulations, there can naturally be no question of a German submarine in connection with the sinking.*

In view of the above remarks made in the German wireless, the Secretary of the Admiralty released a breakdown of those onboard the hospital ship. The *Britannic* crew numbered 625; an additional 500 were medical staff. The latter figure broke down to: Officers twenty-five, nurses seventy-six. This left a balance of 399 comprising sergeants, hospital orderlies, dispensers, laboratory assistants, operating room attendants, nursing orderlies, clerical staff etc. Further weight to his explanation appeared when the Press Bureau on 28 November released the following:

> *With reference to the 'forcible suspicion' stated in the German wireless to have been raised by the large number of persons on board* Britannic, *which was 'extraordinarily striking' and which was stated to be 1,106, it is of interest to note that according to the* Handbuch Fur Die Deutsche Handelsmarine *for 1914, which work is issued by the German Ministry of the Interior, the total compliment of the German* SS Imperator, *which is approximately the same size as the* Britannic, *is 1,184 officers and men.*

During her brief career *Britannic* returned 15,000 wounded and sick members of the armed forces to Britain. The loss of *Britannic* drew parallels to her ill-fated sister ship; almost a century after her demise she remains as much an enigma as *Titanic*. In 1975 the undersea explorer Jacques-Yves Cousteau located the wreck of the great hospital ship. The Cousteau team of divers made seventy dives on the wreck; in close proximity they discovered large weights of a design used to anchor German naval mines. The evidence supported the theory *Britannic* had steamed into a small minefield and was not torpedoed. While preparing for the search expedition Cousteau advertised for survivors of the tragedy, offering an opportunity to descend 360 feet by mini-submarine to the wreck of the hospital ship. Sheila Mitchell [nee MacBeth] survived the sinking; now an eighty-six-year-old grandmother, she contacted Cousteau. She last saw *Britannic* when she was a twenty-six-year-old nurse but despite her advancing years and a replacement hip, took the opportunity to descend to the sea bed to view the rusting remains of *Britannic*; she was the only survivor ever to return. The adventure of Sheila Mitchell will seem very familiar to viewers of the 1997 motion picture *Titanic*.

Alfred Highfield Cox, an eighteen-year-old survivor, who severely injured his leg while getting into a lifeboat. The boat was eventually rescued by a French warship, and before reaching Southampton they had transferred to several different vessels. On arriving home he discovered his calling up notice from the military authorities. Due to his seafaring profession it is assumed he would have been exempted.

A private owner sold the wreck for fifteen thousands pounds in 1996. The new British owners have received permission to grant licenses allowing divers to visit the wreck. To facilitate this, the Greek Government, mindful of the financial benefits of tourism, has diverted a shipping lane clear of the wreck site. A multi-million pound scheme to create an associated complex, comprising a diving school, *Britannic* museum and hotel has received a 2.8 million pound European grant.

One of the survivors, Thomas Walters, who had fourteen years' service with the White Star Company was rescued after nearly an hour in the water. The deck steward survived the wreck of the *Republic* in 1909, and served on the *Baltic* when she went to the assistance of *Titanic*, for which he received a gallantry medal. He also survived the wartime loss of the *Canada*.

Due to the ending of the Gallipoli campaign hospital ship numbers decreased, allowing vessels to be returned to general mercantile use. However, the beginning of the Salonika campaign minimised the number of ships returning to freight use. By early October sixteen hospital ships operated in the Mediterranean. Four hospital ships including the *Formosa* were ordered home, to allow the principle of interchanging hospital ships on long-distance voyages and cross-Channel service. This practice allowed the crews to recuperate from the hectic activity involved with shuttle service crossings. As 2,000 invalids required evacuation from the Mediterranean the War Office proposed to despatch *Aquitania*.

Berlin announced that during October, one hundred and forty-six Allied merchant ships of a total tonnage of 300,500 tons were sunk and seventy-two neutral merchant ships of a tonnage of 87,000. Since the beginning of the war the German announcement claimed to have destroyed Allied merchant ships to a tonnage of 3,332,000 of which 2,550,000 tons were British.

The Dutch cross-Channel ferry *Koningen Regentes* operated on the Tilbury to Flushing route for much of the war. Despite her neutrality she had frequent contact with the belligerents. On 11 November, approximately three hours' steaming from Flushing, a German aircraft circled above the paddle-steamer, much to the amusement of her passengers. The aviators dropped smoke balls ahead of the ship, as a signal for her to stop. On the bridge Captain P Reel appeared unaware of this signal, until the flyers used a megaphone to shout 'Halt your vessel'. Within minutes a German submarine surfaced, then ordered the steamer to head for Zeebrugge. Despite his protestations of neutral ships being immune from attack, Captain Reel was advised 'Go or be torpedoed'. On arrival at Zeebrugge German officials boarded the vessel, the British and French passengers were sent to prison camps and three neutral American citizens were sent home. The ship later resumed its normal service.

An explosion rocks *Braemar Castle*

The *Braemar Castle* was one of the best-known vessels of the Union Castle steamship company. She was built by Barclay Curle and Company, Glasgow, in 1898 and was 450 feet in length and fifty-two in breadth. Her net tonnage was 3,991, and her gross tonnage 6,318. She served as a troop carrier during the South African war and in 1909 underwent conversion to a troopship. Since the outbreak of the Great War the steamer had been entirely in government service, initially employed as a cross-Channel troop ship, she was one of the vessels which transported the naval division to the Dardanelles. After conversion to a hospital ship, with a capacity for 420 beds, she again returned to the Dardanelles coastline. Here she acted as a base hospital ship to which smaller craft transferred their patients; when full to capacity *Braemar Castle* departed.

As the furore over the loss of the *Britannic* continued the Red Cross emblazoned *Braemar Castle,* conveying 400 sick and wounded patients from Salonika to Malta, passed through the channel between the islands of Tenos and Mykenos. At midday a deafening roar rent the air and simultaneously the hull juddered; a mine or torpedo had detonated against the hospital ship. Two days after the loss of *Britannic* Allied minesweepers raced to aid the stricken Union Castle ship. All onboard were saved except for one seaman whose body was recovered; ten of the crew were reported as injured. Some accounts state six patients were killed but these are contrary to contemporary press reports.

The Secretary of the Admiralty announced on 24 November 1916:

> *The British hospital ship* Braemar Castle, *homeward bound from Salonika to Malta with wounded has been mined or torpedoed in the Mykoni Channel in the Aegean Sea. All on board were saved. No further news has yet been heard of* Britannic.

Due to her hull damage the ship's master thought it prudent to beach the vessel and summon aid; she was then towed to Malta for temporary repairs. After three month's repairs at La Spezia *Braemar Castle* returned to service. In 1918

Braemar Castle alongside the quay at Salonika.

she acted as a Murmansk base hospital ship during the Allied intervention in Russia.

The Union Castle Roll of Honour commemorates only one man connected with the hospital ship, Sub Lieutenant G S Holbeck RNR of *Braemar Castle* who died at Haslar Naval Hospital, Gosport. Curiously, enquiries with the Commonwealth War Graves Commission reveal Sub Lieutenant Gilbert Stuart Holbeck [alternative spelling, 'Holbech'] of HMS *Syria* died on 25 August 1916, which predates the mine incident.

Braemar Castle in peacetime.

Notes

1. Statistics from *The Great War*, part 81.
2. National Archives WO 95/4146.
3. On 1 December 1915 *U33* commanded by Gansser captured and sunk by gunfire the *Clan McLeod* while 100 miles east-south-east of Malta. While the crew were abandoning ship they were machine-gunned; a dozen crew died, others were wounded.
4. This date is prior to the commission date of 12 May 1915 stated by John H Plumridge.
5. Source: two documents from the National Archives. A minute sheet containing the three queries, and another listing the personnel and stores onboard.

Chapter Four

1917. Unrestricted Maritime Warfare

One of the smaller and lesser-known hospital ships was the 2,570-GRT Great Eastern Railway Company's *St Denis* [ex *Munich*]. Surviving documentation records that during the first couple of months of 1917, the steamer operated from Tilbury to the Hook of Holland repatriating incapacitated German prisoners of war. On the return trip *St Denis* brought home invalid Allied prisoners. The sailings required a great deal of diplomatic activity to ensure the safety of the hospital ship throughout both voyages. Due to the demand for places on this service, the Transport Department successfully obtained permission from the War Office to increase the amount of passengers by one hundred. Sleeping arrangements for the additional passengers consisted of a mattress on the deck.

Diplomatic correspondence records that on 7 February *St Denis* prepared to receive one officer and ninety-seven other rank German combatants for repatriation. The report described the officer as 'a mental case' and eighty-one of the ranks were cot cases. The British Government, fearing a Germanic uprising on home soil, had interned civilians of German ancestry, and some 2,400 Germans over the military age of forty-five years old wished to return to Germany. During this trip *St Denis* would repatriate 233 ailing civilians including six cot cases.

On the evening of 31 January 1917, the American Ambassador in Berlin was summoned to the Foreign Office. Herr Zimmerman informed him that at

St Denis formerly *Munich* changed for patriotic reasons.

midnight Germany would 'abandon the limitations which she had imposed on herself in the employment of her fighting weapons at sea'. Two major factors prompted the drastic change of policy, namely the failed negotiations for peace and Britain's two and a half year naval blockade of Germany. Henceforth no Allied vessels would be permitted access to a zone between a line drawn from Flamborough Head to Terschelling, an island of the Netherlands, and between Ushant [Isle d'Ouessant] off the Brest coast and Land's End. This effectively barred Channel traffic from the tip of Land's End to as far north as an imaginary line extending eastwards from the vicinity of Grimsby. Territorial waters of the neutral states were observed; however, any vessel entering the prohibited sectors of the North Sea or the Atlantic near the British Isles risked destruction. Neutral ships sailing in the restricted zone now sailed at their own risk. Not wishing to incur the wrath of the neutral United States of America the Germans permitted the regular traffic of American passenger liners, provided they carried no contraband.

American vessels were required to comply with certain conditions. Germany specified any liner's destination should be Falmouth. One steamer may run in each direction every week, arriving at Falmouth on Sundays and leaving on Wednesdays. All vessels were to approach Britain on a specific route devoid of mines. The ships' hull and superstructure required painting in three-metre wide vertical stripes alternating in red and white. Neutral continental passenger traffic also required the same markings as prescribed to American ships. On weekdays during the hours of daylight a Dutch paddle-steamer could sail unobstructed along a defined route.

Germany lost no time in putting their threats into action. The Dutch steamship *Gamma*, the Danish steamer *Lars Kruse* [employed on Belgian relief work], the American steamer *Housatonic*, and other vessels fell victims during the first three days of the new campaign.

The German Government completed its proclamation on 1 February by proclaiming, that it would 'henceforth tolerate no hospital ship' in defined areas, and would treat hospital ships as belligerents. The excuse given for this announcement was that the German Government had conclusive proof that British hospital ships had often been used for the transport of munitions and troops. An allegation that was robustly denied by the British Government who pointed out that the German Government's obvious remedy in any case of suspicion existed within the terms of the Geneva Convention, as any belligerent had the right to board and search any vessel they suspected of breaching the convention a remedy which they have never utilised.

After emphatically denying the German allegations the British replied:

From the German Government's statement that hospital ships will no longer be tolerated within the limits mentioned only one conclusion can be

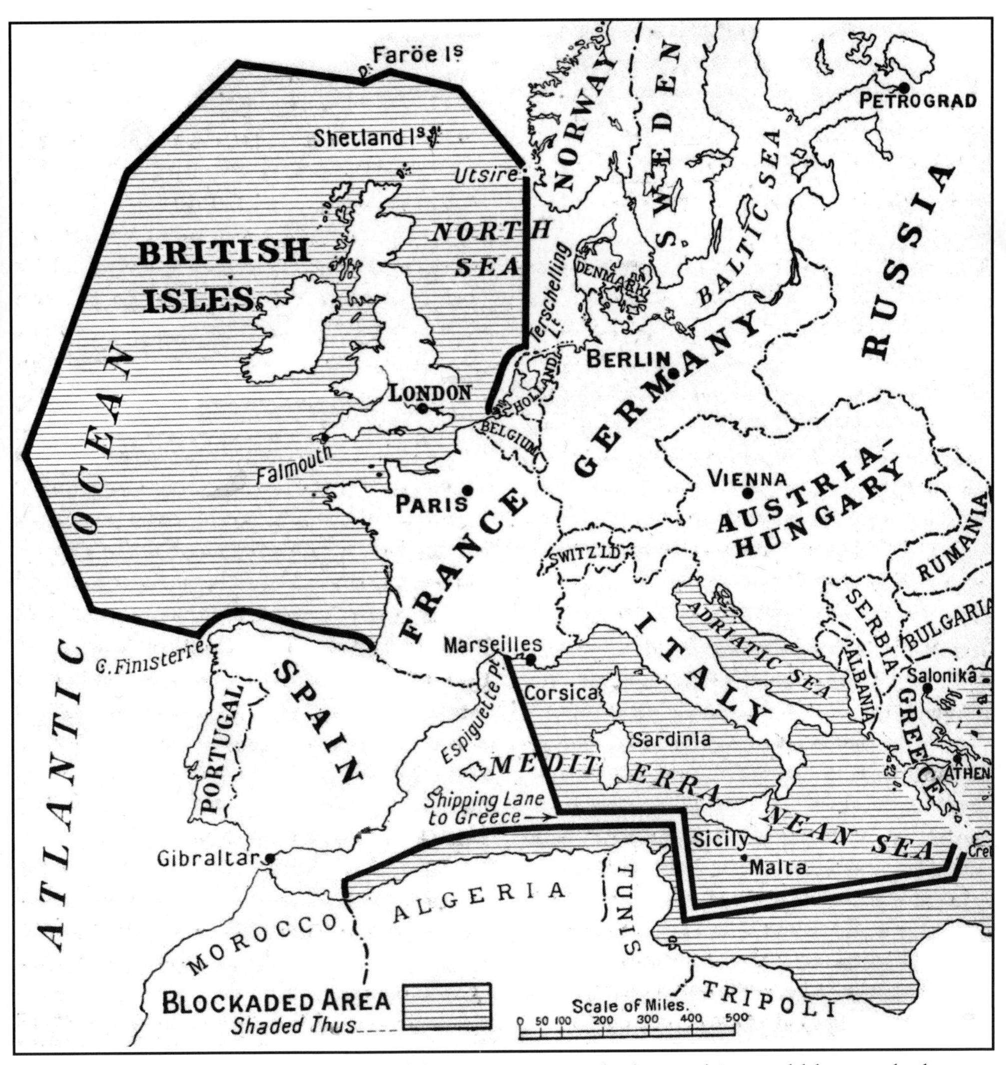

The so-called Barred Zone, declared by Germany, in which any ship would be attacked by the Central Powers.

drawn, viz, that it is the intention of the German Government to add yet other and more unspeakable crimes against law and humanity to the long list which disgraces her record. 'In these circumstances His Majesty's Government have requested the United States Government to inform the German Government that His Majesty's Government has decided that if the threat is carried out reprisals will immediately be taken by the British authorities concerned.'

To substantiate their claims of misuse of hospital ships the enemy referred to the Gallipoli campaign during which, to the fifty-nine hospital ships previously notified Britain added another forty hospital ships. They inferred the additional ships were operating as transports' citing the *Copenhagen* as an example. The vessel served as a transport prior to her registration as a hospital ship on 14 October 1914. Four months later, she reverted to trooping, until 1 January 1916 when Germany claimed she re-registered as a hospital ship. On 4 March of the same year, the Government deleted *Copenhagen* from the hospital ship register. German nationals interned on the Isle of Wight reported hospital ships departing from Southampton left heavily laden. An unidentified Dutch subject advised the German blockade was futile in view of the contraband cargoes loaded in the holds of British cargo ships. France also received condemnation due to several allegations, including the hospital ship *La France* had carried automobiles as deck cargo. For these reasons, hospital ships would no longer be tolerated in the barred zone.

Following her announcement, that neutral merchant ships were now officially legitimate targets, Germany faced severe international condemnation. On 3 February, President Wilson addressed Congress to announce the United States of America had severed diplomatic relations with Germany.

> *On the third of February last I officially laid before you the extraordinary announcement of the Imperial German Government that on and after the first day of February it was its purpose to put aside all restraints of law or of humanity and use its submarines to sink every vessel that sought to approach either the ports of Great Britain and Ireland or the western coasts of Europe or any of the ports controlled by Germany in the Mediterranean. That had seemed to be the object of the German submarine warfare earlier in the year, but since April of last year the Imperial Government had somewhat restrained the commanders of the undersea craft in conformity with its promise then given to us that passenger boats should not be sunk and that due warning would be given to all other vessels which its submarines might destroy, when no resistance was offered or escape attempted, and care taken that their crews were given at least a fair chance to save their lives in their open boats. The precautions were meagre and haphazard enough, as was proved in distressing instance after instance in the progress of the cruel and unmanly business, but a certain amount of restraint was observed. The new policy has swept every restriction aside. Vessels of every kind whatever their flag, their character, their cargo, their destination, their errand, have been ruthlessly sent to the bottom without warning and without thought of help or mercy for those on board, the vessels of friendly neutrals along with those of belligerents. Even hospital ships and ships carrying relief to the*

sorely bereaved and stricken people of Belgium, though the latter were provided with safe conduct through the prescribed areas by the German Government itself and were distinguished by unmistakeable marks of identity, have been sunk with the same reckless lack of compassion or of principle.

...I am not now thinking of the loss of property involved, immense and serious as that is, but only of the wanton and wholesale destruction of the lives of non-combatants, men, women and children, engaged in pursuits, which have always, even in the darkest periods of modern history, been deemed innocent and legitimate. Property can be paid for; the lives of peaceful and innocent people cannot be. The present German submarine warfare against commerce is warfare against mankind.

The German Government had gambled upon Uncle Sam remaining neutral, however, on 6 February the United States declared war upon Germany. It would take some time for America to transfer from a condition of neutrality to belligerency; during this period Germany strove with renewed vigour to complete her submarine blockade of Britain. As an island nation, Britain depended on her Mercantile Marine to deliver foodstuffs and matériel to these shores. If her trade routes were severed, the German submarine blockade would ultimately ensure a Germanic victory.

Enthusiastic crowds greeted the news that the United States had declared war on Germany.

The Royal Navy had no tangible counter-measures for anti-submarine warfare; technology would eventually catch up in the final period of the war. In the meantime, they attempted to counter the unseen menace with ineffective mines and torpedo. Both items were notorious for failing to explode on contact with an enemy vessel. Meanwhile the massacre of merchant ships increased dramatically; in the opening eight weeks of unrestricted naval warfare, over 500 merchant vessels went to the bottom of the sea. British shipyards already burdened by Admiralty work now had to construct vessels quicker than the enemy could sink them: it was a race against time.

Despite Admiralty denials, some U-boat commanders did respect the immunity of the hospital ships. On 23 February as HMHS *Dunluce Castle* [sister ship to the *Dover Castle*] steamed through the Eastern Mediterranean she had an encounter with the enemy. Shortly before sunset, the serenity of a pleasant evening ceased on hearing the unexpected crump of distant gunfire. The firing emanated from a distant U-boat whose series of range-finding shots rapidly closed on the hospital ship. As the shells screamed past her bow, the master telegraphed the engine room to halt all engines. His next command led to the well-rehearsed assembly at boat stations in readiness to abandon ship, prior to the expected sinking of *Dunluce Castle*. Possibly wary of British Q ship tactics, the U-boat stood off a good distance from the ship, and demanded to check the vessels papers. After a rowing boat containing the Chief Officer crossed to the surfaced submarine, a cursory inspection of documentation followed. After satisfying himself that the vessel complied with the terms of the Geneva Convention the submarine commander allowed the vessel to resume its voyage.

Another inspection occurred on 15 March off Ireland when *Kapitanleutnant* Freiherr Von Bothner ordered the Canadian transatlantic hospital ship *Essequibo* to stop engines. Built two years previously for the Royal Mail Steam Packet Company, the 8,489 gross registered tonnage British hospital ship was on loan to the Canadian Government. A boarding party from *U54* inspected the ship's documentation and seeing nothing suspicious sent the ship on its way. These are just two examples of no doubt many unpublished incidents where humanity presided over barbarity; unfortunately matters were about to take a decided turn for the worse.

Harland and Wolff launched the SS *Drina,* an 11,483-GRT Royal Mail Line vessel, in June 1912. The Admiralty requisitioned the twin-screw steamer several days before the declaration of war for use as a 221-bed naval hospital

The *Essequibo* launched July 1914 by Workman Clark & Co, Belfast and survived until 1957.

ship, nonetheless she once carried 900 patients. As an aid to stability *Drina* loaded deep within her hull 1,000 tons of sand as ballast. Her original accommodation appears to have remained in place for she had ten wards of varying sizes, the largest housed forty-six beds while the smallest could accommodate three mental patients. In common with all other vessels; the various ranks were segregated into separate wards, in respect of the social and military hierarchy prevalent during the period. On 1 March, the 500 feet long vessel was off Skokholm Island near Milford Haven when a mine attributed to *UC65* sank her. Fifteen of her crew perished. Her sinking is sometimes referred to as a hospital ship loss; however, *Drina* was a legitimate target. The vessel was an armed passenger cargo ship, on the final leg of her voyage from Buenos Aires to Liverpool, carrying passengers and laden with a cargo of meat and coffee.

Asturias.

Asturias, and the commencement of unrestricted warfare

The 12,002-ton Royal Mail Steam Packet Company vessel *Asturias* slid down the slipway at Harland and Wolff, Belfast on 26 September 1907. She was over 535 feet long with twin propellers whose engines drove her on at a respectable sixteen knots. Three days before hostilities began the Admiralty requisitioned her as a hospital ship for the cross-Channel route. She was reputed to be the largest hospital ship operating cross-Channel. In February 1915, she had successfully evaded an attack by torpedo and gunfire by U-boat.

HMHS *Asturias,* in compliance with the Geneva Convention, was painted white from stem to stern. A broad green band ran the length of the hull interrupted by prominent red crosses signifying her immunity. From dusk to dawn, the hospital ships were brightly illuminated, unlike other wartime shipping which displayed dimmed or no lights. Floodlights highlighted the huge red cross, cabin lights were unscreened and for good measure the entire length of the main deck on both port and starboard sides displayed a chain of appropriate green or red lights. Thus, lit up like a Christmas tree, the hospital ships were unmistakeable, even to someone with murderous intent.

A week earlier *Asturias* had discharged her cargo of some 900 wounded patients but despite being in full hospital colours, she was torpedoed by *U20* at a position approximately five miles north from Start Point, off the Devonshire coast. The weather at the time was fine but dark. Without warning shortly before midnight, one, possibly two, torpedoes struck the quarter of the vessel, damaged the rudder and exploded in the engine room destroying the electrical generators and plunging the ship into darkness. The torpedo exploded with such force *Asturias* had her stern blown off, yet she managed to beach herself at Bolt Head. Distress signals were promptly answered, and a patrol boat towed in a number of boats laden with survivors. Press reports advised between 300 and 400 were landed and local residents cared for many survivors, of which many were thinly clad in night attire. The explosion onboard injured some of those rescued and three died after reaching terra firma. Despite having no wounded on board the press reported forty-three killed and missing; thirty-nine were injured. Among the dead were a nurse, doctor and twelve RAMC orderlies. She had the dubious distinction of being the first hospital ship attacked since the German announcement. Two years previously, the commander of *U20* Walther Schweiger torpedoed and sank the Cunard liner *Lusitania* resulting in the death of 1,198 passengers and crew.

Commander of *U20* *Kapitanleutnant* Walther Schweiger.

On 28 March 1917, British newspapers published the latest announcement from the Secretary of the Admiralty:

> *The British hospital ship* Asturias *whilst steaming with all navigating lights on, and with all the distinguishing Red Cross signs brilliantly illuminated, was torpedoed without warning on the night of 20–21 March. The following casualties occurred:*

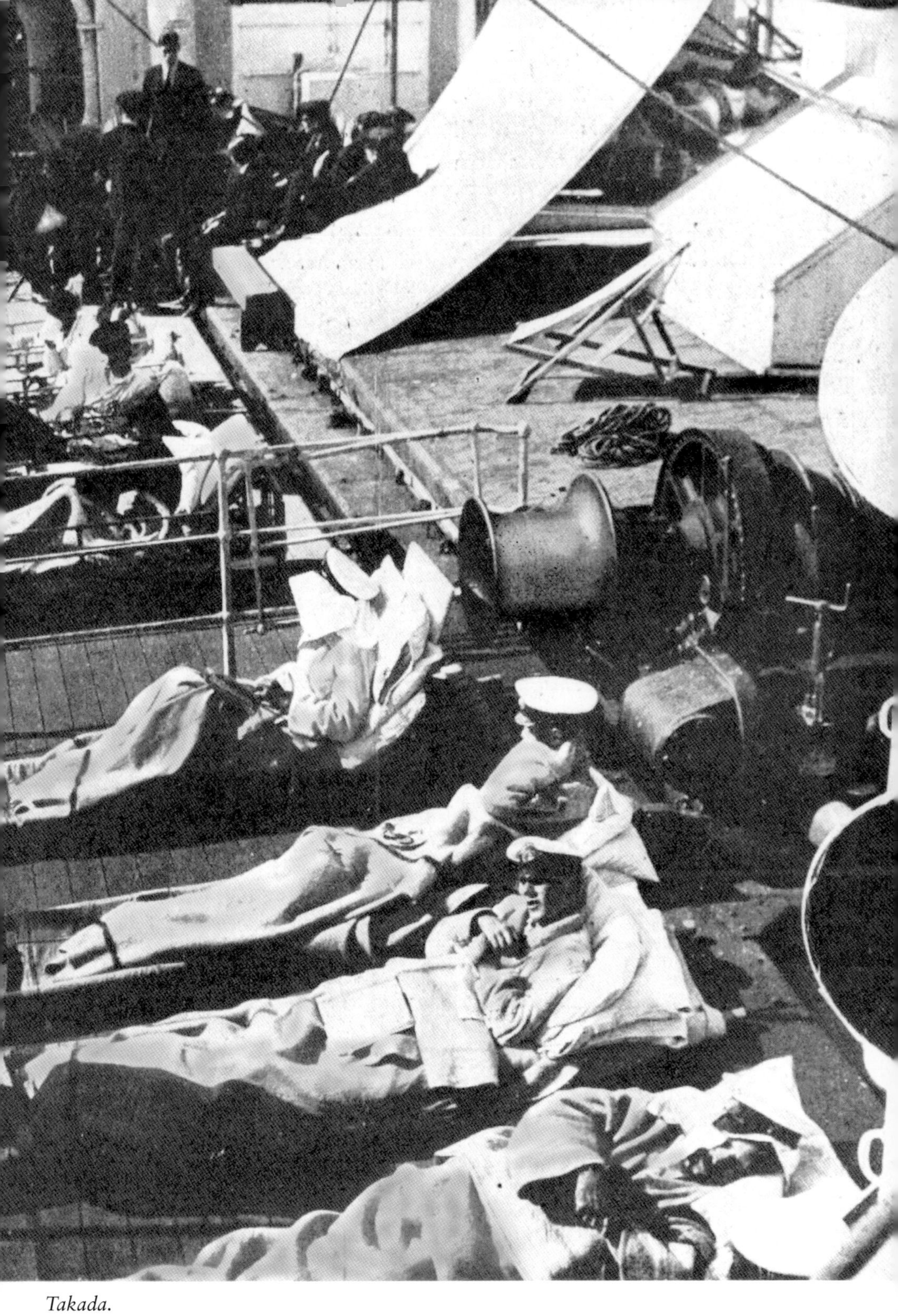

Takada.

> *Military, dead eleven: missing three, including one female staff nurse; injured seventeen.*
>
> *Crew, dead twenty missing nine, including one stewardess; injured twenty-two. The torpedoing of the hospital ship is included in the list of achievements claimed by U-boats as reported in the German Wireless Press message yesterday.*

William T Dobson of Cardiff recalled his escape from the doomed *Asturias*:

> *At about twenty minutes to twelve on the night of 20 March, I was asleep in my bunk when I was suddenly awakened by a loud noise; I dressed in two minutes and hastened on deck. There was an entire absence of panic, and forty-nine persons were coming up the stairs in a quiet manner with their lifebelts on. Everybody went to their stations and awaited orders. Presently several RAMC orderlies and members of the crew arrived with bandaged heads suffering from the effects of the explosion. It was then I noticed that the lights were getting weaker and about ten past midnight they went out.*
>
> *The steamer was still moving, but sinking slowly. An order came to take to the boats, and as there was no room in the one to which I was assigned, I went off and had just time to reach the last boat before it was lowered. The night was dark and cold. After the boat was lowered, it suddenly tipped and threw three men into the water, who I believe were crushed between the boat and the sinking vessel. Attempts were made to push off, but before this could be done, I heard a fearful smashing sound. The boat capsized and everybody was thrown into the water. It was too dark to see who was in the boat with me. There were about twenty people. The boat could hold forty-six.*
>
> *I immediately struck out away from the ship as the propeller was still going. The lights of a small ship a mile away were visible, and after shouting to the others to follow my example, I struck out towards it. I was in the water for over an hour, and the lights of the distant ship seemed as far away as ever, when suddenly a small patrol boat came alongside of me and I was lifted from the sea.*

A commemorative postcard recorded the demise of *Asturias* but more poignantly the Royal Army Medical Corps personnel, evidently comrades of the wordsmith Private W Bennet, who wrote:

> *In loving memory of Sister Phillips, Captain Atkinson, Sergeants Mallot, Kingsland and Fletcher, also Privates Blake, Muir, Rippon, Lloyd, Horsley, Wainman, Foley, Hart, Croft and Barrett, [there is no trace of the latter two names on the CWGC database] who lost their lives in the torpedoing of the* Asturias *on 20 March 1917.*

For King and Country

Twas about the coldest day in March
When the *Asturias* was ploughing her way
Through the waters of the English Channel
Where she had steamed so many a day.

Over 200 lives at the dead of night.
Dreamed of a time they thought so near,
When men would meet their wives
And lads their sweethearts dear.

Then there came a terrible explosion,
A torpedo had found its goal,
And what followed that fatal hour,
Is things that already have been told.

Thirteen of our chums and comrades,
As soldiers, found a sailor's grave
And a sister who we liked so well,
For her dear country, a life she gave.

And we their comrades, Holy Father
Pray to thee, in times so hard,
For all the Mothers, Sweethearts, and Wives
That thou will help them and be their guard.

For humanitarian reasons the Admiralty hoped the *Asturias* had succumbed to a mine, however a detailed investigation confirmed beyond all doubt torpedo damage. An official German wireless message of the 26th confirmed the Admiralty investigation. Three days later a further German message said:

It would, moreover, be remarkable that the English in the case of the Asturias should have abstained from their customary procedure of using hospital ships for the transport of troops and munitions.

The war for *Asturias* was over, the Admiralty towed her to Portsmouth where she became an Admiralty-owned ammunition hulk. In 1919, her former owners bought her back; following a two-year rebuild at her builders she emerged in the summer of 1923 as the cruise liner *Arcadian*. A decade later Japanese ship-breakers purchased the vessel.

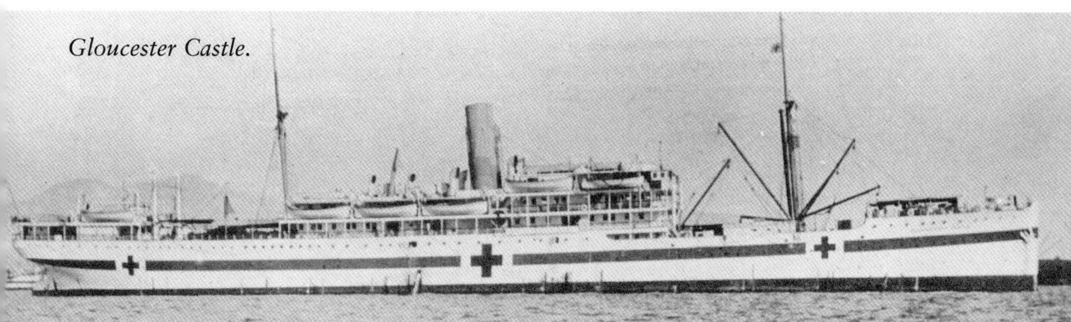

Gloucester Castle.

The *Gloucester Castle* torpedoed

On the night of 30 March, the six-year-old 7,999-ton HMHS *Gloucester Castle,* a veteran of the Dardanelles campaign, departed Le Havre homeward bound for the port of Southampton with 399 casualties onboard, including German wounded. Of these 300 were cot patients, the cot being the naval equivalent to a stretcher.

As the former Union Castle liner steamed towards Blighty across a rolling sea, all hands were in a state of high alert for the third officer had witnessed gun flashes on the horizon. These flashes were explained at 10.20 pm by a passing non-belligerent vessel which signalled she had been fired on by a submarine. The thwarted submarine commander resumed his patrol and soon chanced upon the approaching hospital ship, whose slow turn of speed earned her the nickname of 'Go Slowster Castle'. This time *UB32* launched her primary armament on the defenceless hospital ship, by now in mid Channel. The ship was struck on the starboard side at the forward end of the engine room, and a violent explosion occurred, producing a hole sufficiently wide enough through which four men could walk abreast of each other. A number of the engine room staff were severely scalded by escaping steam. The sea rapidly flooded the engine room and the after stoke-hold, but the Clyde-built ship refused to die.

The conduct of the master Edward John Holl and officers was exemplary during this incident; their calmness at a time of impending death greatly aided the deliverance of the crew and passengers. A well-drilled evacuation procedure now began: the nurses and medical staff brought all the patients to the upper deck allowing the immediate transfer of the wounded to the boats. In instances such as this, the nurses removed the wooden splints from fractured legs, as once immersed in the sea the splinted leg became buoyant and continually forced the man to lay back in the water, increasing the risk of drowning. The ship's wireless transmitter as was often the case in these circumstances had failed. As the abandon ship procedure gathered pace, distress rockets were fired at regular intervals in the hope of attracting rescuers.

Several of the wooden-planked boats were damaged while being lowered into the heavy sea and were taking in water. Lieutenant JB Colvin, commander of *P19* while escorting SS *Duke of Cornwall,* observed the rockets on his port beam, and sped off to investigate. He arrived on the scene to find the stopped and flooded *Gloucester Castle*, whose boats had safely cleared the ship but 150 people still remained on board. They immediately set about transferring the survivors from the lifeboats in their vicinity as they cleared the last boat the 810-ton destroyer HMS *Beaver* arrived. Colvin requested the destroyer to proceed alongside the hospital ship and transfer the survivors, the P boat wireless had also broken down; consequently *Beaver* radioed the naval commander-in-chief of the torpedoing of the hospital ship. The destroyer went alongside the hospital ship and removed sixty-five patients, thirty RAMC including two doctors and ten crew; meanwhile *P19* rescued three further boats of survivors. Colvin estimated he had 350 people on board crammed into every compartment on his ship including engine rooms, boiler rooms and store rooms. They were all accommodated inside as the severely over laden vessel's upper deck was awash, even while travelling slowly.

The Moss Line transport *Karnak* commanded by Charles Ruthven Stewart alerted by the distress rockets hastened to the rescue at top speed. Ladders and ropes were lowered over the sides, prior to the *Karnak* halting two cables astern of the stricken vessel and the occupants of number four boat were rescued.

An aerial view of the sinking *Gloucester Castle*.

Third Officer Cyrus Lloyd:

> *I was in command of number four boat when we abandoned ship. My boat contained forty-three wounded, twenty of which were severe cases, two sisters and three crew members including myself, a total of forty-eight.*
>
> *After getting safely from the ship I pulled to the transport* Karnak *who was lying about a half mile to leeward athwart the sea and rolling heavily. The cot cases were lifted on board in a cane basket slung from one of the ship's davits. No steam was available for lifting purposes so the fall was manhandled by the officers, engineers and the crew of* Karnak. *The operation was a difficult one owing to the heavy sea and the rolling of the*

ship, but was accomplished without incident of any kind. I feel it my duty to call your attention to the skilful and seamanlike way in which the captain and the crew carried out this difficult and dangerous operation. When safely on board we were all treated with great kindness and sympathy ...

A further twenty-one were saved from number twelve boat. Altogether fifty-four wounded, Matron Cashin, two nursing sisters, two RAMC staff and seven members of the crew, a total of sixty-seven were rescued. Captain Stewart wisely lifted the two lifeboats on deck in case an accident befell his vessel. Another vessel the *Bishopstone* also joined in the search for the remainder of the dozen lifeboats progress was slow due to the darkness and the stiff sea.

The emergency evacuation of the patients benefited greatly from the calm orderly conduct of the ship's matron Alice Alana Cashin. The forty-seven-year-old Australian nurse had previously worked in the General Hospital at Calais. After joining the Queen Alexandra's Imperial Nursing Service Reserve in July 1915, she took charge of a large General Hospital in Egypt. During this time, she received two mentions in despatches, including a special mention by Sir Archibald Murray, the Commander-in-Chief of the Egyptian Expeditionary Force. In June 1916, she became matron of the *Gloucester Castle*.

Matron Cashin later wrote:

Having secured my crucifix, prayer book and the cape that had been given me by Her Majesty Queen Alexandra, I checked that all the wounded were safe before I took to the boats.

A commendation noted that 'she showed an example of coolness and devotion to duty, and rendered valuable service'. She was awarded a bar [second award] to the Royal Red Cross medal, becoming the first to receive such an honour. The French also awarded her the Croix de Guerre.

At approximately 1.55 am Captain Holl advised Lieutenant Quinn of *Beaver* there was no immediate danger of the hospital ship sinking. Five minutes later Quinn ordered all vessels to extinguish lights in view of a possible submarine attack. By 3.25 the thorough search of the vicinity ceased, *P19* and *Karnak* were ordered to Portsmouth; but the transport remained until 4.30 when she finally hoisted the last of the survivors on board. The *Bishopstone* should have remained to search for boats at daylight, but at 5.00 am she was found to have left without orders. At 3.40 *Beaver* took the hospital ship in tow but the wire parted immediately. Over an hour later the destroyer *Sandfly* relieved *Beaver* which then proceeded to Portsmouth.

By noon next day, dockyard tugs under Commander Francis I. Carvill had towed the almost sinking hospital ship to safety, successfully beaching the vessel off Stokes Bay.

For reasons best known to themselves the Admiralty delayed their standard announcement of a hospital ship incident. A press cable wired from the Amsterdam office of Reuters at 6.35 pm on 11 April may have prompted the release of their delayed notice.

> *...Following vessels sunk recently in Channel, Atlantic, North Sea, sixteen steamers, seven sailing vessels, two fishing vessels. ... Greek steamer* Katina *[stop] following vessels names which in established convoy steamer with darkened light escorted by war vessel and destroyers [stop] hospital ship in middle Channel between Le Havre and Portsmouth [stop] laden transport steamer escorted by ...*

On 15 April the Secretary of the Admiralty announced: 'the British hospital ship *Gloucester Castle* was torpedoed without warning in mid-Channel during the night of 30/31 March. All the wounded were successfully removed from the ship.'

The Berlin wireless of 11 April proclaims she was torpedoed by a U-boat, thus removing any doubt in the matter.

A fortnight later tugs towed the vessel to the repair yard; however, she remained out of service until 1919. While in a Southampton dry dock, on 26 April an officer from HMS *Vernon*, Plymouth inspected the damaged area. He discovered a piece of steel three inches long by one inch wide, identified as part of the air vessel flange of a German fifty centimetre [19.7 inch] torpedo. The fragment contained a complete radical securing hole with the remains of the securing screw in place. Various identification numbers correlated with an

Gloucester Castle with attendant tug.

example recovered from the ex *UB26* confirmed the torpedo to be of that type.

The ship served during the Second World War until 15 July 1942, when the German commerce raider *Michel* sank her off the Ascension Isles. The thirty-year-old steamer had 154 people on board; of these eighty-two crew, six females, two children, and three male passengers died. The survivors, fifty crew, two women and two children, were transferred to the German supply vessel *Charlotte Schliemann* for internment in Japan. In 1946, a war trials tribunal found the commander of *Michel* guilty of war crimes leading to his imprisonment in Spandau Prison.

Captain Charles Ruthven Stewart [*Karnak*] and Captain Edward John Holl [*Gloucester Castle*] were awarded the Distinguished Service Cross in recognition of their zeal and devotion shown in carrying out the trade of the country during the war [*LG* 14 September 1917]. For their exceptional ability displayed during the *Gloucester Castle* episode the Chief Officer John Vyvyan Watson-Black [after promotion to Captain of *Galeka* he appeared again in the *LG* 29 October 1918] and Chief Engineer Harry Hunt Black were commended by the Admiralty.[1]

Under the Emergency War Programme a class of patrol craft, effectively coastal sloops, were constructed to relieve destroyers from patrol, escort work and anti-submarine work. Forty of these patrol boats each displacing 630 tons were constructed. Their armament usually consisted of one four-inch gun, one 2-pounder, anti-aircraft weaponry and two torpedo tubes of fourteen inch diameter, or suitable tubes salvaged from redundant craft. Two of these P boats were war losses; *P12* sank due to a Channel collision, the other struck a mine. Tyne Iron Shipbuilders launched the latter vessel *P26* on 22 December 1915. Capable of travelling at twenty knots, the almost 245 feet long patrol boats had a mild steel hull with a hardened steel prow for ramming submarines. Designed for high manoeuvrability, fuel economy and ease of construction, and with excellent sea-keeping qualities in all weathers, they proved excellent anti-submarine vessels.

Salta lost in a minefield

Although originally a French vessel, of the Marseilles, based *Société Générale des Transports Maritimes Vapeur* the *Salta* entered Admiralty service, manned by Union Castle personnel. The 7,284-ton vessel had forward and after hatches either side of a lengthy accommodation area. On 10 April despite the bad weather, the twin funnelled *Salta* commanded by sixty-two-year-old Captain Benjamin Thomas Eastaway, departed from Southampton with a cargo of hospital stores destined for Le Havre, where she would embark patients for the return trip. On the outward leg of the voyage she was accompanied by the hospital ships *Lanfranc* and *Western Australia,* all shepherded by a naval escort. During the night, the German minelayer *UC26*[2] sowed a minefield in the Le

Havre roads approximately half a mile north of the Whistle Buoy near Le Havre. The French notified the peril to the Royal Navy who escorted their charges safely past the minefield. At 11.20 am on 10 April, the convoy arrived off Le Havre to await identification prior to the removal of an anti-submarine boom. On receiving, the signal to proceed up the Channel Eastaway ordered a course to the north, the direction of the minefield. The master, concerned by the lack of a pilot in a strong sea, intended to let the rest of the convoy pass. Instead, he placed his ship in dire peril; frantic messages alerted him to his error but the strong wind and choppy sea conspired against him. All attempts to resume his original course failed; buffeted by the heavy seas *Salta* drifted into the minefield. The mine detonated at 11.45 am creating a terrific hole below the waterline, between number three hold and the engine room. The sea rushed in, *Salta* listed to starboard and sank approximately five to ten minutes later.

There were no wounded onboard but fifty-two RAMC personnel including five medical officers, nine nursing sisters and twenty-eight crew were posted missing presumed drowned.

The patrol boat *P26* carried approximately fifty personnel; her commander threw caution to the wind and entered the minefield to rescue survivors. For an hour, her crew pulled survivors from the stormy sea, until she too hit a mine, which claimed sixteen lives on the doomed patrol boat. *P26* broke in two and sank quickly. The casualties may have been higher without the gallant conduct of Lieutenant Commander Charles Carpenter Bolster RN. He fearlessly took his destroyer *Druid* into the danger zone to rescue survivors from the hospital ship, and *P26*. He exhibited a great piece of seamanship by the handling of his destroyer in heavy weather, by taking his warship alongside the wreck of the sinking patrol boat. In recognition of his valour, he received the Distinguished Service Order.[3] The destroyer also came to the aid of a swamped lifeboat full of survivors from *Salta*. The destroyer rescued all the occupants of the boat, excluding a hospital sister and Private Samuel Arnold Bodsworth of the RAMC. The nurse was so exhausted she was unable to grasp the ropes thrown to her; she fell over board but Bodsworth dragged her back into the boat. Private Bodsworth refused rescue; instead, he remained in the boat supporting the unconscious nurse. Due to the rough sea, he took a considerable risk but eventually managed to secure a rope around the nurse; naval ratings then pulled her aboard the *Druid*. Private Dodsworth received the Albert Medal for his role in the rescue.[4]

81853 Private Gwilym Pari Huws of the RAMC attached to HMHS *Warilda* was the son of a Welsh Independent minister in Dolgellau. He studied classics at Bangor University before enlisting into the RAMC in 1916. The twenty-three-year-old medic recorded within a small pocket diary:

> *10 April. Havre –* Salta *and two destroyer's sunk – dreadful night, many lost.*
> *13 April. Havre sailed under escort, ten hospital ships...*

The sea reluctantly gave up some of the lost souls, for weeks later the diarist recorded on 4 June the military funeral at St Marie Cemetery of an officer off the *Salta*. Three days later, he recorded: 'Corpse from *Salta* pulled in today. The following day the sea surrendered another corpse, however the majority have a sailor's grave.'

Two dozen recovered casualties

81853 Private Gwilym Pari Huws RAMC. After demobilisation in 1919, he studied medicine at Liverpool. He became a North Wales GP, later becoming Assistant Surgeon in Chief for North Wales.

from *Salta* and the patrol boat *P26* lie in plot sixty-two of St Marie Cemetery, Le Havre. A memorial also commemorates the following whose bodies were not recovered: sixty-two British soldiers, three unknown men and twenty-two men of the Egyptian Labour Corps. Also commemorated are the missing from *Galeka* mined on 28 October 1916, also the transport ship *Normandy* torpedoed on 25 January 1918.

Hospital ship reprisal air-raids

Number Three Wing of the Royal Naval Air Service [RNAS] arrived in France in the summer of 1916, to provide the British contribution of a Franco-British bombing force charged with raiding German strategic objectives. In reply to the sinking of *Asturias* Number Three Wing now readied themselves for the bombing of Freiburg; or to give it its full title Freiburg-im-Breisgau. The Baden town of 76,000 inhabitants lay on the railway line between Basil and Mannheim. A contemporary account described the town as an important military centre and headquarters of 29 German Artillery Brigade; and a large munitions works.

Seventy miles from Freiburg as the crow flies lay the RNAS Luxeuil base for bombers and Sopwith fighters. For this raid in addition to their four 65 lb bombs they loaded reams of printed paper to be dropped over the objective. Parliamentary papers reveal the leaflets printed in German contained the short sharp message 'As reprisal for the sinking of the hospital ship *Asturias* which took place on the night of 20th/ 21st March 1917'.

Shortly before midday on 14 April 1917, two flights from Number Two Squadron soared into the sky above Luxeuil. Unfortunately, B flight comprising four fighters and seven bombers failed to group in formation and returned to base. A depleted force of eight bombers escorted by four fighters headed for the town. During the inward leg the flight encountered minor anti-aircraft fire yet arrived unscathed above their objective. High above the town centre they released the bombs and leaflets, then set course for base. As the raiders approached the Rhine, six enemy Fokkers rose to intercept them. The enemy machines were superior to the less agile Sopwith; despite this, the RNAS fighters fought gamely thereby allowing the bombers to escape. Despite the technical advantage, one machine claimed two enemy fighters:

> *A short distance after leaving the objective and short of the Rhine we were attacked by six enemy machines coming up from the right and behind under my wing. My gunlayer opened fire at point blank range with both guns. I turned my head and saw a Rowland bank directly over my tail not twenty feet off, the tracer pouring into his fuselage from the three Lewis Guns. I turned inwards towards the next fighter* [Lieutenant Colonel Rathborne] *he was on my level and directly to my left; both of his guns were pouring out tracers. In making this turn, I exposed a Fokker biplane's*

Sopwith two-seater.

> *undertail at very close range. My gunlayer simply riddled this machine and I saw it turn on its nose and spin downwards. My controls gave a tug and went slack sending me into a stall. I put forward my empennage [elevator, vertical fin and rudder] and stick to their full extent and just managed to hold my height, but could only make forty knots, my elevator control on one side being cut and two bracing tails in my tail plane. We were attacked again shortly after I was in this helpless state, my gunlayer RG Kimberley driving this machine off. I saw one more enemy machine, pointed out to me by my gunlayer but it did not come into close range. I was heavily shelled crossing the lines and landed upon a small aerodrome at Corsieux. My gunlayer was slightly wounded in the leg and wrist during the first fight. He showed the gameness of a tiger and his shooting was wonderful. Flight Second Lieutenant WE Flett. Fighter 9654.*

The remaining trio of Sopwiths valiantly engaged the enemy; during the dogfight Flight Lieutenant George R S Fleming had the tail of his aircraft blown off. The aircraft plummeted to the ground; neither Fleming nor his gunlayer Alfred George Lockyer, a former engineering student, survived the crash. Another badly damaged aircraft Sopwith N5171 piloted by Wing Commander Rathborne managed to make an emergency landing. It was irrelevant to his cockney gunlayer, Air Mechanic first class G V Turner now slumped forward dead in his seat. Charles Edward Henry Rathborne survived the crash but became a prisoner of war until his repatriation in 1919.

He received the Distinguished Service Order for his role in the raid, his citation read:

> In recognition of his gallantry and devotion to duty during the course of a long distance air-raid in which he acted as pilot of a fighting machine which formed part of the escort. Wing Commander Rathborne was brought down whilst protecting the bombing machines, his engine having been put out of action. It was owing to the gallantry and self-sacrifice of this officer and those of the other fighting machines that all the bombing machines returned safely from the raid. [*LG* 14 January 1919].

In mid-afternoon B flight, comprising seven bombers and three fighters took off for Freiburg. In their slipstream followed French aircraft comprising five Sopwith fighters, six Sopwith bombers, three Nieuports and one Spad. As the leading British machines crossed the front line, they again encountered enemy aircraft, downing two of the enemy machines. Fires still blazed after the earlier raid, and all seven bombers now released their deadly loads on the burning conurbation below.

> *Five miles north-west of the objective we engaged a fast enemy machine who was attacking another fighter, and observed the fire of my gunlayer* [Petty Officer Herbert JL (Bert) *Hinkler*[5] *hit all along the fuselage whereupon*] *he immediately fell quickly to the ground in a spinning nosedive. After the fight, I observed one of our fighters losing height slowly – Flight Sub Lieutenant H Edwards, I think. Seven miles from the lines, our engine cut out, but we managed to glide two miles into France and landed in the Vosges Mountains. Flight Sub Lieutenant Pattison. Fighter 9708.*

The struggling aircraft observed by Pattison did belong to Edwards whose machine had been hit. Flight Lieutenant Harold Edwards[6] landed in the German

Bert Hinkler, a trailblazer of aviation.

lines and became a captive. Air mechanic Joseph Lawrence Coughlan died in the aircraft. The French fared much better as only one bomber suffered damage, this being on the return when the aircraft attracted heavy shellfire. The pilot landed his machine safely in French territory but his aircraft attracted much artillery fire from batteries sited three kilometres away.

The Secretary to the Admiralty issued this statement:

> *In consequence of the attacks made by German submarines on British hospital ships in direct and flagrant contravention of The Hague Convention number ten, a large squadron composed of British and French aeroplanes carried out a reprisal bombing of the town of Freiburg on Saturday 14 April 1917. Many bombs were dropped with good results. In spite of a number of hostile aeroplanes, all machines returned safely with the exception of three.*

Two days later the Germans published through the wireless message an abusive protest, which 'categorically contested any justification' for this reprisal. According to German reports, the raid resulted in the deaths of seven women and four men, and injuries to twenty-seven others. The Allies were indifferent to these protestations and placed much emphasis on the 'purely military character of the measures adopted'. They defended their action by advising that the airmen who carried out the attack were exposed to and did in fact incur precisely the same dangers from the town defences, as they would have been exposed to in the course of an ordinary action.

Each attack on the hospital ships produced a wave of public indignation, for the sinking of the helpless vessels was contrary to the Edwardian sense of fair play and chivalry. While the armed forces could be decimated fighting for a bitterly contested ridge or ruined village, their casualties were considered by the Staff Officers to be acceptable in a war of attrition. In stark contrast the loss of non-combatants, especially female nursing staff, was deemed abhorrent; each innocent death upon the high seas fuelled the increasing call for reprisals. The Freiburg raid occurred to satiate the demand for retribution; one can only wonder precisely what the raid intended to achieve. It would be reasonable to conclude that after several years of warfare no belligerent would be expected to be brought to heel by such a short sharp shock.

As an immediate reaction to the raid on 12 May, the transfer commenced of French and British officer prisoners of all ranks to Freiburg-im-Breisgau. According to a Berlin telegram, the officers were detained in various hotels situated in the town. This measure was evidently intended to deter the Allies from making further raids on the town; however, intervention came from an unexpected quarter.

Within the House of Commons, serious reservations were voiced concerning reprisal raids. While the policy gained the wholehearted approval of the majority of the population, many ministers disapproved. One member of the house stated 'that to bomb German towns was to punish the wrong people. We were not going to stop German crime by committing crime ourselves. We should keep our hands clean up to the end of the war' [Hear, Hear]. Germany showed her indifference to reprisal raids when three days later the enemy sank two mercy ships in quick succession.

Considering the precious resources and personnel required for the handling of military sick and wounded, it could be argued that German aims would have been better served if the vessels engaged on missions of relief delivered, unmolested, their patients safely to British shores. On the other hand, Germany realised that each lost hospital ship would be replaced from the rapidly diminishing merchant fleet, thereby furthering their objective of isolating Britain.

In April 1917, the U-boat campaign reached its high point: 395 vessels amounting to 881,027 tons sank predominately due to torpedoes. By late April, this amounted to an average of approximately thirteen ships daily, a sobering thought for the men and women of the Mercantile Marine. The Secretary of the Admiralty announced the latest outrage and summed up the situation:

Ward F, on HMHS *Garth Castle*.

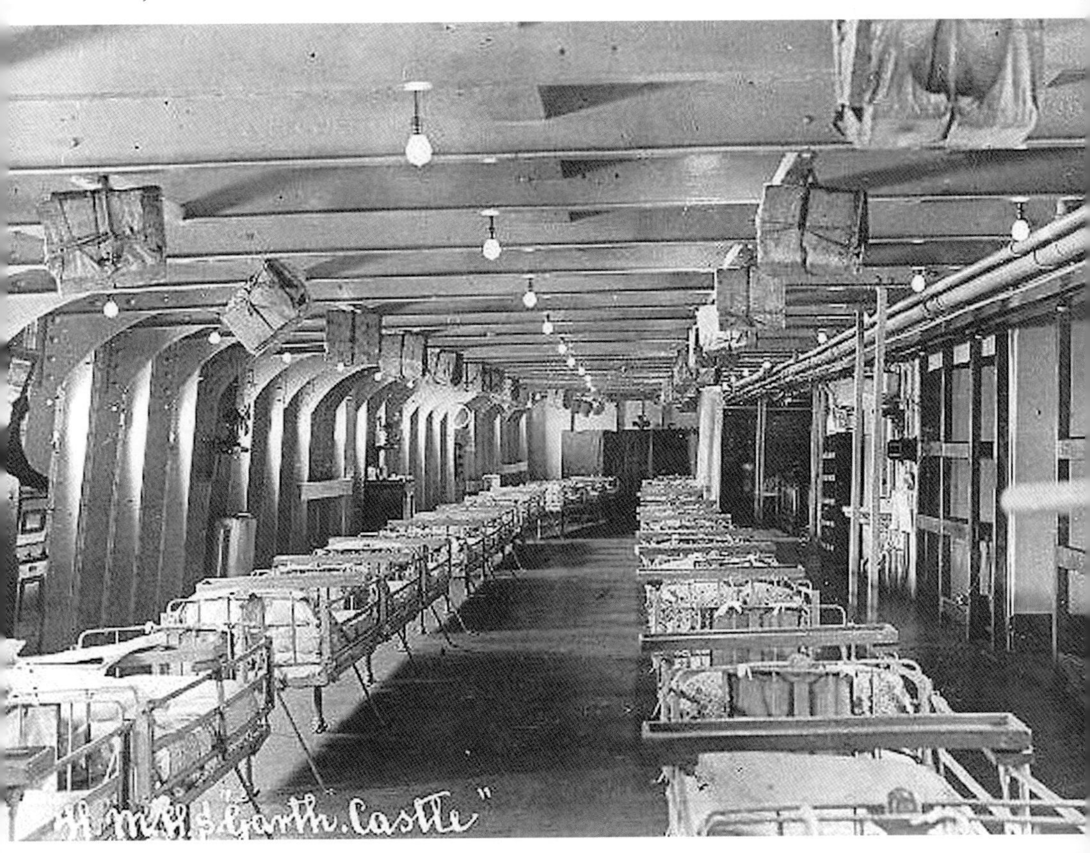

On the evening of April 17th the SS Donegal *and* Lanfranc *while transporting wounded to British ports were torpedoed without warning.*

Owing to the German practice of sinking hospital ships at sight, and to the fact that distinctive marking and lighting of such vessels render them more conspicuous targets for German submarines, it is no longer possible to distinguish our hospital ships in the customary manner. One of these two ships, therefore though carrying wounded, was not in any way outwardly distinguished as a hospital ship. [This refers to the defensively armed *Donegal.*] *Both were provided with an escort for protection.*

The Donegal *carried slightly wounded cases, all British. Of these twenty-nine men, as well as twelve of the crew, are missing and presumed drowned.*

The Lanfranc *in addition to 234 wounded British officers and men carried 167 wounded German prisoners, medical personnel of fifty-two and a crew of 123. Of these, the following are missing and presumed drowned: Two wounded British officers. Eleven wounded British other ranks. One RAMC staff. Five crew. Two wounded German officers. Thirteen wounded German other ranks.*

British patrol vessels at imminent risk of being torpedoed rescued 152 German prisoners. The next of kin are being informed in all cases of loss of life.

Lanfranc attacked and sunk by submarine

The Dundee-built *Lanfranc*, named after an Italian churchman and theologian who became the Archbishop of Canterbury 1070 to 1089, sailed on her maiden voyage on 18 February 1907. She was destined for an uneventful working life conveying passengers to and from Lisbon and North Brazil. The company ran a service from the United Kingdom to Manaus, some 900 miles inland from the Atlantic coast. The city lies on the north bank of the Negro river, eleven miles above its confluence with the Amazon river. The passenger cargo liner operated on the service until late 1915, when the Admiralty requisitioned her from the

Lanfranc in company livery.

Booth Line, and she underwent conversion to a hospital ship.

On 17 April 1917, she had 387 patients on board including twenty-seven German officers and 140 other rank wounded prisoners of war. There were 326 cot cases of severely wounded men who included a number of amputations and fracture cases. The hospital ship cast off her Le Havre moorings and headed for Southampton. She retained her Red Cross livery but now sailed under escort. By five-thirty in the afternoon, the escorted steamer had put Le Havre some forty-two miles behind her stern when without warning *UB40* launched a torpedo with devastating effect. After the disaster, a *Daily Telegraph* journalist interviewed a British officer survivor, whose sensationalised account appeared in the 23rd April edition.

The Lanfranc *was attacked by a submarine about seven-thirty on Tuesday evening, just as we had finished dinner. A few of us were strolling back and forth on the deck, when there was a crash, which shook the liner violently. This was followed by an explosion, and glass and splinters flew in all directions. I had a narrow escape from being pitched overboard, and only regained my feet with difficulty. In a few minutes, the engines had stopped, and the* Lanfranc *appeared to be sinking rapidly, but to our surprise, she steadied herself and, after a while remained motionless. We had on board nearly 200 prisoners belonging to the Prussian Guard and about twice as many British wounded, among the latter being some very bad cases. The moment the torpedo struck the* Lanfranc *the Prussians made a mad dash for the lifeboats. One of their officers came up to a boat close to which I was standing. I shouted to him to go back, whereupon he stood and scowled. 'You must save us,' he begged. I told him to wait his turn. Other Prussians showed their cowardice by dropping on their knees and imploring pity. Some of them cried 'Kamerad' as they do on the battlefield. I allowed none of them to pass me.*

Meanwhile the crew and the staff had gone to their posts. The stretcher cases were brought on deck as quickly as possible, and the first boats were lowered without a delay. Help had been summoned, and many vessels were hurrying to our assistance. In these moments, while wounded Tommies – many of them as helpless as little children – lay in their cots unaided, the Prussian morale dropped to zero. Our cowardly prisoners made another crazy effort to get into a lifeboat. They managed to crowd into one, but no sooner had it been lowered than it toppled over. The Prussians were thrown into the water, and they fought with each other in order to reach another boat containing a number of gravely wounded British soldiers.

The behaviour of our lads I shall never forget. Crippled as many were, they tried to stand at attention while the more serious cases were being looked after. Moreover, those who could lend a hand scurried below to help in saving friend or enemy. I have never seen so many individual illustrations of genuine chivalry and comradeship. One man I saw had had a leg severed, and his head was heavily bandaged. He was lifting himself up a staircase by the hands, and was just as keen on summoning help for Fritz as on saving himself. He whistled to a mate to come and save a Prussian who was unable to move owing to internal injuries. Another Tommy limped painfully along with a Prussian officer on his arm and helped the latter to a boat. It is impossible to give adequate praise to the crew and staff. They were all heroes. They remained at their posts until the last man had been taken off, and some of them took off articles of their clothing and threw them into the lifeboat for the benefit of those in need of warm covering. The same spirit manifested itself as we moved away from the scene of the outrage. I saw a sergeant take off his tunic and make a pillow of it for a wounded German. There was a private who had his arms around an enemy trying hard to make the best of an uncomfortable resting place.

In the midst of all this tragedy, the element of comedy was not wanting. A cockney lad struck up a ditty, and the boat's company joined in the chorus of 'all dressed up with nowhere to go'. Then we had 'Take me back to Blighty', and as a French vessel came along to our rescue the boys sang 'Pack up your troubles in your old kit bag'. The French displayed unforgettable hospitality. As soon as they took our wounded on board they improvised beds and stripped themselves almost bare so that English and German alike might be comfortable. Hot refreshments were provided and cigarettes distributed, and as the ship headed for an English port our fellows, with great gusto, joined in the chorus of 'When we wound up the watch on the Rhine'.

An unidentified YMCA worker described the reception awaiting the rescued victims of *UB40*. This appeared in a 1917 two-penny booklet entitled *The war on the hospital ships*. The following account gives some insight into the impact of a maritime disaster. The shock and trauma for able-bodied passengers would be traumatic enough, yet for wounded personnel the situation must have been far more traumatic, if not life-threatening.

We have had a most stirring and exciting day. We got down to the YMCA hut this morning to find that part of the crew and some of the wounded soldiers rescued from a torpedoed hospital ship had been brought into the dock. They were sent into us to wait for ambulances. The ship HM Hospital Ship Lanfranc *was struck at 8.00 the previous evening. Some French fishing smacks dashed to the rescue and brought them in about eight o' clock this morning. Many of the men were only half dressed, and all were cold and hungry. We made a great horseshoe of our tables round the stove, and got them all a hot breakfast.*

Lanfranc.

Three of them were so badly wounded that they had to be laid on tables. It was awful to see men with their bandages torn off their wounded limbs, and the stories they told bring home to one most forcibly what a shipwreck of wounded soldiers must be like. Some of the crew seemed all right, but after a while, I suppose the shock began to tell, and they looked too dreadful for words. They were all so nice and so brave, for some were clearly in a great deal of pain.

One of those rescued was the officers' mess page, a mere child of about fifteen. We were told that there were 242 British soldiers, only two of which were walking cases, and 130 Germans; thirty-five of these were officers. Two RAMC men were lost, and it is feared, some of the crew.

Some of the less badly German wounded stampeded and jumped into a boat, partly filled with their own wounded. This they swamped, and the only person saved in it was an English boy, brought into us with a crushed hand and leg. A chain down the ship's side caught him, but it held him until he could be removed.

After the dockers had left, and we had got all straight and tidy, some of the wounded went to the piano and began to sing, they are wonderful. It made us feel queer to hear them sing 'Pack up your troubles in your old kit bag' and more.

After a little while Miss Waldegrave went to them and said she felt they ought to give thanks for being safe-would they join in a hymn. Every man came to the piano except one man who was too bad to move [the worse cases had been taken away]. *They then sang most wonderfully, 'O God, our help in ages past'. Then Miss Waldegrave said a short prayer, and before she could move away one of the men said 'might they have "For those in peril on the sea" for their mates, as they did not know where they might be?'*

I have never heard anything like it. Many broke down. In the middle, the cars came to take them away. They finished the hymn and then said goodbye. Many of them ran back two or three times and said 'Thank you, thank you; we shall never forget this morning'. We shall certainly never forget them, and the stories they told. One of those rescued had neither arms nor legs; another, who had lost both hands and both feet managed to get on deck unaided!

It is incredibly difficult if not impossible to disseminate the truth relating to the hospital ship sinkings. Each side released their own versions of events in an attempt to score the maximum points in the propaganda war. The British media continued to portray the enemy as a beast and I see no reason why Germany should not treat our armed forces in a similar manner, after all, it was a war of attrition. Undisputedly Britain trounced Germany in the propaganda war, but were the facts behind the headlines true? That hospital ships sank due to enemy action is fact but some of the detail behind the headlines can be very misleading. After the loss of *Lanfranc* a semi-official statement appeared justifying the German attitude towards hospital ships, in particular the *Lanfranc*.

The statement referred to the seizing of the *Ophelia* in October 1914 by the British on an 'empty pretext', and the fact that *Lanfranc* bore hospital ship markings despite the British Government notifying the German Government, through American channels, of the removal of *Lanfranc* and five other hospital ships from the list of hospital ships. The statement declared:

More convincing proof of British unscrupulousness in misusing the marks of hospital ships could hardly be given. The British procedure of carrying German wounded on these so-called hospital ships in the dangerous barred zone is the crowning criminal English accusation.

The British reply reiterated that *Ophelia* was condemned by a British prize court after its German claimant had every opportunity to present its case fairly. With regard to *Lanfranc*, there had been insufficient time to repaint all the vessels withdrawn from the list. This fact should have made no difference for Germany had already declared her intention of ignoring such markings. In this instance, the vessel served solely as a hospital ship; Great Britain absolutely denies the misuse of hospital ships.

The fine book *With a Camera in My Pocket* by Joyce Mollet, recalls the fascinating life and times of Great War nurse Mary Jane Hughes. Within the book is a photograph of the wrecked German hospital ship *Deborah*, sunk across the Channel to the port of Dar-es-Salaam, and a severe hazard to navigation. According to the Territorial Force Nursing Service [TFNS] nurse on examination, 'the ship was found to be full of ammunition'.

The abandoning of the Red Cross and the loss of the *Donegal*

As the distinctively marked and illuminated hospital ships could no longer rely on the guaranteed immunity offered by The Hague Convention the hospital fleet, excluding the Mediterranean and cross-Atlantic vessels, gradually reverted to a less conspicuous profile. No longer protected by their agreed immunity, the Government decided for their own safety the sick and wounded, together with medical personnel and supplies, would cross the Channel in vessels carrying no distinctive markings. They would also steam without lights in the same manner as other merchant navy ships. After notifying the German Government of their intention, they withdrew from the list of registered hospital ships certain vessels, now designated as hospital transport ships. In common with other merchant ships, they carried at least one artillery piece mounted aft solely for defensive use. One such vessel was the former hospital ship *Donegal*, recently adapted for use as a hospital transport.

Constructed in 1904 in the Greenock shipyard of Caird and Company for the Midland Railway Company, the Belfast registered *Donegal* was one of a quartet of vessels built for the Midland Railway Company to operate from the new port

The ferry *Donegal* in Heysham harbour.

at Heysham, on a regular service to Belfast. The steamer had a tonnage of 1,885 tons and a length of 331 feet, her triple expansion steam engines propelled her at a speed of thirteen knots. After a decade of sea crossings, war service beckoned. Her first encounter with the enemy seems to have occurred on 1 March 1917, in the English Channel, when she was chased by a U-boat, which she managed to outrun and evade.

The former hospital ship now served as His Majesty's Ambulance Transport [HMAT] *Donegal.* Prior to her final voyage, her pronounced white paintwork disappeared under a drab wartime colour scheme, [possibly a dazzle camouflage paint scheme in keeping with countless other merchant vessels], and she had a thirteen-pounder gun mounted on the poop deck. On 17 April, at the port of Le Havre 639 casualties boarded; thirty-three of these were cot cases, a medical officer and four stretcher-bearers also arrived. Any passenger having trepidation about the crossing gained reassurance by the presence of the destroyers *Liffey* and *Jackal* assigned to escort the vessel. Her master ordered a course for Blighty and *Donegal* soon commenced butting her way across the Channel.

Lurking out in the Channel *Oberleutnant* Von Zerboni di Sposetti the commandant of *UC21* watched the approaching vessels. At approximately seven forty-five in the evening, a torpedo hurtled from his craft, possibly aimed for the leading escort. On board *Donegal* Captain John Jackson spotted the track of the torpedo some 375 yards off his port side, and astern of one of the destroyers.

> *I immediately gave the order to the helmsman 'hard to starboard' Jackson later reported, 'However it was too late and my ship was struck near the propeller, with the result the stern was practically blown away, and carried with it the 13-pounder gun, which had only been mounted the day before. One of the gunners standing by it is missing and must be killed.'*

As the seawater cascaded in, *Donegal* rapidly settled in the water speed was vital to avert a great loss of life. However, the port lifeboats prevented the destroyer HMS *Jackal* from coming alongside. After the destroyer crushed the boats against the stricken vessel 500 wounded servicemen and the ship's crew were rescued. Other vessels also came to their aid. *Donegal* was in her death throes; at about eight-thirty, she unexpectedly lurched to starboard catapulting those left onboard into the sea, before she plunged to the sea bed. Gallant deeds were performed around the wreck. Lieutenant H Holehouse RNR received a Royal Humane Society bronze medal, his citation read: 'A wounded soldier was seen in the water; it being nearly dark at the time, Lieutenant Holehouse jumped in and brought the man to his ship, but when got onboard he did not recover.' During the rescue operation, the submarine fired another torpedo at one of the ships, whose officer suddenly swerved the vessel and watched the torpedo pass safely by.

The casualty figures in contemporary newspapers reported eleven crew died and twenty-six to twenty-nine military deaths.

Two people onboard the *Donegal* had a common bond, they had survived the 1912 sinking of the *Titanic*. Fireman Arthur John Priest served on *Olympic* which collided with HMS *Hawke* in 1911; the repairs required by *Olympic* delayed the construction of *Britannic*. Priest survived another sinking and that of *Britannic*. It seems likely this individual gave an account of his latest ordeal to a journalist, who fails to identify his subject but given the similarity in his career, we can assume it is none other than fireman Priest who again survived to tell the tale.

After the loss of *Titanic*, he had frostbite in four toes and an injured leg. In February 1916, he was on His Majesty's auxiliary armed cruiser *Alcantara* [formerly Royal Mail Lines] patrolling the North Sea. After engaging the disguised German raider *Greif* a twenty-minute battle ensued, both opponents were destroyed and sank. This time Priest sustained shrapnel wounds to the leg and suffered burns. Undeterred by his hardship he signed on for *Britannic* and eventually the *Donegal*.

> *I was off duty, and was sleeping aft in my brother's bunk when the explosion came. It was a good thing for me that I was not in my own bunk. That had been given up to a wounded soldier while I was on duty. When the explosion occurred, it blew to pieces that part of the ship where my bunk was. As it was, I was injured. After the crash, part of the deck above my head fell in, and gashed my forehead rather badly. After struggling for a bit in the dark, I got free of the wreckage and managed to get on deck. The blood was streaming down my face so I was ordered into a boat at once. We were picked up by another boat not long afterwards.*

The former ferry *Donegal* was torpedoed by *UC21*in the English Channel.

> *When I saw him, the twenty-nine-year-old fireman's head was swathed in bandages, the eye in his own expressive way was 'bunged up' and his lips and nose were swollen out of all shape. One hand was also wrapped in bandages. Yet he still smiled cheerfully if painfully as he talked and the last thing he told me was he had already fixed up for another boat if he was well enough to go when she sailed.*

Another survivor, Cornwall-born Archibald [Archie] Jewell served as a lookout on the ill-fated *Titanic* from which he escaped in lifeboat seven. He became a key witness in the subsequent maritime investigation into her loss. Several years later the married man, resident in Southampton, signed on as an able-bodied seaman on *Donegal* and was lost at sea.

An unrecorded witness described the arrival ashore of the *Donegal* survivors:

> *One-thirty o'clock on a belated winter's morning. Colder and wretched than it had been at midnight. The waters of the harbour were being whipped to a frenzy in the darkness by a viciously driving sleety rain. A good time enough for those in warm beds, but no sort of a night for seafaring, or for lying on the plains of Picardy, say, trying to get out of a water-logged, sharp-sprayed shell crater. Suddenly the line of watchers at the quay head, their coats all gleaming, jumped into life and animation, for from around the end of the long jetty appeared a masthead light. 'Here they are, at last! How cold and wet they will be.'*
>
> *A second light followed the first, and handled as though they were rubber tyred perambulators on a footpath, two of His Majesty's destroyers were laid gently alongside the stage, their sides just kissing the great rope fenders. The whole operation had been performed in perfect silence; but in that dramatic instant of soundless contact with the wharfside fenders, a full-throated shout rent the rainswept air from the deck of the first destroyer, 'Three cheers for the* Hummingbird *and the* Whipsnake!"
>
> *For a full minute the thunder of cheering rolled out into the night; a very slow moving sound, compact of vivid and varied emotions, and contributed to by men who a day or two earlier had been fighting under the scream of our own and enemy shells, and forcing their way through knee-deep mud and tangles of German barbed wire in the inferno between Vimy Ridge and Arras. There they had been wounded, and passed out for rest and treatment in Blighty. But since then, all unarmed and helpless, they had been suddenly called on to face the Bosche again, and in his vilest and most murderous guise. Yes, the sum of the cheering was moving, its component parts singularly varied. For a full minute the cheering rose and fell athwart the driving rain, and then the* Hummingbird *made the answer with one long blast from her siren; full of defiance and somehow, as it seemed to our ears, of good British cheer.*

Then they began to come ashore; a long stiffly-moving file of shaky, utterly weary souls, wrapped about as to their heads or arms, necks or shoulders, with rain and brine-soaked bandages. Few had had any sleep for several nights; all were newly plucked from the midmost jaws of death among the shell-holes; and all had faced the Bosche again, at his ugliest since leaving France. The fatigue in their eyes, which no man may hide in such a case, was pathetic, but there was a look in the same eyes that overrode anything like pathos – the look of indomitable. Some of the greyness began to fade from out of their faces now, as, warmed and cheered and comforted, they climbed into the waiting train, filling coach after coach in endless succession. As they sank into their seats, one heard short, hard sighs of relief pass their tight-closed lips…

Private Huws RAMC entered in his diary on 18 April Southampton:

> Donegal *and* Lanfranc *torpedoed, parade on quay 12.45 am. We unloaded those saved from* Donegal *and* Lanfranc; *some of us worked through until 6 am.*

Red Cross nurses played a significant role in the war effort.

Articles in 24 April newspapers reported the International Red Cross Committee had addressed a note to the German Government referring to their order issued on 29 January 1917, regarding the sinking of hospital ships and to the torpedoing of the hospital ships *Asturias*, *Britannic* and *Gloucester Castle*. The communiqué read:

> *The International Committee, whose right and duty it is to enforce respect for the principles of the Red Cross and Geneva Convention by reporting violations of them, draws the very serious attention of the German Government to the responsibility which it should assume towards the civilised world, by persisting in a resolution which is in contradiction to the humanitarian conventions which it has pledged itself to solemnly respect. In torpedoing hospital ships it is not attacking combatants but defenceless beings wounded or mutilated in war, and women who are devoting themselves to the work of relief and charity.*
>
> *Every hospital ship is provided with external signs prescribed by international conventions, the use of which has been regularly notified to belligerents, and should be respected by belligerents. The latter may according to the Hague Convention, exercise the right of search, but have in no case any right to sink a ship. The* Asturias *appears to have been torpedoed without any care having been taken to ascertain her character or her destination. Even if the covertness of the facts were admitted, upon which Germany bases the justification of her order, the International Committee considers that nothing can excuse the torpedoing of a hospital ship, and expresses the hope that such an order contrary to international conventions will cease to be carried out.* *Reuters.*

Britain regularly transported German prisoners of war to the United Kingdom for medical treatment, and now sought to capitalise on the situation, by using the enemy wounded as human shields. They made known, through neutral media, of the capture of a significant amount of troops on the Western Front; these wounded officers and men required conveyance to the United Kingdom on hospital ships. 'The prisoners will inevitably share with British wounded, the likelihood of an attack by German submarines. Whether the policy of the German Government is likely to be deflected from its abominable course by the knowledge that it can only be pursued at the expense of their own wounded remains to be seen.'

Due to the onslaught of the submarine campaign and Britain's dilatory adoption of a scientific means to counter the submarines, she intensified her programme of equipping her merchant ships with artillery. In the opening stages of the war rudimentary hydrophones equipment existed for the detection of submarines, but its value as a military asset failed to impress the top brass. By restricting funding for this revolutionary method of submarine detection, Britain suffered a catastrophic loss of tonnage and lives.

Winston Churchill remarked:

> *In April the great approach route to the south-west of Ireland was becoming a veritable cemetery of British shipping; and other cemeteries were small by comparison.*

The scientific solution to the marauding submarines claimed its first victim in March 1916, when the Q ship *Farnborough* sank *U68*. By the following July the first truly effective depth charges were introduced containing 300 lb of explosive; these required a detonation within twenty-eight feet of the hull to destroy the submersible. In May 1917 a well-known firm of Wall Street Brokers offered a reward of £100,000 as a prize to induce any inventor to devise a successful means of combating German submarines – they received one suggestion every four minutes. British shore-based listening systems gradually appeared, but in the uneven war waged on the high seas the submarine retained the advantage of concealment.

For centuries, vulnerable merchantmen had sailed in convoys for protection, a practice that ceased after the elimination of privateers. The navy reluctantly sanctioned an experimental convoy for homeward-bound steamers from Gibraltar. The safe arrival of this convoy led to the introduction of the convoy system, which proved to be Britain's salvation. When the convoys were extended to outward-bound vessels, the tonnage loss fell within a month to below 200,000 tons.

Although armed the merchant ship guns existed purely for the defence of the ship, and by the end of July 1917 the convoy system operated efficiently, and over 3,000 British merchant ships had a defensive capability. Each week this figure increased as more ships received the guns. The master of an armed

Built by William Denny & Bros, *Dumbarton 1905* the *Maheno fulfilled the role of a New Zealand hospital ships.*

merchant ship was not to allow a submarine to approach his vessel within a range of which a torpedo launched without notice might take effect. As the British and French submarines had received instructions not to approach merchant ships at a closer range, any submarine coming within that range must be presumed to be hostile. It was therefore clear it was the duty of the captain of an armed vessel to fire upon any submarine coming within effective torpedo range. This ruling introduced in March of 1916, made the U-boat commander reluctant to surface and declare his intention to a victim whom may or may not be armed. On 26 May, the French Minister of Marine advised by next October all French merchant ships would be armed with two 3.7-inch guns.

Germany continued to insist that British hospital ships routinely carried troops and munitions; understandably there is no confirmation of this in the British media, just vehement denials. Their protestations were to no avail, which inevitably prompted Germany, on 26 May, to extend the barred zones [*sperrgebiete*]. This announcement not only denied safe passage to hospital ships within the barred zone, it now included the Mediterranean Sea, including the route left open for Greece. They would henceforth regard all hospital ships in these waters as enemy vessels of war and would attack on sight. However, they would permit the transport of the sick and wounded from Salonika by Greek railways to Kalamata [now Kalámai] harbour and from there to Gibraltar by hospital ship. This entailed a rail trip of some 650 miles to the embarkation port, an intolerable enough journey for fit travellers but an extremely detrimental one for the sick and wounded. The ships had to travel at a speed previously indicated by the German Government, the name of the vessel and the time of arrival and departure had to be made known to Germany six weeks in advance. A representative of a neutral government representing the interests of Germany had to declare that it was a hospital ship and only carried sick and wounded and nurses, and no other cargo than material for the use and treatment of the sick and wounded. The ink hardly had time to dry on the paper for that same day the enemy torpedoed and sank another hospital ship.

Dover Castle torpedoed

The Government-requisitioned HMHS *Dover Castle* was constructed in 1904 by Barclay Curle and Company, Glasgow, for the Union Castle line. She had a gross tonnage of 8,271 tons, a length just over 476 feet and a service speed of fourteen knots. From 1910, she steamed regularly from London to Mombasa. From the beginning of the war she served as a troopship, until 11 August 1915, when she became employed as a hospital ship with a capacity of over 600 patients. She appeared to have had an uneventful war until 4 October 1916, when she rescued the survivors of the Cunard liner *Franconia*, torpedoed by *UB-47*. The Salonika-bound trooper generally carried 2,700 people, but no troops were on board. The explosion killed a dozen crew, the hospital ship

HMHS *Dover Castle.*

rescued 302 survivors.

A week earlier Germany threatened to attack as war vessels all hospital ships in the Mediterranean, which they were about to implement. The vessel with her precious cargo of 632 wounded patients steamed from Malta to Gibraltar, in company with the British India hospital ship *Karapara*; escorting the ships were the destroyers *Camelon* and *Nemesis*.

Oberleutnant Karl Neumann commanding *UC67* noticed the telltale plumes of smoke belching above the horizon and cautiously maintained a watchful eye

Some of the survivors of the *Dover Castle* caught by an enterprising photographer for a souvenir picture.

Destroyers racing to the rescue of *Dover Castle.*

on the approaching ships. At 6.00 pm on Saturday 26 May, he fired without warning his torpedo, which appears to have struck in the hospital ship's coalbunkers. The devastating explosion claimed the lives of six Southampton coal trimmers, and destroyed three of the lifeboats.

The *Nemesis* laid a protective smoke screen; HMS *Camelon* raced to the stricken vessel and, owing to gallant rescue work while at great risk to herself, managed to take off the majority of the crew and wounded. It is possible this act was observed by the UC II type submarine for she appeared to bide her time, possibly waiting for the warship to depart. The captain T H Wilfred [or Wilford] aided by a skeleton crew set a heroic example. They remained onboard and attempted to sail *Dover Castle* to the nearest port, however Karl Neumann thought otherwise. Two and a half hours had elapsed since the first torpedo, when a second torpedo delivered the *coup de grâce*. The blast sealed her fate and she sank within three minutes, at a position fifty miles north of Bona. Later the wounded survivors from the stricken vessel were transferred to the British India hospital ship *Karapara*, which proceeded under escort to Bona.

The Admiralty statement read:

> *His Majesty's hospital ship* Dover Castle *was torpedoed without warning at 6pm on the 26th instant, in the Mediterranean. At 8.30 she was again torpedoed and subsequently sunk.*
>
> *The whole of the hospital patients and hospital staff were safely transferred to other ships, and the crew were also saved with the exception of six men missing and feared killed by the explosions.*

A proportion of the hospital ships provided sterling service in two world wars, the Bibby line *Oxfordshire* being one of them. In 1950, the thirty-eight-year-old veteran served as a Mediterranean troopship. The two-year-old *Oxfordshire* underwent conversion to a 563-bed hospital ship for the cross-Channel service. At the height of the Dardanelles campaign, she became the base hospital ship at the isle of Mudros until the evacuation of the peninsula. She then provided medical cover in the Persian Gulf and in German East African waters. In her latter role, she dealt more with patients suffering from disease than war wounds. While in East African waters the vessel struck a mine; the details of the incident have passed unrecorded apart from the awards for devotion to duty, which appeared in the 12th June 1917 edition of the *London Gazette*. The King approved the undermentioned awards for gallantry and meritorious service following the mining of a hospital ship.

Major Robert Thornton Meadows RAMC received a DSO, the Royal Red Cross Decoration First Class being awarded to Matron Miss Katherine Conway Jones ARRC, TFNS, Queen Alexandra's Imperial Military Nursing Service [Reserve]. Sister Miss Edith Passmore and Sister Miss Fanny Boulton each received a Second Class Royal Red Cross award. Four men from the RAMC received the Meritorious Service Medal in recognition of devotion to duties. Three men hailed from Halifax including 36729 Private J Sidebottom, 36708 Private J Brockless, and 36717 Private E Iredale. The fourth man, 36719 Private W Jackson originated from Hebden Bridge. All four share an unpublished citation for gallantry.

The war on the hospital ships abated in the latter half of 1917; however, the war slogged out between mercantile traffic and submarines continued to reach new heights of depravity exemplified by the loss of the *Belgian Prince*. The vessel, outward bound from Liverpool laden with a cargo of blue clay destined for Newport News, was torpedoed and sunk in the Atlantic 175 miles from Tory

HMHS *Oxfordshire* the first ship to be requistioned for war service and was converted into Naval Hospital Ship No.1.

Island [near County Donegal]. On 23 July, *U44* torpedoed without warning the cargo ship, an unremarkable action by Great War standards. It was the cold-blooded murders after the event which ensured the victims of the *Belgian Prince* would be remembered.

The crew abandoned the vessel in two lifeboats; the submarine commander *Kapitanleutnant* Paul Wagenfuhr ordered the survivors onto the upper deck of his craft. Under his direction, the boats were destroyed with axes and the crew of *Belgian Prince* were deprived of their life-jackets. Wagenfuhr ordered the merchant ship's master into the submarine and the conning tower hatch closed. The submarine submerged without warning with the shipwrecked seamen standing on her deck. Three men had concealed their life-jackets beneath their coats; they were the only survivors from thirty-three men. One of the survivors Seaman George Saleskia joined the ship at Liverpool on 23 July, the day prior to her departure. After being in the water from nine at night to five next morning, he reached the abandoned ship and managed to board her:

> *I was only aboard about half an hour when the submarine returned to the ship. Three or four Germans came on board and started to gather up the clothes from the officers' quarters. All this time I was hiding at the after end of the ship, but after the Germans had finished pilfering the saloon I saw them coming to the place I was hiding; there was nothing for me to do but jump over the stern into the water. I then swam and held onto the rudder for half an hour, and then as the submarine was coming away from the starboard side I was compelled to swim to the port side to prevent them seeing me.*
>
> *The submarine then fired at the ship to make sure of her sinking, and eventually the ship settled down and I was again compelled to swim about. I managed to get to a dinghy that had floated off the ship, and I picked up the ship's cat, that was floating about on a piece of timber. After about half an hour, I was picked up by a patrol boat and returned to Liverpool. A fortnight after the outrage* U44 *sank with all hands.*

In February, Germany made a specific threat to sink the hospital ship *St Denis*, prompting her withdrawal from the repatriation programme. Due to the Netherlands' neutrality, their shipping companies took over the transportation of exchanged prisoners of war. The Zeeland Company paddle steamers *Zeeland* and *Koningen Regentes* sailed to Hull and back carrying 125 prisoners and ordinary passengers. The Rotterdam Lloyd company operated a private hospital ship, the 5,471-ton *Sindoro*. The company expressed a desire to maintain their service to Hull, providing the Government permitted the export of steering gear components for the 350-persons passenger vessel. Evidently, they received the component for the vessel resumed sailings. Not to be outdone by their competitors the Holland America Company proposed to operate the 12,531-ton

Noordam from Rotterdam to Hull for prisoner of war service; she could carry a maximum of 2,000 passengers per trip.

Meanwhile the events on the Western Front made as dismal reading as the war at sea. In northern Belgium, the town of Ypres remained never far from the newspaper headlines. The Allied-held town stood in a strategic position, dominated by a semicircle of low ridges occupied by the enemy. Germany continually strove to capture the ruins of the heavily shelled town, which the Empire troops defended at tremendous cost to life and limb. On 31 July, the British launched their latest offensive officially named as the Third Battle of Ypres, but better known as the battle of Passchendaele. The Allied objective lay in the capture of the surrounding Messines and Passchendaele ridges, a prerequisite to a decisive breakthrough paving the way to victory. To reach the distant ridges the infantry needed to cross over terrain reclaimed from marshland by generations of Flanders farmers. A network of drainage ditches, which the preliminary artillery bombardments destroyed, intersected the low-lying fields. Constant rain throughout the summer turned the Flanders fields into a quagmire of impenetrable mud. Nature conspired against the advancing troops, for once a man became trapped in the mud few managed to escape, thousands of men disappeared beneath its surface. Some 150,000 troops died in this tortuous campaign, which terminated with the Canadians' capture of the ruins of Passchendaele village on 10 November.

The cross-Channel paddle steamer *Zeeland*.

Letitia on the rocks

The enemy played no part in the loss of the next hospital ship, which once again highlighted the perils of navigation within coastal waters. The hospital ship *Letitia* belonged to the Anchor-Donaldson line. The 470 feet long steamer had quadruple engines, which gave the vessel a service speed of over twelve knots. She displaced 5,763 tons net and 8,991 gross. Her standard complement stood

Canadian hospital ship HMHS *Letitia.*

at 137 crew, seven engineers and four deck officers. Her master had commanded her from new five years earlier. The steamer entered service as a hospital ship on 18 November 1914.

The *Letitia* had served in the Mediterranean where she came under fire while evacuating troops from the Gallipoli peninsula. As the Turks respected the hospital ships, the projectiles were most likely stray shots. Apart from this, her war service appears uneventful until the summer of 1917.

After giving the order to cast off Captain William McNeil departed from the Mersey carrying a full crew, plus seventy-four medical staff and orderlies. She transported 546 wounded personnel, including one hundred cot cases destined for Halifax, Nova Scotia, a province of Canada.

After reaching the far side of the Atlantic the hospital ship sailed through two days of fog, through which the captain steered by dead reckoning towards Halifax. The fog reduced visibility to approximately a quarter of a mile. As the pilot appeared through the mist McNeil signalled for full astern to reduce the vessel's headway. The pilot clambered aboard at about 10.20 on 1 August; minutes later as a dark form loomed astern the pilot failed to react. McNeil issued the order for *Letitia* to make headway to avoid a possible collision. The pilot then took charge of the vessel however, the captain had reservations about the pilot. The sound of the Sambro Island fog signal and, shortly after, the Chebucto Head signal, sounded muffled in the fog. McNeil grew increasingly concerned.

The anxious master looked down from the bridge wing and noticed a line of buoys. Knowing these belonged to the fishermen of the Portugese Shoal McNeil knew the pilot was steering the *Letitia* towards the land. A master for twenty-four years Captain McNeil followed his instincts, leapt across the bridge and slammed the bridge telegraph to full astern. A minute later while making five or six knots *Letitia* struck the rocks, a fatal glancing blow near the break of the forecastle head. The vessel, which drew almost twenty feet forward, had become firmly impaled on the rocks. Twenty minutes after the wreck soundings of her compartments showed number one and two tanks now contained twelve feet of seawater. Due to the direction of the impact *Letitia* had also heeled over twenty-five degrees to starboard. Ten minutes after the pilot joined the ship *Letitia* lay stranded.

After lowering the ship's boats, the captain issued the order to 'abandon ship'. Three pilot boats and assorted steamers arrived to carry away the wounded. Despite the evacuation being conducted in an orderly manner, a greaser named Graham attempted to swim to safety but drowned.

A later attempt to clear the rocks by using the ship's engines assisted by two tugboats failed. Two months later, her Greenock-built hull fractured, her stern sank into deeper water and the owners of *Letitia* abandoned her. An enquiry by the Department of Marine and Fisheries found the pilot guilty of a gross error

HMHS *Letitia* stranded high and dry south of Portugese Cove near Nova Scotia.

of judgement and demoted him.

Speculation abounded on the precise reasons behind the Teutonic revoking of the policy of sinking hospital ships. The concession may well relate to the Spanish decision to refuse submarines access to neutral Spanish waters and German fears that the Spaniards may forsake neutrality and align with the Allies. In early August, the monarch of Spain, Alfonso XIII, sanctioned representations made by the Spanish Government in Berlin, London and Paris. The German Government agreed to the safe passage of hospital ships providing a Spanish naval officer sailed on each vessel, and guaranteed the vessel only transported the sick and wounded. In order to revoke all suspicion Britain and France accepted the arrangements and expressed their thanks to Spain for her humane intervention. Eleven naval commissioners then took up positions in French ports indicated by the Allies.

German contempt for the Red Cross also occurred on land as reported in the *Liverpool Courier* on Thursday 23 August 1917. Viscountess Benoist d'Azy, daughter of the Marquis Vogue, and principal nurse of the hospital at Varennes survived the bombing of the Vaux Varennes Hospital Huts.

> *At ten in the evening German aircraft flew at a height of less than 200 metres in the district behind Verdun over the clearance hospital and another hospital sited on each side of the road and connected by a wooden footbridge. Four incendiary bombs were dropped on the sheds, in which all wounded men occupied the beds. Three sheds started immediately blazing, staff attempted to reach the wounded not reached by the flames.*
>
> *The aircraft returned lower and fired machine guns on the rescuers; number six hospital was also struck by bombs. In order to prevent the spreading of the fire the staff hastened to destroy the footbridge joining the two hospitals. The aviators then fired on them with machine guns, seven of the staff were killed, about twenty were wounded. In the glare of the conflagration the Geneva Red Crosses painted on the roof of the buildings showed up plainly in the night but the aviators came back a third time to bombard the hospital. Seven wounded men were killed in their beds and projectiles struck twelve others. A Red Cross nurse and a male nurse were killed by the bedsides of the wounded. The 180 wounded German patients were all safe.*

On 10 September, a French semi-official statement announced German forces would respect hospital ships in the Mediterranean, which would no longer need an escort by armed vessels. From this date, the German officer prisoners of war were landed from French ships on which they had sailed as hostages. However, navigating the Mediterranean still had its dangers, as enemy submarines routinely sowed minefields.

HMHS *Goorkha* hit a mine off Malta suffering no casualties.

The 6,335-ton Union Castle intermediate steamer *Goorkha* had served as a hospital ship since her commission on 20 October 1914. While conveying 362 patients through the Mediterranean on 10 October 1917 she struck a mine off Malta. All her patients and seventeen nurses were transferred safely from the vessel. The disabled *Ghoorka* was later towed into Malta where on 18 October she became decommissioned; after repairs, she resumed service with the civilian shipping company.

The callous squandering of life during the battles of Third Ypres and a mistrust of General Haig convinced the United Kingdom's Prime Minister Lloyd George to restrict the flow of men to the front. By the following March the strength of the British army on the Western Front diminished by twenty-five per cent. Crucially this coincided with a bolstering of troops available for deployment on the Western Front. After Russia descended into bolshevism Germany agreed a peace treaty, this cessation of hostilities on the eastern front allowed the transference of men across to the Western Front.

From November until the following spring, German fighting strength in France and Flanders increased by approximately thirty per cent. Germany began to prepare for a major spring offensive.

Improved mines and a new concept of minefield prevented the most foolhardy of submarine commanders from accessing the Western Approaches from their base at Zeebrugge. The Allied maritime offensive campaign had reaped dividends, producing a

"Brilliant to the top of his boots!"

Lloyd George about General Haig

rising toll of U-boats. Consequently, by late winter, the threat of starvation disappeared and the submarine menace receded. As the British naval blockade exerted an ever tighter strangle hold on Germany, insufficient vessels carrying essential supplies reached German ports. Her citizens underwent great hardship, as the fighting forces had first claim to food while the civilians eked out an existence on a near starvation diet. Increasingly concerned that the arrival of American troops would tip the numerically balance of combatants in favour of the Allies, Germany prepared for a last ditch offensive in the spring of 1918.

Britain denies hospital ship abuse allegations

In defence of the ongoing allegations of hospital ship misuse, Britain published a white paper [also referred to as the white book]; the Washington embassy received a copy on 21 November. A London Foreign Office memorandum accompanied the document. The contents comprised evidence supplied by the German authorities and the British Government's comments:

> *His Majesty's Government called attention to the fact that German submarines and other warships never once exercised their right of inspecting the holds of British hospital ships to verify their suspicions. Instead, they have relied on conjectural statements of persons who have never had the opportunity of ascertaining whether there was any foundation in their statements. Instead of giving His Majesty's Government an opportunity to rebut these allegations they proceeded to ruthlessly, attack innocent hospital ships engaged in the humane task of serving the sick and wounded. The Government has now investigated the charges contained in the German memorandum as far as they contain British hospital ships... Generally, the charges group themselves under four headings.*
>
> *Alleged excessive use of hospital ships in relation to the Gallipoli campaign.*
>
> *Changes in the list of hospital ships, with supposed intention to deceive.*
>
> *Alleged transport of munitions.*
>
> *Alleged transport of troops.*
>
> *As to [1], the number of hospital ships employed was not excessive having regard to the number of invalids to be evacuated from Gallipoli. On the contrary, the accommodation on hospital ships proved to be inadequate to meet requirements, and it was necessary to employ ordinary transports in addition for the conveyance of sick and wounded. These transports were not protected by the Hague Convention, did not fly the Red Cross flag and were not fitted out as hospital ships.*
>
> *As to [2], no rule exists under which a hospital ship, once notified, must remain in hospital service for the duration of the war. It is perfectly true*

> *that certain ships were notified as hospital ships and later on were removed from the list. This was due to the alterations in the requirements for the various classes of tonnage caused by the sinking of ships by submarines and to changes in the military situation. There are no grounds for the somewhat nebulous suggestion of the Government, that the aim of the changes was to produce uncertainty and confusion about the character of the ships. No evidence is provided to show what military advantages could be gained by such confusion, which, in fact would probably be disadvantageous, since it would be injurious to the safety of the hospital ships themselves.*
> *As to [3] and [4], alleged conveyance of munitions and troops, to which nearly all the evidence relates, A detailed examination of all the particular instances alleged is given below. It may however be stated that British hospital ships have never been used for the carriage of munitions or of combatant troops. Red Cross stores and personnel of the RAMC* [who are protected by the Geneva Convention] *have been embarked. It appears probable that the German Government have been misled by fallacious deductions of their witnesses, who apparently were unable to verify their assumption that cases of Red Cross stores were really munitions of war and bodies of the RAMC in khaki uniform were detachments of combatant troops.*

While the Government denied British hospital ships had carried either munitions or troops, the Admiralty merely denied that troops were carried on hospital ships. The German Government seized on the Admiralty's part denial. The discrepancy in the denials appears to emanate from an Admiralty statement published on 2 February, in which particular notice was taken of the allegations of Albert Messany. His allegation, circulated in a German wireless press message, stated that the hospital ship *Britannia* [he meant *Britannic*] carried 2,000 soldiers who were not invalids. With reference to this allegation, the Admiralty stated that no hospital ship had ever embarked any persons but invalid and hospital staff. There was no reason in that statement to refer to munitions. The play which the German Government makes with this imaginary discrepancy is an illustration of their practice of trying to make capital out of infinitesimal points, a practice that has the appearance of being adopted in order to cover up the weakness of their position.

Britain's repudiations were contrary to a news article published in the *Daily Chronicle* of 11 December after a public declaration that British hospital ships transported troops. Miss Maud Ethel Marsh, a member of the Portsmouth Food Control Committee and a delegate to the Trades and Labour Council attended a war aims meeting at Portsmouth Town Hall Square. At the close of the meeting, during an altercation Miss Marsh stated 'Our hospital ships carry troops, and the Red Cross nurses make red crosses for the troops to sew on their uniform sleeves, and she could prove the allegation'. The enemy claimed this statement corroborated the accusations and justified previous sinking of hospital ships.

The arrested Miss Marsh appeared in court, where she denied ever saying she had proof of her allegation. She refused to repudiate her other claims; the prisoner received a month's imprisonment. The bench said 'If persons of higher position came before them it is probable that they would not have dealt with them so leniently'. The Government considered the allegations so serious, in mid January [post trial] the Secretary of the Admiralty issued a statement denouncing the alleged false statement of Ethel Marsh.

Notes

1. Variations of name of the master of *Gloucester Castle* are Hall, Holt and Holl. The author selected Holl as the name appears in the *London Gazette* and Union Castle honours and awards. The master of *Karnak* appears as Stewart or Steward, again the *London Gazette* surname is the one used.
2. Rammed and sank four weeks later by HMS *Milne*, twenty-four submariners died, two survived.
3. The 22 May 1917 *London Gazette* citation erroneously reports the sinking as 15 April 1917.
4. *London Gazette* 11 January 1918.
5. Petty Officer Herbert John Lewis [Bert] Hinkler had invented an improved dual-control aircraft system that allowed the gunner to relieve a mortally wounded pilot. The gunner claimed six kills. Among the Distinguished Service Medal entries in the 2 February 1917 *LG* is that of ON F 311 [Ch] Leading Mechanic Bert Hinkler. Two other RNAS men ON F 2176 Leading Mechanic Robert William Bager and ON J 26402 Acting Air Mechanic First Gunner Harry George Lovelock also received the DSM. The Australian-born flier went on to become a successful pilot. In 1933 while attempting to circumnavigate the globe in a light aircraft, he disappeared. The Italians discovered the wrecked aircraft in the Apennines mountain range, between Florence and Arezzo. Hinkler had survived the crash but lay dead near his plane. Air crash investigators determined the accident came about due to a lost propeller blade, prompting Hinkler to attempt an emergency landing. Mussolini ordered the aviator to be buried in Florence with full military honours.
6. Flight Lieutenant Harold Edwards of the RCAF became a prisoner of war until his repatriation on 14 January 1919.

Up to 30th November 1917, the Madras War Fund Hospital Ship "MADRAS" has made 50 double voyages and carried 20,791 patients.

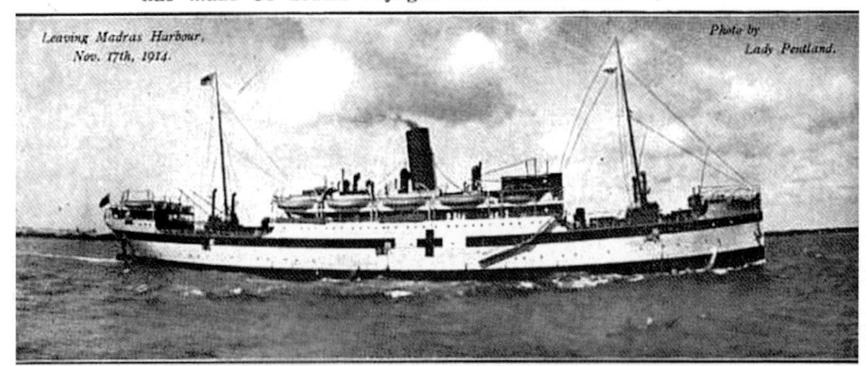

All donations for the maintenance of the "Madras" will be gratefully welcomed and should be sent to the Military Secretary to His Excellency the Governor of Madras, Government House, Madras, INDIA.

Chapter Five

1918. Victory Hangs in the Balance

A growing dissatisfaction among the U-boat crews who were concerned over the increasing amount of boats failing to return from patrols began to ferment sedition within the German and Austrian Navies. All the glamour attached to the submarine service during the height of the campaign had long gone. Due to a lack of volunteers men were drafted in from the surface fleet. In an attempt to popularise the service submariners were given a fuller diet than the men on capital ships, and were allowed to loot torpedoed ships prior to the deliverance of the *coup de grâce*; in view of the shortages and rationing in the nation this would have been quite a bonus. Since September rumours had circulated of mutinous outbreaks initiated by submariners at Kiel and subsequently spread to the local crews of cruisers. Unwillingness of men to do duty on submarines was given as one reason for the outbreak. The American press contained accounts of sailors on the battleship *Kronzprinz* [complement 1,150 men] throwing Admiral Schmidt overboard, and stabbing and throwing overboard the Admiral's aide Lieutenant Raul and another officer. During a fight on the ship's deck three of the officers and a number of sailors were allegedly killed. Similar scenes occurred on the smaller *Schleswig-Holstein,* also moored at Kiel. All surviving mutineers were arrested. Despatches between Amsterdam and London reported

German Fleet unrest at Kiel.

the crews of four battleships of the German Fleet had taken part in a mutiny at Wilhelmshaven. Three of the ringleaders were shot while heavy sentences were imposed on the others. Admiral Eduard von Capelle, head of the *Reichsmarinearmt*, accused three Radical Socialist Deputies of involvement in the plot, but the German Government took no action against the Reichstag.

The Kiel newspaper *Neueste Nachrichsten* of 2 November reported a torpedo explosion in the submarine yards at Kiel. A submarine was badly damaged and ten people were either wounded or killed. All other reports of extensive mutinies were reported as being without foundation. A fresh mutiny erupted in mid January involving several of the earlier mutineers. Official diplomatic despatches received in Washington also confirmed several others, including clashes between Austrian sailors and German submariners at Pola, in which officers on both sides were killed. Military discipline swiftly asserted itself over the idle and disillusioned sailors whose vessels were confined to the great German naval bases; the threat of a disastrous mutiny was merely postponed.

Hospital ship *Rewa* sunk in torpedo attack

In 2003 sub-aquarist enthusiasts discovered and identified the wreck of HMHS *Rewa* situated about thirty-three miles off Newquay on the Cornish coast. The former British India steam navigation vessel lying on a sea bed littered with wrecks is reputed to be the largest wreck in the area. The divers identified her by her six boilers, recovered artefacts including a 1918 vintage bottle of champagne and inspected her mangled stern, testimony of her death. Launched in 1906 at the Dumbarton yard of William Denny and Brothers, she had a hull length of 456 feet with a fifty-six foot beam; single stage Parsons Compound steam engines powered her three propellers producing a speed of eighteen knots. Originally designed to carry a combination of 165 first- and second-class passengers during the Great War the 7,305 gross tonnage steamer, the sister to *Rohilla,* became a naval hospital ship.

She began her new career on 29 January 1915, bearing the naval pennant number *YA5*. The *Rewa* played a significant part in the Dardanelles campaign by treating and conveying almost 7,500 patients; of these some 3,600 were taken to the advance base, the remainder arrived in hospitals at Alexandria, Malta and Plymouth. As she approached the third anniversary of her commissioning *Rewa* departed from Greece, calling at Malta and Gibraltar to collect patients. She then headed for Blighty with a total of 560 souls onboard, including thirty cot cases, and a number of soldiers suffering from malaria. Bad weather encountered in the Mediterranean delayed by four days the vessel's arrival in home waters.

After dark on Friday 4 January she lit up in accordance with hospital ship practice. As she proceeded at the sluggish pace of four knots, Wilhelm Werner, the commandant of *U55* observed the sedately moving illuminated mercy ship.

A few miles south-west of Lundy island Wilhelm Werner after briefly surfacing fired a torpedo, the time was 11.15 pm. Contemporary accounts report the torpedo struck the vessel on the Red Cross mark amidships on the port side abreast the funnel. The explosion destroyed the lighting system and the sick and wounded had to grope around in the dark for their clothing. Many failed in their search and arrived on deck clad only in underwear, not ideal on a cold January night, while in the boats they had little comfort from the piercing cold wind.

Under the calm directions of Captain JE Drake fourteen lifeboats were lowered without mishap; all except for three men escaped the shipwreck. As the sea water engulfed *Rewa* she settled lower, while maintaining an even keel. No sooner had the boats departed from her, the steamer suddenly dipped her bows and disappeared. Captain Drake ensured all the lifeboats remained together. After igniting a succession of distress flares two trawlers and a tanker were attracted to the flotilla of lifeboats who rescued the survivors at about 3.00 am.

The Press Association's Swansea correspondent, where most of the survivors arrived, reported on the vessel's demise:

> *She had arrived within measurable distance of her destination with lights burning brightly when two lights suddenly appeared on the water belonging to a low sized craft. This was for the moment thought to be a pilot craft, and the captain immediately acquainted by the look out decided to take no notice but to go right ahead. Then within a minute there was a loud explosion, the engine room lights went out, and it was apparent the* Rewa *had been torpedoed. The submarine disappeared as quickly as she had made her appearance.*
>
> *There was no commotion aboard for everybody had been drilled in readiness for any eventualities. Firstly care was taken of the wounded below, and they were brought upon the deck. The great majority aboard joined in singing hymns, SOS signals were quickly responded to, and another steamer and three trawlers were speedily on the scene.*
>
> *One difficulty was that all the illumination had gone, but fortunately a member of the crew found a candle in his locker, and this small find brought into requisition the task of attending the patients proved invaluable. In twenty minutes all the wounded as well as the crew and others onboard were safely in the boats and floating on the sea. As luck had it, the night was calm, though deadly cold. One or two of the boats were so heavily loaded that baling became necessary.*
>
> *Accounts related afterwards showed that many deeds of quiet heroism were performed. Solicitude for the wounded was general. One of the nurses gave all her heavy garments to cover the men who were very ill and remarking on this an officer transferred to her his overcoat. Men of all*

ranks gave every rag they could spare in order to keep the wounded as warm and comfortable as possible.

The members of the crew as well as the officers had rushed to their posts with such alacrity that they had very little clothing for themselves. Some were without boots and socks, others without shirts and again others without trousers; while several others appeared in underpants and minus other garments.

It was eight hours after the wounded had been transferred to the rescue ships [*Paul Paix* and two drifters] *that they reached port. Red Cross motor vans and a fleet of motor omnibuses speedily conveyed the more serious cases to the local Red Cross hospitals. Dock men arriving at business rushed down to the quayside, and in the chilly morning divested themselves of their overcoats to cloak those being landed.*

Then a procession of maimed and limping men, some on the backs of others and all without boots, wended its way under the willing hands of helpers to the Coal Exchange which was adapted to their reception, all business being suspended. Others were taken to the leading hotels, such as the Metropole, and cared for.

All aboard were landed except three Lascars, who were listed as missing. Some of the survivors were taken charge of by members of the Chamber of Commerce and local officials of the Shipwrecked Mariners'

HMHS *Rewa* within Malta harbour.

> *Society. Later all but the serious cases were despatched to various centres in England.*

On the 11 January 1918, the Admiralty released the following statement:

> *His Majesty's hospital ship* Rewa *was torpedoed and sunk in the Bristol Channel about midnight on 4 January, on her way home from Gibraltar. All the wounded were safely transferred to patrol vessels, and there were only three casualties among the crew, three Lascars being missing. She was displaying all the lights and markings required by the Hague convention, and she was not, and had not been, within the so-called barred zone, as delimited in the statement issued by the German Government on 29 January 1917.*

Germany attempted to explain the heinous action by claiming the ship may have hit a mine. Once more the enemy raised the subject of British hospital ships carrying munitions and troops, accusations which were robustly denied throughout the Great War. However, German claims appear in this instance to have some basis of fact. In 2004 sub-aqua divers, while exploring the wreck, discovered a large number of ammunition boxes in the collapsed hold of HMHS *Rewa*. The dive team recovered one shell to prove their claim, but left the remainder of the munitions intact.

Disturbingly, if the reports are true, the discovery verifies, certainly in this instance, the enemy's claims of British violations of the Geneva Convention. Precisely why an ambulance ship should have munitions in her hold will probably remain a mystery. She may have been returning ammunition from Salonika, or a far less controversial explanation may be that the shells provided a convenient means of weighting the canvas body bags used for internment at sea.

Further allegations and rebuttals

In early February the American press published the British Government's latest denunciation of enemy allegations; four charges referred to in the 'white book' were repeated. The khaki-clad personnel onboard were again explained as RAMC. German civilians interned on the Isle of Wight had reported through their embassy that outward bound hospital ships were lower in the water than on their return. A witness reported 'it was noticeable that the hospital ships on their voyage to France were submerged to the load line; they were evidently carrying munitions'. The Admiralty answer was that the prisoners were not in a position to judge the draft of the ships with much accuracy. The difference noticed was due to the fact that ships carried sufficient coal in their bunkers to make both voyages.

In response to the statement of an Austrian officer who claimed while a prisoner at Naples in March 1916, to have seen the *Mauretania* sail for Salonika with troops and munitions under the Red Cross flag the Government replied, 'at the time *Mauretania* was not at Naples and that during her previous visit neutral diplomats had inspected the vessel'.

A Russian from Riga named Alexander Buttler swore before the court of the Russian 23rd Infantry Brigade that in the summer of 1915 he was a seaman on the Belgian steamer *Escaut*. The ship steamed from Brooklyn to La Rochelle and carried nothing but munitions of war. He alleged to have assisted in the transference of munitions to the hold of a hospital ship, which he assumed to be British as all the officers wore English naval uniforms and spoke English. British investigations revealed the absence of a British hospital ship at La Rochelle during July 1915. The credibility of the witness collapsed when the log of the *Escaut* revealed the vessel neither called at La Rochelle nor at La Pallice in June, July or August 1915. During that period the ship was fitted out for the transport of horses. Buttler could not have been in the position to know the ship he purported to sail on carried no cargo but munitions of war.

The Vienna opera singer Adalbert Franz Messany was interned in Egypt at the outbreak of hostilities. He was transferred to Malta onboard *Britannic* and eventually returned home. The singer informed a Vienna court that contrary to the Hague Convention 2,000 healthy men were transported on the huge liner. Evidence provided by the British revealed the men were non-cot cases recovering from illness or not badly wounded and still wore their uniforms.

In reply to the German submarine commander who said 'in February last, while on a sixteen-day cruise of the Aegean, he saw nothing but hospital ships in the day time'. The Government replied there was no proof that any of these hospital ships were engaged in illegal action. If he had any suspicions why did he not exercise the right of examination and control given by Article Four of the Tenth Hague Convention?

HMS *Boxer,* an Ardent class torpedo boat destroyer, was completed by Thorneycroft at Chiswick, London in 1898. Measuring 200 feet long by

St Patrick.

nineteen feet, the lightly armed vessel displaced a mere 260 tons. Evidently classified as surplus to requirements the Portsmouth-based *Boxer* appeared in a 1914 Navy List of vessels for sale, but the outbreak of war gave her a reprieve. She was Britain's oldest serving destroyer.

On 8 February during bad weather *Boxer,* commanded by Lieutenant Commander J K Chaplin, steamed through the English Channel unaware she lay in the path of the ambulance transport *St Patrick,* a former ferry. The collision mortally damaged *Boxer* whose commander attempted unsuccessfully to beach *Boxer* in the shallows of Sandown Bay, Isle of Wight; the vessel sank over two miles from the shore. As a result of the collision, one boy was posted missing.

The damage to *St Patrick* may have been slight for she remained in service until her decommissioning in 1919.

The Royal Navy had gained the upper hand in the submarine war but the German navy, far from being cowed, became increasingly audacious. During the darkness hours of 15 February the enemy attempted to breach the anti-submarine nets straddling the English Channel. A flotilla of enemy destroyers fell upon the patrolling drifters, sinking eight before retiring to the north. Similar raids continued in the Channel and North Sea and despite the protection of convoy stragglers fell prey to the prowling U-boats.

Formerly *German*, the *Glenart Castle* is sunk by Germany

Prior to the Union and Castle lines merger, two of the Union steamships G class liners were launched with Germanic names, namely the *German* and *Galician.* Following the onset of hostilities both names were deemed unsuitable under the prevailing circumstances consequently, in the autumn of 1914, the liner *German* adopted the name of *Glengorm Castle.* The name distanced the company from any Teutonic connections, whilst adopting a name more in keeping with the Union Castle steamship profile. The Galicians were part of the Austrian-Hungarian Empire, now one of Britain's adversaries, thus the ship *Galician* became the *Glenart Castle* but not before she had a close encounter with the enemy.

Before requisition the *Galician* continued to operate the Cape Town to Southampton mail service. On 15 August 1914, near Tenerife, the voyage was interrupted by the intervention of the cruiser *Kaiser Wilhelm der Grosse.* Refitted in 1908 the warship bristled with armament including four 9.4-inch guns and fourteen of 6-inch calibre, therefore the merchantman unhesitatingly obeyed the German orders to sail south. After inspection the warship scrutinised her progress until the following morning when they signalled 'due to you having women and children onboard I will not sink the ship, you are released. Bon voyage'.

Six weeks later the Government requisitioned the 6,824 gross tonnage vessel now renamed *Glenart Castle* for duty as a hospital ship on the cross-Channel run. On one occasion she left Le Havre with patients destined for Southampton; on 1 March 1917, she either struck a mine or was torpedoed off the Owers light vessel off Sussex. The unusually mild weather and a dead calm sea inevitably contributed to the rescue operation. Mercifully no lives were lost; all of her human cargo was safely transferred to other craft. The holed and sinking hospital ship was taken in tow, successfully reaching a Portsmouth graving dock just in the nick of time. After repairs she served as a cross Atlantic hospital ship. Uneventful service in the Mediterranean followed, but the following year she again made the newspapers.

The sinking of the hospital ship was announced by the Admiralty on Wednesday 27 February 1918:

> *His Majest'ys hospital ship* Glenart Castle *was sunk in the Bristol Channel at 4 am on 26 February. There were no patients onboard she was outward bound and had all her lights burning. Survivors have been landed by an American torpedo boat destroyer. Eight boats are still adrift. Further information will be published as soon as it is received.*
>
> *The vessel which had about 200 onboard including medical staff and nurses sank in the Bristol Channel on Tuesday in seven minutes. Up to last night thirty-eight survivors had been landed, twenty-two at Swansea, nine at Milford and seven at Pembroke. There were 182 persons onboard, so 144 are still unaccounted for.*

A second statement swiftly followed:

> *The outward bound ship was torpedoed and sunk at 4 am on 26 February. Of the 182 onboard, comprising 120 crew, eight female nurses and fifty-four members of RAMC, 153 are missing feared dead. Some of the survivors were rescued by an American torpedo boat destroyer.*

On returning from the Mediterranean the *Glenart Castle* underwent three weeks of repairs prior to departing for France. On a pitch dark night a westerly wind blew across a moderate sea. With her hospital ship lights brightly burning *Glenart Castle* steamed out of Newport, Monmouthshire bound for Brest to embark Portuguese sick on what became far from a routine voyage. Lit from stem to stern the hospital ship dimmed her accommodation lights to make the

Glenart Castle.

hospital ship lighting scheme more pronounced. Her course did not zigzag instead she sailed straight as a die at a speed of eleven knots, perhaps assuming her otter boards would protect her from mines. Despite having no invalids on board she carried 186 people, comprising a crew of 122 including officers, about fifty medical staff, also nurses and chaplains. About three in the morning Jacob Sheler, the quartermaster, was at the ship's helm when he observed a bright light on the starboard bow. A half hour later both he and the lookout again saw the light now considerably closer. The light transpired to be the surfaced *UC56* commanded by Wilhelm Kieswetter manoeuvring for the kill. By four in the morning the hospital ship had a position of fifty-one degrees and seven minutes north by four degrees and forty-nine minutes west. As the crew prepared to change watch, a torpedo exploded into the starboard side of number three hatch aft of the engine room, destroying the engines and plunging the ship into darkness. Simultaneously the electrical generators failed rendering the wireless equipment useless. Most of the boats on the starboard side were destroyed and the deck was ripped by the explosion.

Captain Bernard Burt [a retired Lieutenant Commander RNR] raced onto the bridge, blew the ship's whistle several times, the signal to lower the lifeboats. Without any hope of rescue and the ship rapidly sinking by the stern approximately fifty miles west of Lundy Island, the chief officer ordered 'every man for himself'. Fifty-five-year-old Captain Burt remained cool and resourceful and ordered the quartermaster to get away the boats; turning to Sheler he said 'now my lad jump into the boat or you will get drowned'. The survivors spoke highly of the captain, who once his duties were completed returned to the bridge and in true mercantile tradition went down with his ship.

Most of the stern was awash and it was evident the ship was rapidly sinking [1]. Excluding those on duty the men and women were attired in night clothes and attempted in the darkness to launch the remaining lifeboats. They had less than seven minutes to evacuate the ship before *Glenart Castle* went down stern first, her bows lingering briefly in the air before sliding beneath the waves. The rapid demise of the vessel was attributed to the probability of a propeller shaft tunnel door being open, but understandably no one accepted responsibility for their careless action. The loss of life might have been more severe if the crew had not practised boat stations on average twice a week.

During the 27 February Admiralty enquiry into the ship's loss one of the vessel's greasers Alfred Bale, who endured ten hours adrift before being rescued by an American destroyer, stated:

> *After hearing the order 'every man for himself' I then slid down the boat's fall with two other men, but before we could cast the falls adrift, the ship sank and I was thrown out the lifeboat. When I came to the surface I saw a boat, bottom up with three men clinging to it and made my way towards*

it and hauled myself up on the keel. Soon after I saw what I took to be a schooner coming towards us and we all shouted together, a lot of men close to us in the water also shouted. A minute or two after, I saw it was not a schooner but a submarine on the surface and I said to the man next to me 'we can expect nothing off him, it's the submarine'. The submarine was not more than a hundred yards away then and I could distinctly see the outline of the hull and the conning tower. About a half an hour later a raft drifted alongside and I got on board to make more room for the men on the boat. I held on to the boat for a time but had to let go. I did not see the men on the boat again.

Seven out of nine lifeboats were successfully launched but some of them were only partially occupied. A large number of men were compelled to jump into the sea with lifebelts and few of them survived, for the sea was so rough it was impossible to rescue them from the lifeboats. Waves twenty feet high churned up by a nasty cross-current dashed over the boats continuously. The boats shipped water continually, requiring the occupants to continually bale out the boats to avoid swamping. Flimsily clad in such adverse conditions the survivors stood little chance of survival before hypothermia set in. All around the wreck site the night air was filled with the heart rending cries of those struggling in the bitterly cold water; gradually these calls faded away as the victims perished. Approximately ten hours after the sinking the French schooner *Feon* [spelt *Faon* in some accounts] came to the aid of number eight lifeboat, coxwained by the bosun's mate. Despite scouring the area no further boats were found, for it was the only surviving lifeboat. Thomas Mathews, the bosun's mate on board *Glenart Castle,* informed the enquiry:

Seven lifeboats got away with people in them and two more empty ones floated off the poop. My boat remained in the neighbourhood of the sinking for about three quarters of an hour but I saw nothing of the other boats. Our boat contained twenty-two survivors, comprising nineteen crew and three RAMC and was landed at Swansea having been picked up by a French yawl [Feon] *six miles north of Lundy.*

Asked if there were any orders for the nurses to be put in the boat first he said there was no time to do anything, the ship sank in seven or eight minutes and there was no time to rescue anybody– they merely had the order to lower boats. Another witness Thomas Casey, (fireman), was turned in when the ship was struck:

I went along the alley but I had to come back again because the explosion had blown up all the after hatches – I had to return. I went up to the saloon deck. When I ran along to get to my boat station I asked the Bosun "How is it Tom!" He said "Stand by!" He sang out asking where the Sister

A tactless intrusion. *Punch* cartoon dated 16 January 1918.

was. He told me to stand by the after fall. Then we waited until he gave orders, and when the whistle blew we were told to lower the falls. We were told to get the boat halfway down – to lower it down to the next deck. She had two decks. We lowered it down to the saloon deck to take in people. He [the Bosun] *then saw that the blocks were alright and we lowered away then. I chucked the fall clear and I went on the falls and shinned down. I saw three boats floating on the sea ahead of me on the port side. The suction of the ship sinking forced my boat away and I could not be certain if the other boats carried lights. My boat was picked up at about half past ten next morning. "There was such a heavy sea running that I doubt if the other boats have lived in it."*

The following men rescued by the French schooner were landed at Swansea:

R Moss, Harold Road, Tottenham. HW Wooley, Cobham Road, Leytonstone. RA Howes, Aldeby Beeches, Norfolk. FE Davies, Ice House Hill, Spring Road, Southampton. CS Dear, Derby Road, Southampton. WJ Kelly, St Margaret's Place, Southampton. P Jacobean, Malshar Street, Poplar, SE. EH Langdon, Ashurst, Lyndhurst Road, near Southampton. J Brannan, Shafterburg Road, Bournemouth. F Fish, Beckley, near Christchurch, Hants. T Cassey, Alexander Road, Newport. A Holden, Bartram Road, Tatton. J Burton, Cranbury Avenue, Southampton. T Mathews, James Street, Southampton. J Spiller, Cambridge House, Brook Road. A Phillips, Bond Street, Northans, Southampton. C Wilson, Marke Road, Southampton. D Davies, Eastleigh, near Southampton. T Tuzzian, Upper Marsh, Lambeth. The three RAMC survivors were SR Pratt, Trinity Lane, Hinckley, Leicestershire; Corporal H Fulcher, Princess Avenue, Hull and Corporal W Forbes, Leightank, Craigellachie, Banffshire.

A second set of distressed mariners owed their salvation to the men of the American destroyer USS *Parker* [Commander Halsey Powell USN.] The heroic endeavour of two of the Americans prompted calls in the House of Commons during mid March for an official recognition of their gallantry. Ten hours after the sinking the USS *Parker* came to the aid of a raft bearing survivors. Possibly through fear of swamping the raft, the warship stood some distance off. Two naval ratings plunged into the sea, ignoring the temperature of the water and heavy seas and swam to the raft, while other ratings jumped onto small rafts and wreckage to facilitate the rescue. Nine immensely relieved survivors, including the four navigation officers, were hauled onboard, though one died onboard. The deceased was Fireman Jessie White, a twenty-five year old married Southampton man. Attempts to acknowledge the gallantry of the pair of naval ratings by the Union Castle and Government departments appear to have been politely declined by the American Government. An expression of gratitude by the House of Commons appears to have sufficed.

During the enquiry into the loss of *Glenart Castle* an independent witness

John Hill, 2nd hand of the fishing trawler *Swansea Castle,* gave a graphic account of the sudden and unexpected disappearance of the hospital ship:

> *We were coming into Lundy Island. When we sighted Lundy, I called the skipper and he told me to keep her in N by E and said that if I saw any lights I was to call him or when I got the light of the Lundy North Light bearing E by N. I was also to awake him if I saw any trawlers. As we were steaming along I looked around with the glasses and away in the starboard rigging I saw the Hospital Ship with green lights all around her – around the saloon. She had her red side lights showing and mast-head light, and also another red light which I suppose was the Red Cross light. We were steaming North and she was going West by North. As we were steaming along I did not know whether to alter course, but her speed took her across our head clear of us – she crossed our bow. When she got right ahead all her lights went out. When the lights went out, I turned around with the glasses in my hand to see that she went clear of us and I saw the vessel in the moonlight. Every light on board had suddenly disappeared. Of course that made me think that something was wrong and I remarked to my mate at the wheel that it was funny. Therefore, after I spoke to him, I picked up my glasses and looked around the horizon in order to see whether I could discover anything at all. As I came around with my glasses to about the North East I saw something on the water, so also did my mate, with no lights. As I looked at it, my mate said, 'What is that, Jack?' I replied 'I do not know', but that it was rather funny. It looked like a Noah's Ark. After speaking to him I put the glasses down. I said a few more words and when I looked again the object had disappeared. As soon as I saw that object disappear such a thing as a submarine was far from my mind, but my mate said to me instantly "A submarine, Jack – call the Skipper". I then shouted down to the Skipper "Submarine, Skipper". As soon as he got his eyes open, which was done very quickly, he said "Over here". I left the wheel and ran aft to call all hands to man the gun. "Submarine" I sang out. Everyone was at his post very quickly and the gun was trained right round at once. Before I left the bridge, the Skipper said, "Keep her east north east". By going east north east it was impossible to go past that object* [the submarine] *without seeing it. As soon as I had warned everyone, I returned to the Skipper. I looked at the compass and I said to him that she was on the port bow. After I had altered her course, I said to the Skipper "Poor look-out, Skipper, she will not give us another chance". We proceeded afterwards to Lundy.*

The *Liverpool Courier* of 1 March published the following announcement by the Secretary of Admiralty:

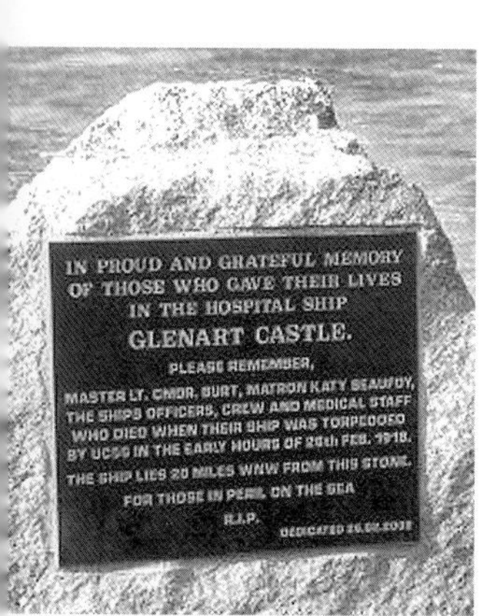

The *Glenart Castle* memorial.

Sworn statements by two survivors of the Glenart Castle *make it quite clear that she was struck by a submarine, which was sighted within hailing distance within ten minutes of being struck. It is to be noted she was in 'the free area' and was sunk even in breach of the German pledge given as to spare hospital ships from attack in that area.*

The total number saved so far reported is twenty-nine, and the total number missing 153. The numbers are as follows: total crew 120, RAMC officers seven, female nurses eight, other ranks RAMC 47, total on board 182. Saved crew 25, RAMC ranks four, total saved twenty-nine. Total missing feared drowned 153. A search is being made for ship's boats carried out to sea, either in the Irish Sea or the Atlantic. The coast is being watched on both sides of the Bristol Channel for wreckage. Several men in the engine room and attending the boilers were killed or injured by the explosion. Two of the lifeboats were rendered useless.

Sir Eric Geddes, formerly Director-General of Military Railways and Inspector of Transportation became first Lord of the Admiralty in 1918.

Invalidated press reports claimed the submarine may have surfaced as bodies were discovered with firearm wounds. This malicious factor combined with the high death toll, in particular the eight nurses, prompted the Bishop of London to declare:

The cries of the drowning nurses will echo in our ears forever and could well brand us as a nation of cowards if we ever cease to strive that such appalling wickedness may be made impossible for all time.

Among those presumed drowned on *Glenart Castle* were two nurses who for almost a year had nursed German prisoners of war, at Belmont, Surrey. Sister Beresford joined the *Glenart Castle* on 24 February, and Australian nurse Sister Blake joined in November. The *British Journal of Nursing* summarised their deaths as 'brutal ingratitude that their work for the enemy wounded should be requited with foul murder at the hands of the German navy'.

On 26 February 2002, at Hartland Point, North Devon a memorial commemorating those who perished on the *Glenart Castle* was unveiled.

On 5 March Sir Eric Geddes, by now the First Lord of the Admiralty, reported in the House of Commons on the continued success of the convoy system, advising over 35,000 ships had been convoyed, and losses to either mine, submarine or surface craft were very low. He stated in recent months the chances of a submarine returning from its voyage in home waters were one in five or fewer. British and American forces in home waters were believed to be destroying submarines as fast as they could be built. However, the introduction of convoy duties reduced the amount of warships available for submarine duties and U-boat commanders became increasingly bolder when attacking ships. Despite this, advances in depth charges and visual spotting of submarines from airships or sea planes had turned the hunter into the hunted. Late the previous November the Admiralty ordered all British merchant vessels of 2,500 or greater were to employ four men solely for the task of masthead lookouts. While employed in this role the men were rewarded with an additional payment of fifteen shillings a month. This safeguard followed the patriotic gesture of Sir Alfred Yarrow, the founder of a shipbuilding dynasty and great philanthropist who offered a twenty pound prize to anyone on a merchant ship who sighted a submarine. Open to both passengers and crew, by October 172 prizes were awarded, as a result over eighty-five percent of the vessels reached port safely, while half reached port without being attacked. These losses were now sustainable, unlike the devastating losses of the previous spring.

A lucky day for the *Guildford Castle*

Built in 1911 the intermediate steamer *Guildford Castle* was one of three sister ships; her siblings were the *Galway Castle* and the *Gloucester Castle*. During the opening phase of hostilities *Guildford Castle* acted as a troopship for the first wave of the BEF. Weeks later she was converted to a 427-bed hospital ship and entered service on 22 September 1914. The ship served in the German war zones of East and West Africa, a theatre where illness and disease far outweighed battle casualties. On 10 March 1918 the steamer, with 438 patients onboard, sailed off Lundy Island, in the Bristol Channel. Lightly laden the hospital ship stood well out of the water; visibility was reported to be in the region of five miles, and the ship's Red Cross markings had recently been repainted. All too aware of the dangers of the Western Approaches the navigating officers remained vigilant for clues of any imminent attack. When a submersed

Guildford Castle took part in the first troop convoy to Europe in 1914. Was commissioned as a hospital ship in September of that year.

submarine launched a torpedo, the track of the first was seen by the captain; the fourth officer observed the wake of the torpedo for six hundred yards before it passed harmlessly by. A minute later a second torpedo was fired and struck *Guildford Castle* a heavy blow on the port side abreast the mainmast, causing her to vibrate considerably fore and aft. Lady Luck intervened for the torpedo failed to explode.

The Admiralty issued the following announcement on 14 March 1918:

> *His Majesty's hospital ship* Guildford Castle [Captain Thomas M Lang, RNR], *homeward bound was unsuccessfully attacked by a submarine at the entrance to the Bristol Channel at 5.35 pm on the 10th instant. She was flying the Red Cross flag, and in addition had her hospital lights on. We are informed that the officers of* Guildford Castle *stated on arrival at Avonmouth, that the vessel was attacked in much the same position of the outer Bristol Channel as where the* Rewa *and* Glenart Castle *were sunk.*

The vessel was struck by a torpedo which, however, did not explode, and the prompt arrival of patrol vessels compelled the submarine to give up the attack.

The *Guildford Castle* had a large number of wounded on board. Captain Lang had commanded the *Guildford Castle* for some nineteen months, and this was the first time the 8,036-ton Union Castle liner had been attacked by a submarine. With the loss of merchant ships now a daily occurrence it normally required an attack on a Red Cross ship to generate media interest. The fortuitous escape of the *Guildford Castle* prompted a journalist to interview Captain Lang; the following account appeared a few days after the incident:

> *About 5.35 pm on 10 March, the* Guilford Castle *was nearing the entrance to the Bristol Channel flying her Red Cross flags, and in addition showing all her hospital lights. I was on the bridge with the fourth officer. He called my attention to a torpedo which started on the forequarters of the vessel about 600 yards away. It crossed the ship's wake at right angles, passing the stern from thirty to forty yards distant. At this time all the hospital lights were on, and also the largest sized Red Cross flag and ensign were displayed. The reason for the lights being on was the low visibility, although it was still daylight.*
>
> *About ninety seconds after the torpedo had passed the stern the ship received a very violent blow. The helm was put hard to starboard to avoid exposing the whole length of the ship to another torpedo, as I assumed at the time there was another submarine acting in co-operation with the first one. At the same time I placed the ship in a better position for manoeuvring. The moment the blow was received the wireless was put in operation and I received two replies, one from Land's End and the other from another station. There were no other ships in sight. I could not form*

any opinion as to what was the cause of the blow until the ship was dry-docked and examined.

We at once signalled for boat stations, and the RAMC set to work to bring up the patients including cot cases, for the boats. These patients were smartly brought up on deck, the staff working admirably together. The crew, ship's company, RAMC, and patients all behaved splendidly. There was no rushing about or trouble of any kind, their stations being taken, and all remained quietly at the boats awaiting orders.

As soon as I found the ship was not making water I dismissed them from their boat stations, and had the patients placed in the companion-ways and spots adjacent to the boats to protect them from the weather and placed in readiness in case of another attack. They were kept in that position until we were well up channel, off Bull Point, when the patients were sent back to their respective wards.

Captain Lang expressed great pride in the manner those onboard behaved, then continued,

The vessel had a full complement of patients on board, and was capable of making eleven knots an hour. Although we never sighted the submarine there was a patch of oil from where the torpedo was fired.

The 30 April *New York Times* reported after dry-docking the vessel an examination of her hull occurred. After taking into consideration the ship was on a steady course at the time of attack, the description of the blow proved the *Guildford Castle* was struck by a torpedo, which did not explode. The torpedo apparently rebounded after first striking the vessel, and returning, bumped along the ship's side until it was finally struck by one of the ship's propellers. One of the blades was found to be marked and slightly bent. A detailed examination of the marks showed they were not made by the vessel striking a submarine.

The unsuccessful torpedo assault fuelled a spate of signatories to the Tower Hill petition whose signatories included baronets, clergy and authors campaigning for protection from U-boat murders. The petition called for

HMHS *Guildford Castle*, survived the war but was declared a total loss following a collision in 1933.

German prisoners and wealthy interned Germans to be carried as hostages on British merchant vessels. This movement arose from the mistaken belief that French hospital ships had secured immunity for their hospital ships plying between Marseilles and Salonika by including enemy officers among their passengers. Mr Bonar Law assured the House of Commons the reports were erroneous and Britain had no intention of adopting such an odious measure, and would not respond to calls for reprisals.

Under International Law belligerents had the right to stop and search vessels they deemed to be in breach of the Geneva Convention, yet German naval sources appear to have seldom taken this option. Instead in late April they intensified their protestations by claiming American aviators were travelling to Europe onboard hospital ships. The claims were based on shot down American airmen whom they alleged freely admitted 'it was general practice for aviators to enter the American Ambulance service for their passage to Europe, and to cross on hospital ships. After they landed in France they immediately transferred to the Automobile Corps and thence into the air service'. German intelligence cited an American flyer brought down in the region of the army of General Oskar von Hutier. The aviator carried a pass which referred to him as a member of the American Ambulance Service in France. Another carried a certificate in which the dates of several transfers were officially indicated.

As an explanation the American naval authorities advised they had several aviators who were in the Allied ambulance service before the United States of America entered the war. These men had crossed the Atlantic in ordinary ships, taking the risk of being torpedoed, while the British again asserted 'no hospital ship, British or American, has ever carried anyone but invalids and the necessary medical staff'.

America considered the probable reason for the false charges as Germany laying the foundation for the justification of the torpedoing later of American hospital ships, in case any were put on the transatlantic service to carry home invalided soldiers. The reasoning behind this was similar abuse claims made against British hospital ships as a prelude to torpedoing them. Weeks later the German claims were used as an excuse for one of the worst maritime atrocities of the war.

Proposals to abandon long-haul maritime evacuation

The escalation in hospital ship attacks prompted the Government to consider an alternative scheme for the long-haul transportation of the sick and wounded to and from the British Isles. Since the introduction of Spanish commissioners on hospital ships operating in the Mediterranean the enemy had not attacked any hospital ships. With this point in mind, and the requirement of keeping invalids out of the dangerous waters of the Western Approaches for as long as it was possible, it was proposed in early March that the following scheme be adopted.

[1] All invalids [hospital ship cases] from the Mediterranean were to be conveyed to Marseilles by hospital ship. On arrival they would disembark into ambulance trains for Le Havre [requiring a rail journey across the length of France] and cross the Channel in ambulance transports.

[2] All invalids [hospital ship cases] from India should be conveyed to Egypt by hospital ships. Then transported as above.

[3] All invalids [hospital ship cases] from the African Cape to be conveyed to Egypt in hospital ships, then as in point one.

Additionally the proposals included alternative arrangements for vessels leaving British ports laden with incapacitated colonial troops.

[4] Invalids [hospital ship cases] for Australia, New Zealand and South Africa should be conveyed to Le Havre in Ambulance Transports. From there they would travel by rail to Marseilles, by hospital ships to Egypt and then by connecting hospital ships to their destinations.

[5] Invalids [hospital ship cases] for Canada should be conveyed in ambulance transports sailing with an escort.

In response to the proposals, the Ministry of Shipping advised on the estimated monthly numbers of sick and wounded evacuated from the Mediterranean. The campaigns in Egypt and Salonika each produced an average of seventy-five officers and 1,200 patients. A further fifty officers and 900 other ranks from India arrived via Egypt. This figure of 3,500 per month could escalate if severe fighting occurred in Salonika. The ships involved in this operation ran from the Mediterranean to Avonmouth: they comprised *Braemar Castle*, *Dunluce Castle*, *Formosa*, *Glengorm Castle*, *Guildford Castle*, *Kalyan* and *Wandilla* with a total accommodation of 230 officers and 3,400 other ranks. Two additional vessels *Goorkha* and *Valdivia* were expected to be available in the near future.

Canadian wounded embarking.

As the Italians refused to allow hospital ships carrying neutral delegates to enter Taranto, it was only possible to utilise Marseilles. The new arrangements would throw an additional strain on the cross-Channel service and would necessitate one or two additional large ships being put on the Southampton to Le Havre route. To do this would require transferring ships currently on the Mediterranean to United Kingdom run. The proposed new arrangements would result in a saving of tonnage thereby allowing vessels to be released for other work. Furthermore the ships still engaged on the services would perform more voyages than they then did.

Another Government department in reply considered the scheme an excellent method of evading enemy submarines, but it would considerably increase the rail traffic in France and the cross-Channel transport work. If Britain adopted the scheme we would appear to be conceding our right of sailing hospital ships under the Hague Convention. Furthermore once we abandoned this protection the nation might find it very difficult to exercise that right at a later date. As an alternative to the proposed scheme it was suggested:

> *[A]To route all hospital ships leaving the United Kingdom, so that they sail clear of the known positions of enemy submarines. In the case of hospital ships homeward-bound to the United Kingdom, to intercept them by patrols, and order them to steer a course that will take them clear of the known positions of enemy submarines. This scheme is by no means infallible.*
>
> *[B] To extend the Spanish Commissioner system to the Atlantic, and to arrange that a Spanish Commissioner sails in every hospital ship on every voyage in the Atlantic as well as in the Mediterranean.*
>
> *Doubts were also raised over the logistics of transporting the wounded on an already over-capacity French rail network, and the calculated level of saved tonnage as a result of the scheme. Consequently the War Office proposed to take no further action. The complacency appears to arise from the mistaken belief the last three lost hospital ships fell victim to a rogue submarine commander. The German Government were requested to prevent a reoccurrence of these attacks. In an effort to reduce hospital ship attacks the Admiralty attempted, in mid April, to persuade Canadian hospital ships from embarking patients at Liverpool. Major S M Bosworth the Director of Supplies and Transport considered it would be desirable, on the grounds of safety, that the hospital ships should make Avonmouth the port of embarkation. The objections to the use of Liverpool were due to hostile minefields which not infrequently closed the port. A passage to Liverpool required a lengthier sailing in the danger zone compared to that of Avonmouth. As the* Llandovery Castle *was at Barry undergoing a refit scheduled for completion in ten days time, Bosworth required confirmation if arrangements could be completed in sufficient time for her to embark patients at Avonmouth.*
>
> *The General Officer commanding the Overseas Military forces of Canada replied the relocation could not be done without the complete*

dislocation of hospital ship embarkation, as the whole system revolved around the use of Liverpool as a port. Within Liverpool and its immediate vicinity a total of 1,375 hospital beds were available for clearing station purposes, of which 175 were for mental patients, the latter being the hardest accommodation to duplicate. Should the War Office insist on the use of the port of Avonmouth they will need to provide similar clearing accommodation at that port. Should the Liverpool accommodation be retained hospital trains will be required to convey hundreds of wounded on a specific date to the proposed embarkation port. In view of the above points if the Admiralty does not consider the Avonmouth embarkations essential we propose to retain Liverpool as the port of embarkation, and successfully argued their case.

Originally known as the *Mongolia* when her Trieste builders completed her for the Russian Government the single stack steamer was purchased by a Danish company, who in turn sold her to the Government of Western Australia. Renamed the *Western Australia* she operated on the North West coast of that state. Unfortunately, she proved unsuitable for her new role and in July 1915 her owners decided to sell the vessel in Britain where there would be no difficulty in finding a buyer. On arrival in the United Kingdom her Australian crew were paid off when the Admiralty agreed a charter for the duration of hostilities. After conversion to a 305 bed hospital ship she entered service on 21 October 1915 manned by a Union Castle Crew. Three years later while serving as an ambulance transport the *Western Australia* was attacked by a submarine, fortunately the torpedo missed.

The Kaiser's spring offensive

Germanic attempts to gain a victory attained by submarine warfare had failed and her leaders looked elsewhere for a great military triumph. Inevitably the plans involved the Western Front where the first indications of spring heralded a new round of fighting. The British offensives in late 1917 had incurred some 320,000 casualties, and since the beginning of 1918, the army continued to disband infantry battalions. Lloyd George's restrictions on fresh drafts for the front severely weakened the army, while on the other hand Germany utilised resources released from the former Eastern Front. For Germany to take full advantage of the situation, she had to abandon her defensive strategy and attack before American troops arrived in sufficient strength to negate Germany's superior reserves of manpower.

Throughout one of the coldest winters on record Germany made intensive preparations for a major offensive intended to break the deadlock on the Western Front. General Ludendorff masterminded Operation MICHAEL which would strike on a sixty-mile frontage from near Arras extending in a southerly direction to La Frere on the River Oise. Beyond the river lay the boundary of

the French and British sectors: Ludendorff believed a breakthrough in the weakened British sector would drive a wedge between the Allied armies. For in the event of a breakthrough the Anglo-French forces had different priorities, Britain would attempt to protect the routes to the Channel ports while the French would safeguard Paris. Imperial Germany was about to gamble all her resources in manpower and matériel in a desperate attempt to destroy the BEF once and for all.

On 21 March Operation MICHAEL, the opening phase of the *Kaiserschlacht* [Kaiser's Battle], began. A thunderous earth shaking barrage supplemented by poison gas and smoke shells preceded the infantry attack, successfully destroying lines of communication. A thick fog concealed the advancing field grey clad troops, and at the vanguard of the assault were specially trained storm troopers. Using innovative infantry tactics they bypassed isolated points of key resistance, successive waves encircled the strongpoints and eliminated the resistance. The weakened British divisions crumbled before the onslaught and fell back in disarray and the situation became critical. By 27 March the enemy had punched a forty-mile indent into the Allied line, and reached Montdidier where French reserves halted the advance. On 9 April Ludendorff launched the second phase of the attack, codenamed Operation GEORGETTE; further blows were now directed on the Allied frontage between Ypres and La Bassee. Again the Allies reeled under the pressure, ceding a ten mile bulge in the front line before the stiffened resistance prevented further inroads. The British had suffered almost 100,000 casualties, prompting an urgent recall of several infantry divisions from Italy, Palestine and Salonika. A further 140,000 fresh troops were despatched from Britain.

Warilda and the Paramount clause

In the congested harbour shipping channels maritime accidents were not uncommon. One such incident, concerning the *Warilda,* recorded in the diary of Private Gwilym Pari Huws, surprisingly became the topic of debate in the House of Lords.

The *Warilda* departed Le Havre at 11.00 pm on 23 March; at an illegible location *Warilda* collided with an unnamed possibly much smaller vessel – the diarist noted six people died as a result of the collision. The hospital ship reached Southampton and commenced disembarking patients late the following afternoon. On 25 March the damaged steamer lay moored at berth 31; subsequent moves occurred until the vessel entered graving dock for repairs to her damaged bow. She returned to service on Saturday 25 May.

To avoid problems arising from the legal case Attorney General v Adelaide Steam Ship Company Limited, which dealt specifically with the collision liability and the sue and labour clause, the House of Lords Admiralty debated the matter. The Lords held that the Admiralty-chartered *Warilda* had collided with

Left: The bow of *Warilda.*

vessel *P* which was proceeding with only dimmed sidelights. The collision was due to the negligence of the master of *Warilda* in not giving way or reducing speed, and was engaged on a war-like operation of which the collision was a direct consequence. As the Admiralty hire charter agreed to be responsible for war risks, they were deemed liable for the damage caused by *Warilda*. As damage arising from negligent navigation was not excluded by the policy on marine risks, the marine underwriters were liable for the loss under what was then the running down clause. The incident led to the insertion of 'The Paramount Clause' into the Law of Marine Assurance.

The Royal Navy had received much criticism over their inability to defend Allied merchant shipping from the marauding submarines. All attempts to mine the waters surrounding German naval bases in the Heligoland Bight were thwarted by German minesweepers which quickly cleared the Channel from danger. The only alternatives were to destroy the submarines as they passed around the tip of Scotland or through the English Channel heading for the Atlantic. The English Channel route reduced by eight days the time required for a submarine to reach its patrol area; the saving in fuel also permitted the craft a lengthier patrol duration, thereby increasing its chance of a kill. In an attempt to prevent belligerent vessels from slipping through the English Channel the Admiralty had constructed anti-submarine nets and minefields which they considered to be almost impossible to bypass; they were unaware that thirty submarines a month crossed over the nets.

Towards the latter end of the previous year, while laying mines off the Waterford coast, *UC44* struck a mine. The Admiralty raised the vessel and discovered amongst their freshly acquired intelligence, papers revealing the U-boats routinely negotiated the Dover net barrage. Consequently, the minefields and nets were extensively modified. To prevent the submarines passing over the nets under cover of darkness, patrols were doubled and the minefields were illuminated by night. As the Admiralty believed the main U-boat threat emanated from the submarines based at Bruges in occupied Belgium, they sanctioned approval for a block ship operation on two outlets allowing egress for submarines to the North Sea. On St George's Day, 23 April 1918, Royal Navy and Royal Marine raiding parties attacked the heavily defended Zeebrugge Mole, a vast concrete breakwater. It proved a costly and almost suicidal raid, but while the defenders were repulsing the seaborne attackers, three concrete-filled obsolete British cruisers scuttled themselves across the main channel. As a result only small submarines with a shallow draft could bypass the obstructions, until dredging work permitted larger craft to scrape by the block ships. Two attempts to block Ostend failed; both harbours remained operational, but egress became dependent on the tide, limiting their use as an effective naval base. This action, combined with the improved Channel barrage and a more aggressive Dover Patrol force, severely curtailed submarine activity.

The English Channel route became too dangerous for hostile submarines, and as the methods of detection improved U-boat losses increased. The submarine war was now almost won, but victory elsewhere seemed as distant as ever.

The loss of the 6,953-GRT *Kyarra* is occasionally erroneously described as a hospital ship or ambulance transport loss [she had a gun mounted on her after deck]. The confusion arises due to the Australian United Steam Navigation vessel having 100 wounded Australians onboard. The steamer departed from London carrying a general cargo destined for Sydney, New South Wales. After clearing the Thames *Kyarra* was to proceed to Devonport to collect Australian wounded to be disembarked at Sydney.

Despite her having wounded onboard the steamer was a legitimate target and was not in hospital ship livery. As she navigated off the Dorset coast on 26 May the fifteen-year-old ship was struck by a torpedo launched from *UB57* commanded by *Oberleutnant* Johann Lohs. The passenger and cargo liner sank a couple of miles off Anvil Point; six lives were lost in the incident.

Late in May two surprise diversionary attacks broke through the French lines between Soissons and Reims, ultimately reaching the Marne on 30 May when the impetus ebbed away. At this juncture the first of the American divisions received their baptism of fire, on the Marne at Belleau Wood and Château-Thierry where they counter-attacked. Ludendorff's strategic gains created two great bulges and a lesser one in the Allied front line. A fourth offensive launched against the French on 12–13 June intending to straighten the undulating German front line failed. The enemy now paused to consolidate their gains and give a welcome respite to their exhausted troops; the delay proved catastrophic. The French and British regrouped and American reinforcements flooded in: by mid July seven American divisions were immediately available, while many more were learning front-line survival. Now out-manned and out-gunned, the chances of a German victory looked increasingly slender.

PS *Koningin Regentes.*

In early June a British delegation headed by Sir George Cave boarded the earlier mentioned Rotterdam Lloyd mail paddle steamer SS *Sindoro,* destined for Rotterdam to attend a conference at The Hague on the exchange of prisoners of war. The 5,471 ton *Sindoro*, in convoy with the paddle steamers *Zeeland* and the hospital ship *Koningin Regentes,* sailed from Boston at four-thirty on Thursday 6 June. It was a fine day with a smooth sea yet the delegates were shortly to witness the sudden and dramatic loss of a hospital ship.

At precisely eight minutes past one, the *Koningin Regentes* was about five hundred yards astern of *Sindoro* when those onboard heard a terrific explosion. The captain of *Sindoro* immediately swung his ship around, for the *Koningin Regentes* had been struck amidships, and broke up and sank within five minutes, fifty miles east of the Leman Bank. Sir George and the other delegates were in the saloon at the time of the explosion; they arrived on deck to witness the ship sink. After searching the sea in the vicinity of the wreck the two remaining ships continued their voyage without incident. Four firemen were killed by the explosion and the ship's paymaster succumbed to exposure when he reached the *Sindoro*. The remainder of the crew, the Red Cross doctors, nurses, and the nineteen returning German civilian prisoners were rescued by the *Sindoro*.

When interviewed Captain Redecker of the *Koningen Regentes* claimed his ship was torpedoed, basing his belief on the testimony of the lookout, the carpenter and a seaman. The first two assured a naval officer representing the Dutch government that they saw the track of a torpedo, while the seaman claimed he had briefly seen the torpedo.

A Berlin telegraph, after declaring no prisoners of war were aboard stated that on the safe lane for hospital ships no mines had been laid from the German side; talk of a torpedo attack was nonsense. Witnesses on the *Sindoro* claimed three mines were seen shortly before the hospital ship exploded. However, the testimony of three crew members supported an attack by submarine. The *Nieuw Rotterdamsche Courant* left its readers in no doubt that the ship was torpedoed, pointing out... the ship was a paddle steamer and that the Germans insisted on the use of such ships, because they could easily be identified from a distance by submarine commanders. On the shoulders of the ruffian who has done this 'there falls a heavy responsibility on the eve of fresh negotiations over the exchange of unhappy prisoners'.

The heinous sinking of the *Llandovery Castle*

The Royal Mail line took over the Union Castle line in 1912, yet allowed the company to manage its own operations. In 1914, the Clyde built 11,423-ton *Llandovery Castle* arrived from the Barclay Curle shipyard. She had the distinction of being the first passenger cargo liner ordered for the considerably expanded shipping line. The steamer would not be remembered for this

Sindoro.

milestone in nautical affairs, but for one of the most barbaric acts perpetrated upon the high seas.

The increased level of requisition of the company vessels led to the disruption of the mail service, which despite the war still operated. During 1915, the company assigned the *Llandovery Castle* to operate on the mail service. On 8 June, the vessel cleared the Bay of Biscay and approached Cape Finisterre, Spain, where she was almost intercepted by an enemy submarine. The mail ship, which had a maximum speed of fifteen knots, managed to outrun the surfaced U-boat, and escape.

During December 1915, she was requisitioned by the Government as a troopship on the cross-Channel run. During one of the crossings as she approached Dover, prisoners of war caused a fire on the liner. Fortunately the assistance of the naval and local fire service extinguished the flames. On 2 March 1916, the 11th East Lancashire regiment [Accrington Pals] boarded at Port Said for Boulogne to take part in the Big Push. On 1 July they went over the top for the attack on Serre; in less than twenty minutes 235 were dead and 350 were wounded. A fortunate few may have seen the vessel again, for on 26 July 1916 the Union Castle liner was chartered by the Canadian government to convey their sick and wounded military personnel from England to Halifax. She

Llandovery Castle.

could accommodate 622 patients and made five voyages during which she carried a total of 3,223 patients. In accordance with the Geneva Convention the vessel bore the appropriate markings; the authorities registered her as a hospital ship with the belligerents.

On 17 June 1918, the *Llandovery Castle* reached Halifax harbour, Nova Scotia, where she disembarked 644 military patients. Three days later the hospital ship commenced her return voyage. On board were 161 crew and members of the ship's hospital unit. The Canadian Army Medical Corps [CAMC] unit numbered seven officers, fourteen nursing sisters, and seventy-six other ranks. A number of the nurses had stoically endured several years' active service, primarily in the First Canadian Division casualty clearing stations in France. They were assigned to the hospital ship as a respite from the stress and ever-present dangers of the Western Front. Due to the empty hospital wards and pleasant weather the medical staff now anticipated a relatively relaxing cross Atlantic return voyage to Liverpool. The captain set a course for England then proceeded at a speed of fourteen knots into the wide expanses of the Atlantic Ocean on the 2,509 nautical miles voyage to Liverpool. Brightly illuminated with her regulation hospital lights, a huge electric cross over the bridge and red crosses on either side, illuminated by electric lights, she steamed onwards under an overcast sky, unmistakeably a defenceless hospital ship. All went well until the vessel reached the Western Approaches, the favoured killing ground for U-boats, currently being patrolled by *U86*.[2] Approximately 115 miles south-west of the Fastnet Rock the German submersible attacked.

Major Lyon [RAMC] recalled:

At 9.30 pm the night was clear. All lights were burning, with the large Red Cross signal prominently displayed amidships. Most of the medical personnel had not yet retired. Without previous warning or sight of any submarine the ship was struck just abaft the engines at number four hold. There was a terrific explosion, badly wrecking the after part of the ship. Immediately all lights went out. The signal to stop and reverse the engines was without response, all the engine room crew evidently being killed or wounded. Consequently the ship forged forward, but was gradually forced down by the head.

While the carpenter went aft to inspect the damage, in his wireless cabin the Marconi operator tried in vain to transmit the ship's position, for the explosion had brought all the top hamper (including the wireless rigging) down. The carpenter reported to the bridge that number four hold was blown in and she could not remain afloat. Many of the engine crew were dead, even so damage to the after end of the engine room made it impossible to put the engines astern and halt the headway. Following a well-rehearsed drill Lieutenant Colonel TH MacDonald marshalled his staff at the various boat stations and confirmed all his staff were present prior to boarding the lifeboats. As the ship continued steaming ahead the launching of the lifeboats was fraught with danger, but as the vessel rapidly settled in the water Captain Sylvester had no option but to order the lowering of the boats on each side of the ship. There were nineteen boats on board, although some of the port boats were destroyed by the explosion. Excluding two smaller cutters, the others had a maximum capacity of fifty-two persons. The forward motion of the ship and the extreme slope of the sinking ship's deck made the launching extremely difficult, survivors report five boats were lowered from the starboard side, two of which were swamped, so only three got away safely. On the port side two boats escaped; great emphasis would later be paid to the number of boats surviving the foundering.

Sergeant Knight took charge of the starboard [all odd numbered] number five lifeboat which, apart from him, contained fourteen nurses and eight crew. After quickly lowering the boat they had great difficulty in getting free of the fall ropes. They were securely fastened to the ship, two axes were broken in an attempt to free the boat without success. The ship's forward momentum and the choppy sea continually pounded the lifeboat against the ship's hull. Fearing the destruction of the boat the oars were used to hold the boat away, but soon every oar broke. Almost ten minutes after their launch the ropes came free, allowing the boat to drift away towards the stern. Unexpectedly the poop deck sheared off and plunged into the sea, precipitating a great suction which drew the lifeboat towards the vortex.

Unflinchingly and calmly, as steady and collected as if on parade, without a complaint or a single sign of emotion, our fourteen devoted nursing sisters faced the terrible ordeal of certain death– now only a matter of minutes away as our lifeboat neared that mad whirlpool of waters where all human power was helpless. A few seconds later we were drawn into the whirlpool of the submerged afterdeck, and the last I saw of the nursing sisters was as they were thrown over the side of the boat. All were wearing lifebelts, and of the fourteen two were in their nightdresses, the others in uniform. Sergeant Knight doubted if any of them came to the surface again.'

Union Castle cap badge.

Three times the eddy sucked Sergeant Knight under; he was the lifeboat's sole survivor. After the boat overturned he found himself sitting on the keel, bruised and dazed, until the captain's boat came to his aid.

Within a few days of the incident the national press published the following account of possibly one of the most despicable outrages of the Great War:

... A small accident boat should have remained onboard for the last men off the ship. When all the boats had left the captain went to his cabin for a torch and on returning to the deck discovered the boat had also gone. Chapman the second officer found a lifeboat hanging in the falls with her stern in the water and bows in the air. He and a steward succeeded in placing her in the water the remaining crew swarmed sixty feet down a two inch rope to board the boat. They pulled away from the ship and were fifty feet clear when Llandovery Castle*'s stern went down leaving her long bows standing perpendicular from the sea. A boiler within her seemed to blow up as the water reached it, and her funnel leaned aside as she slowly listed to starboard, tore loose and fell away. Then stern first she slid under and disappeared. She sank in not more than ten minutes of the explosion.*

Huge quantities of wreckage floated around on the quiet sea including rafts and large gratings on which the mooring hawsers had been coiled. Among them men were floundering and calling out, one was even walking around on one of the gratings. The captain's boat recovered eleven men from the wreckage, and then pulled over towards a voice that called from help in the water in the dark, hearing at the same time two others that called from another direction. It was then that there appeared from the night gliding through the debris the long black shape of a submarine. Its conning tower was opened and there were vaguely seen figures along her deck.

It hailed the boat in English: "Come alongside", it ordered. The boat was pulling down to pick up the drowning man. The second officer stood up, and shouted back, "We are picking up a man from the water". "Come alongside", repeated the brusque order from the submarine. The boat held on its way, and forthwith two revolver shots were fired at or over it. "Come alongside or I will shoot with my big gun", shouted the submarine commander.

The boat lay alongside the submarine, and the captain was ordered on board. In case he should be made prisoner and kept onboard he gave the second officer, who remained in the boat, the course to steer. He was then taken to the conning tower of the submarine, where two officers awaited him. [The dazed Sergeant Knight thought this was a rescue ship and before he could be stopped he clambered upon the submarine. As soon as the German seamen saw him they picked him up bodily and threw him back in the boat.]

The commander asked him sharply "What ship was that?" "It was the hospital ship Llandovery Castle," *answered the captain. "Yes"– the commander did not attempt to appear surprised. "But you are carrying eight American flight officers." "We are not," replied the captain. "We have seven Canadian medical officers on board, and the ship was chartered by the Canadian Government to carry sick and wounded Canadians from England to Canada." To this the submarine commander reiterated "You have been carrying American flight officers". The captain added "I have been returning to Canada for six months with wounded, and I give you my word of honour that we have carried none, except patients, medical staff, crew and sisters". The commander then demanded to know if there were any Canadian medical officers in the boat, and was told there was one. He ordered him to come onboard.*

"Where are your other boats?" asked the captain then. The commander did not answer, he was watching the Canadian medical officer being roughly handled on board and thrust along the deck. This was done so violently and with such plain intention to injure that the Canadian, Major T Lyon, CAMC actually had a small bone in his foot broken by the handling he received.

But there was another German officer in the conning tower, the second in command, who had not yet spoken. In reply to the captain's question, he motioned over his shoulder with his field glasses to the northwards. Major Lyon was interrogated, and after protesting his character as a medical officer, was ordered back into the boat. The captain was also allowed to go. The boat was cast off and pulled away from the submarine.

The submarine then began to circle round the wreckage at full speed. Several times she shaved the boat narrowly, once sweeping past within two feet of it, and then she stopped again, took the second and fourth officers on board and questioned them. By this time the submarine commander had invented a new excuse, and stated that there was a big explosion aft as the vessel sank, and that therefore she must have been carrying ammunition. The second officer explained patiently the explosion of the boiler and the falling of the funnel, and they were allowed to return to the boat which then made sail and proceeded. Again for a while the submarine circled and threatened her by stopping close to her, then moved off and seemed to come to a stop.

"From this position," says the captain's official statement, "she opened fire at an unseen target, firing about twelve shells."... The captain's boat had been towed for some distance while alongside the submarine; there was nothing to be seen, and since no wireless had been sent out there was no hope of assistance arriving from the north. The captain therefore decided to make for the Irish coast to send help, and after sailing and pulling for about seventy miles, they were picked up by His Majesty's destroyer Lysander, *which immediately sent out wireless that search should be made for the other survivors, and carried the occupants of the captain's boat into Queenstown.*

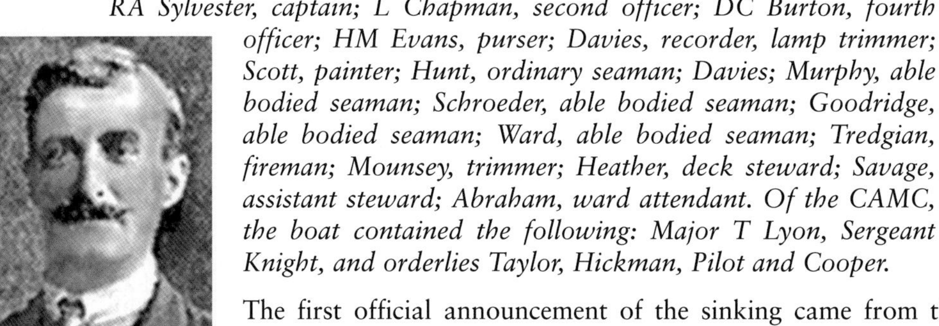

The following survivors from the captain's boat are the only ones accounted for at present; eleven of them were picked up from the water: RA Sylvester, captain; L Chapman, second officer; DC Burton, fourth officer; HM Evans, purser; Davies, recorder, lamp trimmer; Scott, painter; Hunt, ordinary seaman; Davies; Murphy, able bodied seaman; Schroeder, able bodied seaman; Goodridge, able bodied seaman; Ward, able bodied seaman; Tredgian, fireman; Mounsey, trimmer; Heather, deck steward; Savage, assistant steward; Abraham, ward attendant. Of the CAMC, the boat contained the following: Major T Lyon, Sergeant Knight, and orderlies Taylor, Hickman, Pilot and Cooper.

Fireman Bruce Bradley, drowned.

The first official announcement of the sinking came from the Secretary of the Admiralty who announced:

At 9.30 pm, ship time ie 10.30 British Summer Time, on 27 June, when 116 miles south-west of the Fastnet, His Majesty's hospital ship Llandovery Castle [Captain RA Sylvester] *was torpedoed by an enemy submarine, whilst showing all her navigation and regulation ship lights, and sank in about ten minutes. She was homeward-bound from Canada and therefore had no sick or wounded onboard, but her crew consisted of 164 officers and men, and she carried eighty Canadian army medical and fourteen female nurses. Of this total of 258 only one boat containing twenty-four survivors has so far reached port. Search is still being made, and there is a bare possibility that others may yet be found.*

It should be remembered that in this, as indeed in all other instances, under the Hague Convention the German submarine captain had a every right to stop and search the hospital ship. However, he chose to torpedo the *Llandovery Castle.*

The survivors were in the boat for thirty-six hours with only biscuits and water to sustain them. Their chief comfort seems to have been due to the captain's foresight in running to his cabin for his pipe before leaving the vessel. This was the only tobacco on board and the pipe was passed around in turn. On 29 June the discovery of the captain's boat prompted a sea search for the remaining survivors; the searchers were optimistic for the weather had remained fine. A systematic search by the British sloop *Snowdrop* and four American destroyers emanated from the position where *Lysander* rescued the captain's lifeboat. Nine miles from this position *Snowdrop* found an empty *Llandovery Castle* lifeboat; the position of the lifeboat sail indicated she had carried survivors. The search continued until 1 July; no further boats or survivors were found despite the good weather conditions. Two days later a figure of 234 lives lost appeared in the press only the fortuitous escape of the captain's boat prevented the submariners' cover-up of the atrocity. With the exception of six survivors– Major Lyon, Sergeant Knight, Privates Hickman, Pilot, Cooper and Taylor – the list of casualties included the entire medical personnel.

Numbered among those lost at sea was Robert Sharp, the son of William Sharp and Helen Sharp nee Anderson. He was born in 1867 at Cuppister, Shetland Islands. Due to the isolation of the Shetland Islands employment opportunities were limited; the Sharps relied on the sea for their income, and several of Robert's brothers and nephews were master mariners. Robert emigrated to Adelaide, Southern Australia [where some of his descendants live to this day]; now married to Rosina Grace Sharp, they resided in Carson Street. In true family tradition Robert become a master mariner. During the height of the U-boat campaign he returned to his native country to visit his Shetland relations. It is not known why at Liverpool the fifty-one-year-old [aged forty-five on CWGC records] signed the ship's articles as a boatswain [bosun]. Robert Sharp is one of the 12,000 Great War Mercantile Marine casualties who have no known grave but the sea, commemorated on the Tower Hill memorial, London.

Robert Sharp.

The 3 July edition of the *New York Times* published an article headed 'Retribution for Germany'. If there can be any degrees of fiendishness in sinking hospital ships and murdering their helpless people, the submarine commander who torpedoed *Llandovery Castle* deserves the most coveted decoration... The news this morning gives evidence of our determination to win in the announcement by Secretary Baker to the President that we now have more than a million men of our army in France and on the way there. More than a half a million men have been sent overseas in the last two months... The British Seaman's Union has blazed the way by proclaiming a boycott against Germans after the war for their misdeeds at sea. Mister Joseph Havelock Wilson declared in a speech at the Albert Hall that 25,000 men in the shipping industry have determined not to tolerate a German in a British ship. They would also not take a British vessel into any German port for a term of years in retaliation for the shameful assassination of 15,000 non-combatant seamen.[3]

The vessel had expected to carry eight medical officers, but at the last moment the passage of one was cancelled; she took only seven medical officers. Enemy intelligence knew of the eight officers they expected to find onboard, only they were medical not flying officers. Evidently the vessel was torpedoed due to information received from a Halifax informant. World condemnation followed the ruthless massacre of the hospital ship survivors, but the German government denied all knowledge of the act. There appears to be some substance in this claim for Patzig failed to enter the sinking in the vessel's log book. He also marked on the charts a different route for the patrol of his craft, thereby distancing *U86* from the scene of the crime. If his superiors decided to investigate the slaughter of unarmed survivors Patzig considered he had sufficiently covered his tracks. After hostilities ended the German authorities arrayed the absent First Lieutenant Patzig on charges of war crimes.

Naturally the Canadians took the massacre of innocents personally and at the first opportunity they sought to avenge the deaths of their compatriots. The official history of the Canadian Army in the First World War refers to their troops preparations for the victorious Battle of Amiens which commenced on 8 August 1918. Six weeks after the sinking each division reported assembly completed, by sending Corps headquarters the code word *Llandovery Castle*. All the operational instructions for the attack bore the initials LC. Brigadier George Tuxford, a native of Moose Jaw, Saskatchewan [recruiting area for 229 battalion and home town of two of the nurses]. When issuing instructions to the brigade he added: 'the battle cry on the 8th August should be "Llandovery Castle", and that the cry should be the last thing to ring in the ears of the Hun as the bayonet is driven home'[4].

Commemorated on the Halifax memorial to the missing are three members of the Canadian Machine Gun Corps [CMGC] who perished on the hospital ship. The Veterans Affair Canada website reveals service in the CMGC also the *Llandovery Castle*. They may have recently transferred to the medical corps, for they are recorded as CAMC personnel in the 'Book of Remembrance'.

The *South African Nursing Record* summed up the world's revulsion of the atrocity:

> *The Hun has committed such revolting outrages that sometimes one wonders if one has any capacity for horror left; but an affair like the sinking of the hospital ship* Llandovery Castle *was so unspeakable as still*

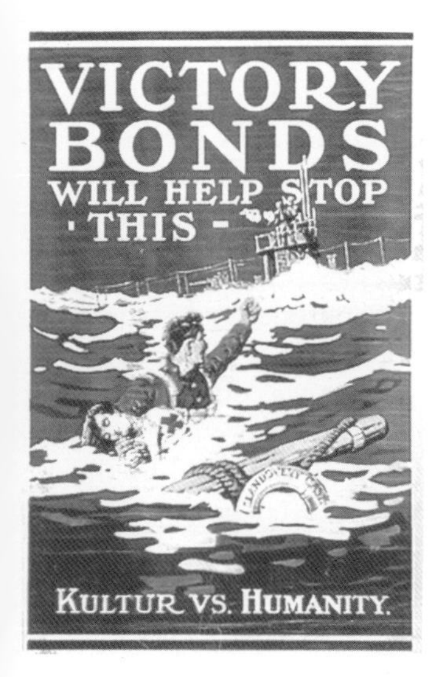

to bring a gasp of surprise from all around the world. Surely, there is nothing to do with a beast like that but annihilate him completely.

The German papers supported a mine theory or maintained the ship was justifiably torpedoed. The *Kolnische Volkszeitung* considered it 'superfluous to reproduce details of the commander's conduct, as published in England, and regarded it as significant that the vessel carried such a large crew as 164'. The Essen newspaper *Rheinische Westfalische Zeitung* asserted 'the vessel probably struck a mine, but even if she was torpedoed it was probably rightly done, as most overseas hospital ships are armed'.

A poignant footnote appeared in the Western Front Association bulletin number seventy-seven, within the obituary of Captain Kenneth Cummins. As a seventeen-year-old youth he found himself on the P&O *Morea*, a converted armed merchant cruiser employed on convoy duties. The vessel previously spent six months as a hospital ship:

Marama was launched at Greenock in 1907, when converted she carried 550 cot patents.

During his first voyage out he saw, south-west of Fastnet Rock the floating bodies of nurses from the Llandovery Castle. *Cummins recalled the corpses being driven across the sea by their billowing aprons and skirts which had dried in the hot sun to form sails, but the risk of being torpedoed prevented the recovery of the bodies.*

The German navy denied while sinking ships they ever purposely destroyed lifeboats with their passengers. While the facts of the *Llandover Castle* were fresh in people's minds the French armed steamer *Lyndiane* was sunk off the north coast of Spain on 16 July. The crew managed to launch two whaleboats and a raft; nevertheless all three were successively rammed at full speed by the U-boat. The boats were sliced in half; the raft finally broke up after six ferocious attacks. Part of one boat still remained afloat, with men hanging on to it, and the submarine again returned and rammed the wreckage. The U-boat eventually disappeared without helping the survivors. Only nine of the *Lyndiane*'s crew of forty-two were eventually picked up.[4]

Stunned by the atrocities committed by Patzig of *U86* the British authorities reconsidered the earlier proposal to rail the wounded across France. On the third of July the Fourth Sea Lord during the initial discussion of the proposals advised,

As the situation on the Western Front is, and will remain for at least the next three months critical, I think it would be unwise to rail the individuals across France. I have also given instructions that the transport of invalid and wounded Australians, New Zealanders and South Africans shall be temporarily suspended and have requested the Transport Department to ascertain the views of the New Zealand, Australian and Canadian Military Authorities on the matter.

The *Neuralia* when serving as a troop transport post war, seen here passing through the Kiel Kanal.

At Avonmouth, the *Wandilla* and *Neuralia* carrying Australian invalids were scheduled to sail on 8 and 9 July for Australia, connecting with Australian hospital ships at Egypt. Under the new proposal the Adelaide Steam Ship Company's *Wandilla* was to disembark her invalids and send them overland to Marseilles, the 7,784-GRT *Wandilla* would sail empty to Marseilles where the invalids would then board her for conveyance to Egypt. The proposals suggested *Neuralia* should halt embarkation of Australian invalids who should be transported overland. The Fourth Sea Lord dismissed both proposals and the vessels sailed, evidently safely reaching their destinations.

The turning of the tide

On 15 July, in the vicinity of Reims, Ludendorff launched his final great offensive but made little progress. Three days later Marshal Foch launched a Franco-American counter-attack supported by masses of light tanks. The Germans managed to extricate their troops and straighten their line. Depleted of reserves and weakened by 500,000 casualties, on 20 July Ludendorff abandoned his Flanders offensive and went on the defensive.

Over one and a quarter million men of the American Expeditionary Force were now in France. The arrival of the inexperienced but eager troops had a considerable demoralising effect on the German war machine, all too aware of the vast resources and manpower at American disposal. A series of counter-strokes swiftly broke against the enemy positions, the most significant being a surprise Anglo-French attack near Amiens on 8 August involving a great number of tanks. By now totally demoralised the enemy fought without conviction and some units offered only token resistance. General Ludendorff later said 'August 8 was the black day of the German army in the history of the war... it put the decline of our fighting power beyond all doubt'. The tide had finally turned in favour of the Allies; the advance to victory had begun.

The loss of the ambulance transport *Warilda*

Built in 1912 for the Adelaide Steam Ship Company by the Clydebank firm of William Beardmore and Company, yard number 505 slid down the launch ways as the *Warilda*. Displacing 7,713 gross tons the 412 feet long steamer originally served on the east-west Australian coastal service. A brief civilian career terminated with her 1915 requisitioning as a troopship for the Australian Imperial Forces, prior to becoming a hospital ship from 25 July 1916. The vessel with an official capacity of 546 patients [she often carried more] safely plied the Le Havre to Southampton route for almost two years. In May 1917 her Australian crew excluding the officers and engineers returned to their homeland; a British crew then signed on. After the introduction of unrestricted naval warfare the *Warilda* became an ambulance transport, equipped with a 4-inch gun which served as a deterrent to marauding submarines, rather than an effective counter-measure.

While berthed at Le Havre the vessel embarked 600 sick and wounded including seven Americans, the majority of which were cot cases. This was her first trip without wounded German prisoners on board which caused some concern among her crew, later claiming this had a sinister significance. Also onboard were eighty-nine nurses and members of the Women's Army Auxiliary Corps [WAAC] and approximately 120 crew. The vessel commanded by Captain Sim, set sail for England escorted by HMS *P35* and *P45*. In the darkness of the early hours of Saturday 3 August 1918, *Warilda* was torpedoed in mid-Channel. At the time of the incident, about twenty minutes to one in the morning, most of her crew were in their bunks, their dreams abruptly shattered by the detonation of one, some say two torpedoes. A submarine had stalked the vessel and while the moon was overshadowed by a black cloud *UC49* commander Kukenthal seized his opportunity and launched her primary armament. [Some press reports state *Warilda* attempted to ram the surfaced submarine.] The self-propelled missile impacted on the starboard side of the ambulance transport in the after part of the engine room, killing the third engineer and two engine room workers. The dynamos were destroyed, plunging the vessel into darkness and greatly adding to the rescue problems. Above the dynamos was a ward containing ten patients; most were killed by the explosion, and the others received fresh wounds. Tragically the explosion also wrecked a communication ladder to the lower deck, thereby destroying the escape route for between ninety and one hundred souls. Water engulfed the lower bowels of the ship; rescuers struggled through the rising water in pitch blackness attempting to rescue the trapped men. All attempts were futile and over ninety trapped patients drowned.

The command 'abandon ship – patients first' heralded the vessel's evacuation. The vessel remained afloat for two hours which gave the survivors more time to abandon ship, thereby reducing the death toll. However, the survivors feared the imminent demise of the ship. The vessel continued to make headway as her engines could not be stopped. Her momentum hampered the launching of the lifeboats at least three boats were smashed while lowering, throwing their occupants into the choppy sea. One boat containing six women impacted against another just before reaching the sea and overturned. Three of the ladies from the overturned boat were rescued by another boat containing five soldiers who each had an arm in a sling. Steward TE Redman occupied the first lifeboat containing six women; he described how one woman became entangled in the ropes as she was being placed in a lifeboat, and became trapped between the boat and the side of the ship. The badly crushed lady pleaded to be released but no help was possible; when the weight came off the line the woman fell into the sea and drowned.

Immediately after the attack both escorts depth-charged the area in an

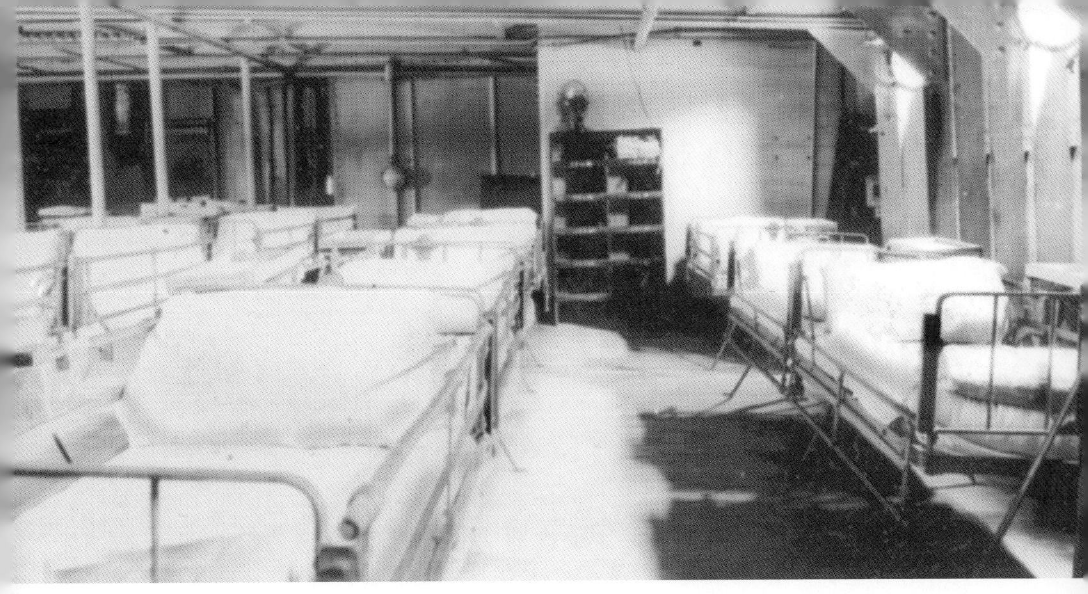

One of the hospital wards on *Warilda*.

unsuccessful attempt to destroy the submarine. In response to her distress calls other warships arrived on the scene to rescue survivors. The *Warilda* crew, under the direction of the officers, went coolly about their difficult task of locating in the dark and bringing the wounded up on deck. Despite the rough weather a destroyer managed to come alongside allowing the wounded to be lowered in slings to the rescuer.

The Secretary of the Admiralty issued the following announcement:

> *On 2 August two of HM torpedo boat destroyers were sunk by enemy mines with the loss of five officers and ninety-two ratings. All the next of kin have been informed.*
>
> *The homeward bound ambulance transport* Warilda, *Captain James Sim master, was torpedoed and sunk on 3 August.*
>
> *The following are missing presumed drowned: Military officers, two, Commandant Queen Mary's Army Auxiliary Corps, one, other ranks 112, total 115. US troops, other ranks one, total 116. Casualties among crew, officers one, crew six, total 123. The next of kin are being informed.*

Meanwhile a far less prominent cog in the enormous war machine, Private Gwilym Pari Huws, a medic onboard *Warilda*, entered in his diary:

> *August 3. Struck by a torpedo about 1.45 am. Dreadful– many lives lost. Went on the* P45. *To the test chambers, had breakfast and lunch there.*

Warilda.

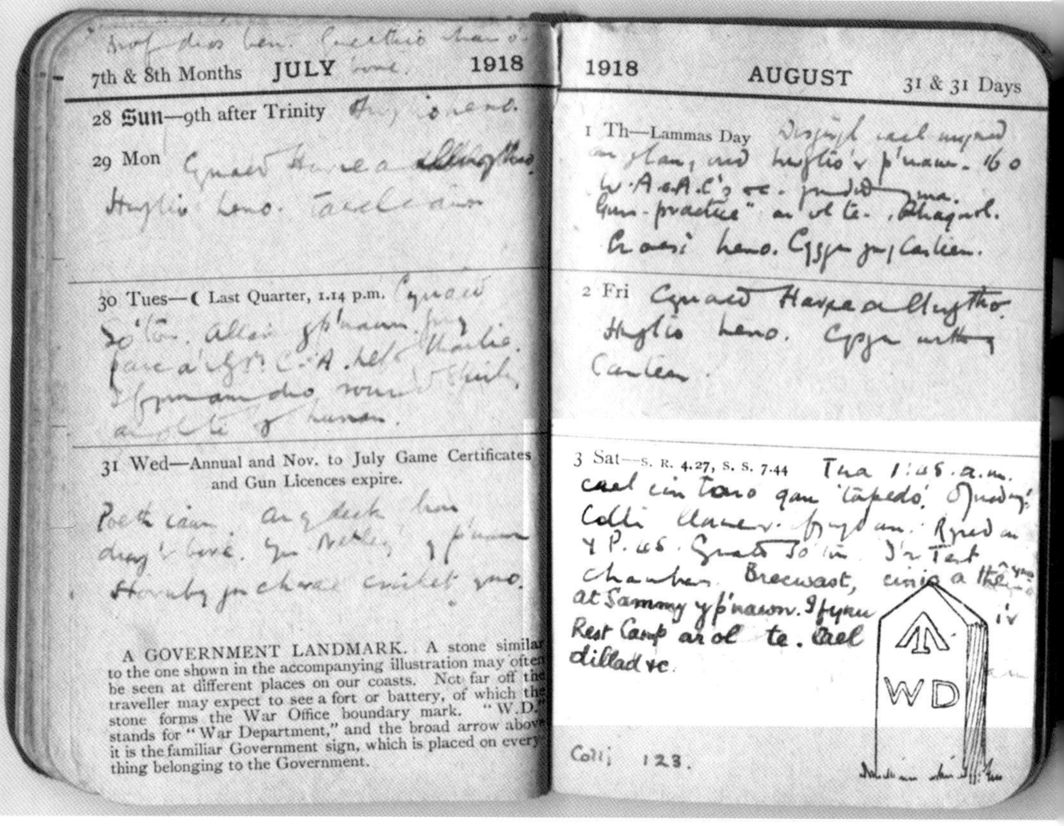
7th & 8th Months JULY 1918

28 Sun—9th after Trinity

29 Mon

30 Tues—(Last Quarter, 1.14 p.m.

31 Wed—Annual and Nov. to July Game Certificates and Gun Licences expire.

A GOVERNMENT LANDMARK. A stone similar to the one shown in the accompanying illustration may often be seen at different places on our coasts. Not far off the traveller may expect to see a fort or battery, of which the stone forms the War Office boundary mark. "W.D." stands for "War Department," and the broad arrow above it is the familiar Government sign, which is placed on everything belonging to the Government.

1918 AUGUST 31 & 31 Days

1 Th—Lammas Day

2 Fri

3 Sat—S. R. 4.27, S. S. 7.44

The Welsh-written diary of Private G P Huws.

> *To Sammy in the afternoon. Up to rest camp after tea. Got clothing etc, 123 lost…*

The stated reason for the loss of 116 servicemen is attributed to the fact that the damage caused by the explosion prevented the rescuers, despite their gallant efforts, from reaching the long rows of men who were in a ward, in close proximity to where the torpedo impacted. One witness said 'the torpedo crashed into the engine room on the starboard side, and most of the casualties were caused in what was known as the eye ward where ninety to one hundred men were drowned by the in-rush of water'.

Only one female appeared among the missing, Mrs Violet Long, the Deputy Chief Controller of the QMAAC, who with Mrs Burleigh Leach founded the movement. Mrs Long, described as a very attractive woman with a fine head of bright brown hair, had been on a tour of the members in France and was returning to England. She was formerly Controller of Administration of the Women's Army Auxiliary Corps raised in 1917. In May 1918, when Queen Mary became Colonel-in-Chief of the Corps the unit became the Queen Mary's Army Auxiliary Corps [QMAAC].

Miss Charlotte Allen Trowell QMAAC, who was on the *Warilda* travelling home on special leave to be married described her experiences to a journalist.

39857 Private William Arthur Boggis of the East Surrey Regiment. He was posted to the 1/21st [First Surrey Rifles] Battalion, the London Regiment. He was born at Hasketon, Suffolk. He enlisted at Bury St Edmonds, Suffolk. He died as a result of *Warilda* sinking.

> *I was acting as orderly to Mrs Long, Deputy Chief Controller of the QMAAC. Mrs Long came to my bunk just before midnight to inquire if I was comfortable and to give me some chocolate. When the torpedo struck the vessel I was thrown out of my bunk. I hurried on deck, and just as I got there, the stairway was blown up. There was no panic. I was put with a number of wounded into a boat, but it capsized and we were thrown into the water. I clung to a rope, and a wounded American officer and an Australian pulled me into another boat. The wounded soldiers who were in that boat insisted on wrapping their wet blankets around me.*
>
> *I shall never forget the end of Mrs Long, who had been so kind to me. She clung to the boat into which I had been dragged, and I caught hold of her by the hair. She exclaimed "Oh save me, my feet are fastened. I have lost a foot". Her feet had become entangled in some rope. Strenuous efforts succeeded in freeing her limbs, and a Southampton sailor tried to get her into the boat, but she collapsed, suddenly fell back and was drowned. We were about two hours in the boat before we were picked up. When the rescuing vessel came alongside an officer on her called out "lift up wounded first", but the wounded soldiers shouted in reply, "There is a girl on board. You go up missy". It was quite impossible,* [said Miss Trowell] *to reach some of the cot cases in the lower part of the ship. The groans of the dying men were terrible. She would never forget the heroism and self sacrifice of the wounded men. All who survived,* [she said] *deserved the Victoria Cross.*

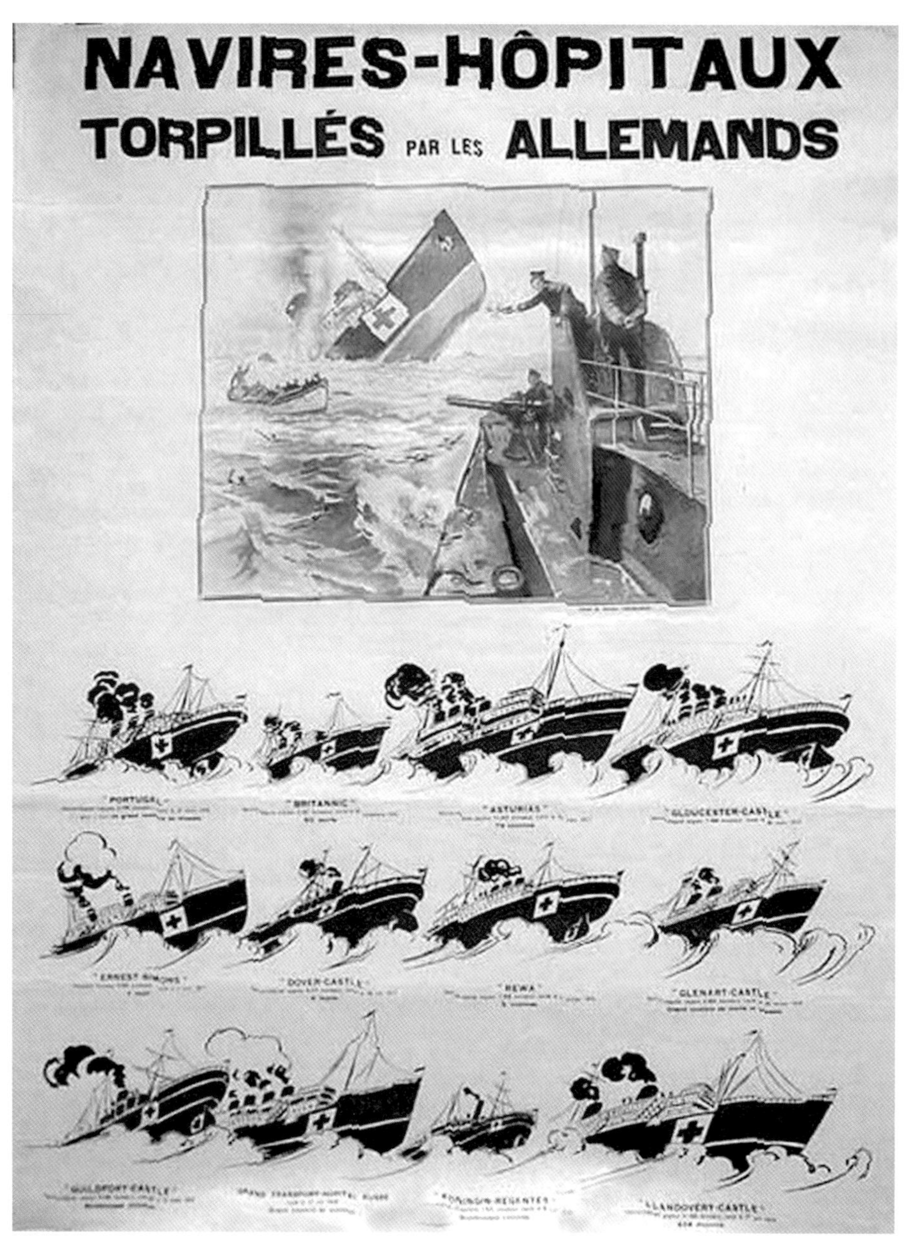

A French poster denouncing the sinking of Allied hospital ships.

A private in the London regiment who was among the rescued survivors told a Daily News correspondent:

> *After the ship was struck by a torpedo she listed a little, but her engines continued to run for some time, until rescuing destroyers came alongside. Shortly after the explosion an orderly came into my ward with the order "All on top who can walk". Those who could did so, helping the less fortunate up the stairs while the RAMC men attended to the cot cases. Some men who had splints on their legs limped or crawled to the top deck. Here I lost consciousness. When I opened my eyes a destroyer was alongside and a second destroyer alongside that. I gripped two ropes running from our ship down to the first destroyer, and with assistance reached the deck of the warship.*
>
> *The ship was struck amidships as far as I can learn and the explosion appears to have wrecked the bottom ward where some convalescent Australians and Jocks* [Scots] *were accommodated. Usually German prisoners were carried in that ward, and this seems to be the first occasion for some time in which none were travelling across the Channel. It was in that ward that the chief casualties occurred, and I understand that the inrush of water prevented rescue.*

Walter Long. At the age of seventeen, he joined the Royal Navy as a cabin boy. By 1912, he had attained the rank of petty officer. While serving on HMS *Perseus*, he qualified for the Naval General Service Medal, with a bar Persian Gulf 1909–1914 in operations suppressing the arms traffic. Married in 1912, he left the navy a year later, and transferred to HM Coastguard. Following the outbreak of hostilities he was recalled to the navy. He was awarded the Meritorious Service Medal for saving life, during the *Warilda* rescue operation. After demobilisation he returned to the Coastguard service.

Although evidently in a perilous condition a destroyer attempted to tow the stricken *Warilda* to port; however, she progressively sank lower. When she was almost on the verge of sinking the tow ropes were cut and two and three quarter hours after the explosion she slid down into oblivion. An eyewitness described her final minutes:

> *The* Warilda *settled slowly at the stern and then up-ended. When the water reached the boilers they blew up in a terrifying column of fire and steam, and then darkness fell again.*

Up to the time of her loss the ship had carried over 7,000 troops and hospital patients. The *Warilda,* now an official war grave, lies in fifty metres of water thirty-two miles south-south-west from the Owers light vessel. Her precise location remained unknown until August 1992 when divers discovered the wreck, thirty-six nautical miles offshore. The rusting remains of *Warilda* sit on the sea bed with a forty-five degree list to port. Two days after sinking *Warilda UC49* attacked the *Tuscan Prince* two of the crew died, however the holed vessel reached port. A sustained depth-charge attack by HMS *Opossum* and seven motor launches then ensued. The hunter became the hunted and descended to the sea bed to avoid detection but the listening hydrophones located the marauder. After several near escapes the hunters sank the U-boat off Berry Head, Torbay, Devon.

The beginning of the end

Throughout the war at sea the British authorities restricted detailed information on counter-measures employed against hostile submarines. While mercantile losses were reported, very few facts emerged about the Admiralty's elimination of their unseen adversary. The imbalance in information had a detrimental effect on the general public. Once the submarine peril had been undisputedly averted the Government issued a statement on 7 August 1918. Lloyd George announced 'at least 150 of these ocean pests have been destroyed'. Germany challenged the statement, prompting the British to issue the names of 150 commanders of boats which had been accounted for. Three others known for particular outrages were named including *Kapitanleutnant* Wilhelm Werner who they claimed excelled in sinking hospital ships.[6] Despite being on their wanted list the bold Werner survived and returned to his deadly trade during the Second World War.

In the final phase of the war the submarines were barred from the oceans by a vast mine barrage laid chiefly by the American navy. Approximately 70,000 mines were dispersed across the 180-mile expanse of the North Sea between the Orkney Islands and the limit of Norwegian territorial waters. Vessels now had to negotiate three vast minefields to gain access to the shipping lanes; however, as Norway neither mined or defended her territorial waters vessels were able to bypass the great Northern Barrage. An unexpected mine victim was the hospital ship *China* which struck a mine at Scapa Flow. At least three of the medical staff died 10 August 1918 as a result of the explosion. The vessel survived the incident and was decommissioned in 1919.

The *London Gazette* of 29 October 1918 published the following list of names brought to the notice of the Secretary of State for War for invaluable services rendered on the occasion of the sinking or damage by enemy action of military ships and transports:

> *Captain Gilbert Berry* [Transport *Norseman*], *Captain Edmund Weatherstone Day* [HMHS *Glenart Castle*], *Captain William Edward Pontet* [HMHS *Lanfranc*], *Captain John Barry Whitton* [HMHS Goorkha], *Captain John Vyvyan Watson-Black* [HMHS *Galeka*],
> *Chief Officer Robert Henderson Horner* [HMHS *Anglia*], *Chief Officer James Disraeli Kerridge* [HMHS Glenart Castle], *Chief Officer Geoffrey Handfield Purcell* [HMHS *Lanfranc*], *Chief Officer Sidney Godolphin Symons* [HMHS *Goorkha*].
> *First Officer Hugh Wilson Douglas Wilson* [HMHS *Galeka*], *Third Officer Mathew Henry Williams* [HMHS *Galeka*], *Head Saloon Steward George Thomas* [HMHS *Lanfranc*] *Second Steward Henry Walsh* [HMHS Galeka], *First Cook J L Griffin* [HMHS *Lanfranc*].

In a series of bitterly contested engagements the Allies reversed German fortunes on the Western Front. By August the German tide began to ebb; they fought tenaciously to retain their occupied ground but gradually withdrew in the direction of the Fatherland. Ludendorff admitted the war could not be won, but wished to maintain a strong military position in order to negotiate favourable terms in the inevitable peace treaty, ideally retaining possession of Belgium and Luxemburg. Austria promised to send reinforcements to France but a few weeks later attempted to broker a peace deal with the United States; it was declined. On 27 September Bulgaria also sought an armistice, followed by the abdication of their monarch.

Carisbrook Castle was built in 1898 and served as both hospital ship and troop transport.

Late September also saw the defeat of the Turkish armies in Palestine. Faced with the collapse of the alliance between the Central Powers, Germany became increasingly isolated prompting Ludendorff to demand an immediate armistice, to which the Kaiser agreed.

In an address to Congress on 8 January President Wilson had announced fourteen precise points which specified his demands for peace, and formed the basis of any armistice. Britain and France objected to the proposed ban on blockades, while France sought more severe reparations on her almost vanquished foe. Wilson compromised and accepted both objections while threatening to negotiate a separate peace policy on behalf of the United States. As neither of the Allies wanted to prolong the war they fell in with American aims. On 4 October Germany initiated armistice negotiations and reviewed the conditions contained within the fourteen points.

Meanwhile the submarine attacks continued; the Canadian Pacific *Montford* was lost with five crew members on 1 October, the following day fifty-two mariners perished when the Portishead-bound benzene-laden tanker *Arca* fell prey to *U118*. Two further losses in the Western Approaches threatened to stall the peace process. On the very day German diplomats broached the subject of an armistice, Germany added another victim to her long list of sea crimes.

The 7,700-ton Japanese liner *Hirano Maru* was built in Nagasaki in 1908 and was owned by the Nippon Yusen Kabushiki Kaisha [now known as NYK] of Tokyo. On Saturday night 4 October the liner was braving a violent storm off the Irish coast when she was torpedoed and sunk. Onboard were about 320 people including 120 crew, only twenty-nine were rescued. Among the drowned passengers were two European female nurses, three Japanese women and seven children. Some of the survivors reported as they were attempting to launch the boats into the raging sea a second torpedo struck the doomed liner. A nearby American destroyer USS *Sterrett* alerted by the explosion dashed to the rescue of those struggling in the sea; the submarine evidently watching its victims now fired at the destroyer. Two torpedoes were averted; the *Sterrett* now broke off from rescue work and attempted to depth charge the submarine. After driving off the submarine the rescue work resumed but valuable time had slipped by for the victims, who succumbed to the rolling waves and icy water. The ship's master Captain Frazer and all his officers perished, along with many neutrals including nine Dutchmen.

Another submersible the *UB123* commenced her patrol by sailing north of Scotland to enter the North Atlantic; days later she entered the Irish Sea. The city of Dublin Steam Packet Company steamer RMS *Leinster* had departed Kingston [now Dun Laoghaire] for Holyhead she carried 687 passengers, predominantly military personnel returning to duty or on leave, plus a crew of seventy. Robert Ramm the commander of *UB123* ordered the launching of two torpedoes, both found their target. One hit the engine room and the other

RMS *Leinster*.

detonated in the vicinity of the mail room where twenty-one postal clerks were sorting mail. One clerk was blown through the side of the ship and recovered later, his twenty colleagues died in the blast. The engine room rapidly flooded, and the ship is reported to have sunk in thirteen minutes. The torpedo boat destroyers *Lively* and *Mallard* came to the rescue but the casualties were extremely severe, 501 souls perished. Of the 150 women and children onboard only fifteen were accounted for and several died after their rescue.[7]

Admiral Reinhard Scheer.

On hearing of the two latest mercantile losses President Wilson demanded the end of the U-boat campaign. On 14 October Wilson let it be known to the German Government 'There can be no peace as long as Germans attack passenger ships'. Seven days later Reinhard Scheer, Admiral of the German High Seas Fleet signalled an order to all U-boats. 'Commence return from patrol at once. Because of continued negotiations any hostile acts against merchant ships are prohibited. Returning U-boats are only allowed to attack warships in daylight'. The U-boat war was over.

In the face of imminent defeat the German military planned one final throw of the dice, a suicidal attack against the British Grand Fleet. When ordered to sail to the North Sea to engage the British, sailors in Kiel refused and took up arms, setting off a mutiny on 29 October. Within several days the mutiny spread throughout German bases; only the submariners remained loyal to the Kaiser. To cries of 'Bread and Peace' the disaffection spread to the civilian populace triggering the German Revolution which led to the establishment of the Weimar Republic. The naval mutiny effectively ended the war at sea. After the armistice the humiliated German navy sailed under heavy escort to Scapa Flow. In a final act of defiance on 21 June 1919 the fleet scuttled itself rather than be distributed as spoils of war amongst the victorious Allies.

On 5 November the Admiralty announced they had successfully defeated the submarines and maintained a huge convoy system. Of the 85,772 merchant ships convoyed only 433 were lost. Germany's key allies Turkey and Austrio-Hungary signed armistices on 30 October and 3 November respectively. Her own peace negotiations stalled over Wilson's insistence on the abdication of Kaiser Wilhelm II. Exasperated by the Kaiser's reluctance, the German Chancellor forced the hand of Wilhelm by announcing his abdication on 9

HMHS *Berbice* in a Malta graving dock.

November [he officially abdicated on 28 November]. Two days later Germany signed an armistice signifying a ceasefire. The Great War for civilisation was over.

Gradually the requisitioned liners returned to their owners. Approximately three dozen vessels remained on charter for three to six months after the armistice. These ships were utilised for the repatriation of debilitated prisoners of war and servicemen who succumbed to illness during the considerable delays in the demobilisation process. A worldwide influenza pandemic would not have helped matters. Some of the more modern Great War hospital ships reprised their role in the Second World War.

Notes

1. Some accounts refer to a second torpedo which blew out the side of the ship. Considering the dire condition of the victim it seems doubtful a precious torpedo would be expended on a rapidly sinking vessel.
2. Built in the *Germaniawerft* Kiel shipyard *U86* was a Mittel U-style craft. After the armistice she surrendered; in 1921 while on a passage to the breakers' yard *U86* sank in the English Channel.
3. After a meeting in Liverpool of 600 seamen and stewards, Joseph Havelock Wilson, President of the British Seaman's and Fireman's Union added another five years to the boycott. The Liberal politician remained president of the Union he established until his death in 1929.
4. Page 31. *Amiens dawn of victory* by James McWilliams and R James Steel.
5. As reported in *The Daily News* Tuesday 22 October 1918.
6. The commander of *U55* had sunk the *Carpathia* [in 1912 the vessel rescued *Titanic* survivors] outward bound for Boston in convoy. His two torpedoes were followed by a third which hit the ship as the boats were being manned. The ship sank some 120 miles west of Fastnet on 17 July 1918. Werner received the *Pour le Mérite* on 18 August.
7. HMSO British Merchant Vessels Lost at Sea lists 176 dead including the master. However, as indicated in the book the figures do not include troops onboard; given the significant amount of troops onboard this explains the disparity with the usually quoted figure of *Leinster* deaths. On 18 October, while returning to base, *UB123* struck a North Sea mine. The entire crew perished.

Chapter Six

Post Armistice

The terms of the Armistice initially ran for thirty days but were regularly renewed. After six months of negotiations at the Paris Peace Conference the key allied delegates produced a peace treaty. On 7 May, the anniversary of the sinking of the *Lusitania,* Germany received the humiliating peace terms, which they initially rejected. Eventually the defeated nation signed the Treaty of Versailles on 28 June 1919, thereby officially ending the war.

Inserted in the treaty were three articles relevant to this work:

> ***Article 228.*** *The German Government recognises the right of the Allied and Associated Powers to bring before military tribunals persons accused of having committed acts in violation of the laws and customs of war. Such persons shall, if found guilty, be sentenced to punishments laid down by law. This provision will apply notwithstanding any proceedings or prosecution before a tribunal in Germany or in the territory of her allies. The German Government shall hand over to the Allied and Associated Powers, or to such one of them as shall so request, all persons accused of having committed an act in violation of the laws and customs of war, who are specified either by name or by the rank, office or employment which they held under the German authorities.*
>
> ***Article 229.*** *Persons guilty of criminal acts against the nationals of one of the Allied and Associated powers will be brought before the military tribunals of that Power. Persons guilty of criminal acts against the nationals of more than one of the Allied and Associated Powers will be brought before military tribunals composed of members of the military tribunals of the Powers concerned. In every case the accused will be entitled to name his counsel.*
>
> ***Article 230.*** *The German Government undertakes to furnish all documents and information of every kind, the production of which may be considered necessary to ensure the full knowledge of the incriminating acts, the discovery of offenders and the just appreciation of responsibility.*

A committee of lawyers formed at the Peace Conference investigated the legal position and available evidence for the prosecution of war criminals. Owing to delays, the clauses of the Treaty appertaining to Military Tribunals and the trial of persons accused of committing acts of violation against the Laws and Customs of War could not be implemented until 10 January 1920. The considerable delay allowed suspected war criminals an opportunity to disappear. Vital witnesses no longer in military service had returned to their homes throughout the globe and would prove exceedingly difficult to locate.

The Allies presented the German Government with a considerable listing of men they viewed as war criminals, ranging from the Kaiser to prison camp guards. Germany considered prosecution of many of the names on the list would bring down an already weak Government. Instead they suggested placing before the Supreme Court [equivalent to our House of Lords or Privy Council] at Leipzig forty-five defendants to be tried by way of an experiment. The Allies accepted the proposal, advising they would supply the evidence and leave the trials to the German legal system. Although being in a position to interfere with the trials they refrained from doing so, as they were unfamiliar with the workings of the German legal system. Unlike the aftermath of the fall of the Third Reich the Allies were not an occupying power and preferred Germany to conduct her own legal affairs.

The Leipzig war crime trials took place in the Kaiserhalle of the magnificent Supreme Court building in Leipzig. The walls were lined with panels of carved oak illuminated by stained glass windows. Suspended at intervals upon the walls were full size portraits of Kaiser Wilhelm I and Kaiser Freidrich II. The portrait of Wilhelm II had been removed. The seven judges known as the Punishment Senate of the Reichsgericht wore dull crimson robes and coordinating headwear, large white bow ties completed their ensemble.

The Leipzig war criminal trials

The case against Lieutenant Karl Neumann, the ex-submarine commander responsible for the sinking of HMHS *Dover Castle,* came to trial on 31 May 1921. The proceedings were temporarily adjourned as according to the German authorities a preliminary examination established the innocence of Neumann. The counsel for the defence, Dr Hahnemann of Leipzig, had presented a blanket defence of the submarine war in general, with particular regard to hospital ships. The upper echelons of naval command were the true culprits of the crimes, but the Punishment Senate shrewdly returned no verdict on this line of defence. Neumann admitted twice torpedoing the hospital ship in good weather. In fact he had allowed a captured British captain, held prisoner onboard, to observe his approach to *Dover Castle.* Despite the prisoner witnessing the sinking, as Neumann was going ashore, the prisoner requested a certificate. Neumann duly signed one with his full name, giving his rank in the service. He would not have complied with this request if he considered his orders or execution of them were illegal. He simply complied with orders from his superiors, who had directed that hospital ships failing to comply with German conditions forfeited immunity.

Contrary to the preliminary findings Neumann appeared on trial on 4 June when the public prosecutor demanded his acquittal. In the dock Neumann again admitted his crime while acting under orders, as the hospital ship was not keeping to the specific channel dictated by Germany. The prisoner stated he believed the vessel was carrying munitions, but as he could not substantiate his claim Chief Justice Schmidt, the court president, refused to accept the claim as evidence. The president acquitted Lieutenant Karl Neumann with costs against the German Government on the grounds he had to obey the orders of his superiors. Afterwards the presiding officer said:

> *That all civilised nations recognised the principle that a subordinate is covered by the orders of his superiors. The accused had carried out orders without in any way exceeding them, and that there was nothing to prove that he had been guilty of particular cruelty, as alleged in the Allies 'accusations.*

During the trial the prosecutor stated in his view, the hospital ships were employed for purposes in breach of the Hague Convention, if they were used for the transportation of soldiers wounded on the field of battle. They could only be used in connection with naval operations he concluded.

The officials of the Triple Entente had expected a ruling on the German submarine policy in relation to war crimes; understandably they were severely disappointed by the verdict. The case did set a legal standard for obedience to military orders.

OH WHAT WILL THE ANSWER BE?

What did you do in the war daddy?

The name of Walter Schwieger, responsible for the sinking of *Lusitania,* had appeared on the list of wanted war criminals, but he and the entire crew of *U-88* died on 17 September 1917, when the craft hit a mine. At the Second Criminal Senate of the Imperial Court of Justice, Britain selected another six for war crime trials, the accused were equally divided between prison camp and perpetrators of the *Llandovery Castle* atrocity. The latter was in some respects the most significant of the British trials.

Great Britain had demanded the trial of Commander Helmut Patzig, formerly a first lieutenant when commanding *U86,* the submarine which torpedoed the *Llandovery Castle.* Fearing he may have been brought to book, Patzig had fled Germany, allegedly returning to his home town of Danzig [now Gdansk]. Due to the Treaty of Versailles, Germany no longer had jurisdiction over Poland, consequently Patzig evaded trial for murder. However the German authorities thoroughly investigated the atrocity and collected sufficient evidence to support the British allegation. The German authorities arrested two officers present on *U86* during the incident. Lieutenant Dithmar was the first officer of the watch and had remained in the navy, Boldt the second officer of *U86* had retired, the fourth accused Meissner, the best gun layer, was implicated but died prior to the trial. Captain Sylvester, the master of the hospital ship, also died before the committal.

The case came to trial on Saturday 16 July 1921, Ludwig Dithmar now aged twenty-nine appeared in uniform as he served as First Lieutenant and commander of the Cuxhaven Command. His co-defendant twenty-six-year-old John Boldt, now a merchant, wore an overcoat with his Iron Cross pinned to the lapel. The facts regarding the sinking on the evening of 27 June 1918 were presented to the court. In accordance with International Law belligerent submarines were forbidden to attack hospital ships. Both Britain and Germany interpreted the Hague Convention ruling on hospital ships transporting ill servicemen or those wounded in land battles as binding. Nonetheless, the German naval command had directed hospital ships were only to be sunk if operating within the German designated barred zone. Patzig disobeyed orders by sinking the hospital ship 116 miles south-west of Fastnet, but felt justified due to the continual reports of British abuse of hospital ships. Believing she carried American airmen he decided to torpedo the ship alongside him in the conning tower were Dithmar and a witness named Popitz. Dithmar advised against the attack, the other defendant Boldt was at the depth rudder. The torpedo struck the *Llandovery Castle* amidships on the port side; in ten minutes she disappeared beneath the Atlantic waves.

The court accepted the testimony of second officer Chapman, described as a quiet, clear-headed and reliable witness. He saw five boats lowered from the starboard side, two of which capsized, so only three got away safely. Two boats got away from the starboard side; the one containing the late Captain Sylvester contained two dozen men, the only survivors of the tragedy. A cutter from the port side containing the first officer and five or six men also cleared the sinking ship. Witnesses confirmed the captain's boat, the port cutter and boat number three rowed clear of the stricken ship. Confirmation of the successful lowering of boat three was proved by a man taken from it while alongside the submarine and returned to the captain's boat, a lucky man.

The court then heard of the attempts by Patzig to secure evidence supporting his assumption that the hospital ship carried troops or munitions. The prosecution called Kass, Knoche, Ney, Tegtmeier and Popitz, all members of *U86* as prosecution witnesses, who all confirmed the British evidence. Popitz and Knoche were involved in the interrogation on the deck of the submarine and confirmed they obtained no proof of unlawful hospital ship use. After Patzig gave the order to 'make ready for submerging' all the crew went below. Patzig, the two accused and the late Meissner, the first boatswain's mate and (significantly) an experienced gun-layer, remained on deck. Minutes later firing commenced, within the submersible the crew heard the gunfire and feared for the fate of the lifeboats. This was confirmed to the court by Popitz, the third officer of the watch, who lay on his bunk listening to the gunfire, while the submarine cruised around on the surface. Knoche the chief engineer supported the evidence of the third officer.

After the incident Patzig summoned the crew and officers to the control room where he swore the complement to a vow of secrecy. He also extracted promises of secrecy until the end of the war from two captured British merchant navy officers who were also called as witnesses at the trial. Both Boldt and Dithmar honoured their vow and refused to give evidence to the court. Their silence was interpreted as damming evidence of the atrocity committed against the lifeboats. Furthermore Patzig had failed to enter details in the log book and entered on the chart an incorrect route taken by the ship, thereby distancing *U86* from any enquiry into the loss of *Llandovery Castle*.

During the proceedings the defence called a series of witnesses who attempted to prove the Admiralty had committed atrocities at sea and the immunity of British hospital ships was abused. A former German prisoner of war stated 'while at Tilbury he witnessed hundreds of uniformed men embark on the *Llandovery Castle*'. The fact was probably true, for the khaki clad British RAMC soldiers wore the same attire as combatant troops. Evidence of a similar nature continued to be presented. Sir Ernest Pollock, the British Solicitor General, protested vehemently to the assistant State Attorney, prompting a court adjournment.

The next morning the State Attorney and the Presiding Judge repeated his opinion of the previous day stating the unsubstantiated misuse of hospital ship evidence was irrelevant and of no value. If the defence continued to make such claims a further adjournment would be required to allow the British to prepare an answer. Such counter-charges have previously not been submitted to the British authorities. A sheepish looking counsel concurred no further such charges would be made. A court judgement read:

With regard to the question of the guilt of the accused, no importance is to be attached to the statements put forward by the defence, that the enemies of Germany were making improper use of hospital ships for military purposes, and that they had repeatedly fired on German lifeboats and shipwrecked people. The President of the Court had refused to call the witnesses on these points named by the defence. The defence, therefore, called them direct. In accordance with the rules laid down by law the Court was obliged to grant them a hearing. What the witnesses have testified cannot, in the absence of the general and exhaustive examination of the events spoken to them, be taken as evidence of actual facts. The defence refused a proposal for a thorough investigation of the evidence thus put forward.

For the defence, Dr Trofer asserted German naval officers were convinced in the latter stages of the war hospital ships were abused, and should be regarded as ships of war. Furthermore German submarine commanders firmly believed that any destruction of enemy vessels was fully justified. Another witness, Vice Admiral von Trotha, declared that as the severity of the U-boat campaign increased, submarine commanders were convinced that no feelings of humanity should interfere with their efforts.

The defence naval expert Corvette Captain Saalwachter addressed the court; he made no attempt to justify the brutality and placed no importance on the severity of the explosion when the ship was sunk by torpedo. He dismissed claims the severity of the explosion resulted from the ignition of munitions allegedly carried by such vessels. The naval expert admitted it was impossible to determine if such an explosion emanated from the boilers or an explosion of munitions. He conjectured the missing lifeboats may have been sunk by wreckage shooting up to the surface from the submerged ship, which the court dismissed. The naval expert emphasised the submarine commanders exercised extreme caution of lifeboats due to the British mystery ship practice involving 'panic parties', a successful ruse in attacking surfaced U-boats. He acknowledged the loyalty of the accused to their absent commander and disputed claims the accused officers should have refused to obey Patzig.

The State Attorney opened his summary of the case by saying 'in his forty years' experience he had never to shoulder so difficult a task, to accuse two German officers of the most serious charge known to our German code'. He reiterated the story of the sinking and firing and accepted nearly all the evidence and expressed a belief at least three boats fully loaded had reached comparative safety when the ship sank, and it was quite clear that beside the captain's boat, at least one other was investigated by the submarine. He said 'The legality of the sinking of *Llandovery Castle* was not a matter at issue during this trial', adding the Court was also not concerned with whether Britain had ever misused hospital ships, 'we are only concerned with the events after the sinking.' He was convinced the object of the firing was to exterminate the survivors of the ship. This decision arose only after the investigation of the examination of the lifeboats concluded. There was no need to determine exactly who fired the weapon as Patzig and the accused had acted jointly and therefore were jointly responsible. He was convinced the absence of Patzig meant that all three officers were guilty. As it was not proved any of the deaths occurred as a result of the gunfire, he only called for a verdict of 'attempted murder'.

His speech incensed the defending counsel; both made political speeches denouncing Britain for her 'hunger blockade', the other stated 'it was necessary to destroy the men and women in the lifeboats in order to prevent them from reaching their homes and rejoining the war against the Fatherland'. The Court showed considerable irritation during these outbursts.

Despite the views of the State Attorney the court determined 'the act of Patzig is homicide, as the lifeboats were hit and their occupants killed by gunfire'. As the wind and sea were calm, there was no reason why the three boats should not have remained seaworthy and their occupants rescued by search vessels. The State Attorney may have convinced himself if news of the sinking reached London great difficulties may arise for the German Government. The announcement of a further hospital ship sinking may have brought remaining neutrals into the field against Germany.

By sinking the lifeboats Patzig purposely killed the people who were in them, yet no evidence appeared to show he carried out this killing with deliberation. The Court determined Patzig decided to exterminate the survivors, only after the fruitless efforts to obtain evidence to justify torpedoing the vessel. This finding posed the question whether the crime was one of homicide or manslaughter. The Court determined murder had not been committed, as the officers acted on the impulse of the moment, and the dastardly deed was not premeditated. A direct killing, following a deliberate intention to kill was not proven against both officers. They were, therefore, only liable to punishment as accessories to the crime. As naval officers both defendants knew they were not legally authorised to kill defenceless people, they should have refused their order; as they did not do so they should be punished.

In assessing the sentence the Court acknowledged the principal guilt rested on the absent Patzig, under whose orders the accused acted. The co-defendants had acquired the habit of military authority, and to refuse the commander on the submarine would have been so unusual that it is humanly possible to understand that the defendants could not bring themselves to disobey. This justifies the recognition of mitigating circumstances. A severe sentence must be passed as the killing of defenceless shipwrecked people is an act in the highest degree contrary to ethical principles. It must also not be left out of consideration that the deed throws a dark shadow on the German fleet, and especially on the submarine weapon which did so much in the fight for the Fatherland. For this reason a sentence of four years' imprisonment on both the accused was considered appropriate. The court refused the public prosecutor's demand for a sentence of four years hard labour. Dithmar would also be dismissed from the *Reichswehr* defence force. The recently retired Boldt was deprived of the right to wear officer's uniform and stripped of his civil rights.

Had Dithmar given evidence he may have reduced his sentence, for Major Lyon the doctor who was ordered out of the captain's boat, reported Dithmar had given him the hint 'to clear off at once'. However, had this been confirmed during the trial it would have proved foreknowledge of Patzig's intentions.

On hearing the sentence there was a commotion in the courtroom, but the police locked the doors and prevented demonstrations. The British Mission quietly left to avoid any unpleasant demonstrations. The guilty officers' loss of liberty lasted only a few months for both escaped from detention in suspicious circumstances. The pair may have been under house arrest for Boldt gave the jail director his word of honour he would not try to escape, but only for three months. The period expired on 15 November 1921 and Boldt warned the director of the expiration of his agreement. Possibly while in transit to Hamburg jail and with the connivance of the wardens the pair escaped. Boldt fled to Sweden and Dithmar disappeared without trace, having served a mere four months of their sentence.

After the Allied observers departed from Leipzig the German authorities investigated some 800 war crimes; each hearing was dismissed on the grounds of insufficient evidence. In January 1922 a Commission of Allied jurists assembled to enquire into the entire fiasco; they unanimously agreed the Leipzig Court should discontinue war trials. In accordance with Article 28, they insisted Germany should hand over the accused for trial. The recommendation prompted protest meetings, during which senior German officers reminded the Triple Entente that 25,000 servicemen and the Reichsweir police would take steps to halt any deliverance of their countrymen to the Allied courts. Unlike after the fall of the Third Reich, the Allies did not occupy Germany, and not wishing to provoke a situation which may have led to further conflict the Allies backed down. However, in the aftermath of the Second World War the Nuremberg War Trials ensured the fiasco of Leipzig was not repeated.

Roll of Honour

Abbreviations used in the Roll of Honour

A.	Army
A/	Acting
A & S High.	Argyll & Sutherland Highlanders
ACC.	Army Cyclist Corps
ASC.	Army Service Corps
AIF.	Australian Imperial Forces
Att.	Attendant
CAMC.	Canadian Army Medical Corps
E.	East
Engrs.	Engineers
Fusl.	Fusiliers
Gds.	Guards
HAC.	Honourable Artillery Company
High.	Highlanders
IMS.	Indian Merchant Service
Inf.	Infantry
KOSB.	King's Own Scottish Borderers
KOYLI.	King's Own Yorkshire Light Infantry
L/Cpl	Lance Corporal
L.I.	Light Infantry
MCG.	Machine Gun Corps
MM.	Mercantile Marine
Northant.	Northamptonshire Regiment
Northum'd Fusil.	Northumberland Fusiliers
QAIMNS.	Queen Alexandra's Imperial Military Nursing Service
R.	Royal
Reg or Regt.	Regiment
RN.	Royal Navy
RNASBR.	Royal Navy Auxiliary Sick Berth Reserve
RNSBR.	Royal Navy Sick Berth Reserve
RNR.	Royal Naval Reserve
RWF.	Royal Welsh Fusiliers
S.	South
W.	West

Name of Vessel	Company	Built	Requisition Period	Beds approx
Aberdonian	Aberdeen	1909	16 October 1915 to 16 June 1919	245
Agadir	Royal Mail	1907		
Anglia	London & North Western Rail	1900	25 April 1915 to 17 November 1915	275
Aquitania	Cunard	1913	4 September 1915 to 27 December 1917	4,182
Araguaya	Royal Mail	1906	2 May 1917 to 8 November 1919	840
Assaye	Peninsular & Orientalal	1899	16 May 1915 to 2 March 1920	490
Asturias	Royal Mail	1907	1 August 1914 to 21 March 1917	895
Balantia	Royal Mail & Nelson Lines. see St Margaret of Scotland.	1909	1916 to 1918	
Berbice	Royal Mail	1909	1915	
Braemar Castle	Union Castle	1898	7 October 1915 to 1 August 1918	420
Brighton	London, Brighton & South Coast Railway	1903	18 March 1915 to 19 March 1918	530
Britannic	White Star	1914	1915 to 21 November 1916	3,310
Cambria	London & North Western Rail	1897	8 August 1915 to 20 January 1919	190
Carisbrook Castle	Union Castle	1898	3 September 1914 to 26 August 1919	440
Catania	Duke of Sutherland steam yacht			
Cecilia	Sir Charles W Murray's yacht		From 1914	
China	Peninsula & Oriental	1896	4 August 1914 to 1919	
Copenhagen	Great Eastern Railways	1907	1 January 1916 to 5 March 1917	255
Delta	Peninsular & Oriental	1905	4 January 1915 to 19 March 1918	530
Devanha	Peninsular & Oriental	1906	22 August 1914 to 28 February 1919	525
Devantia				
Dieppe	London, Brighton & South Coast Railway	1905	6 May 1915 to 17 November 1917	165
Donegal	Midland Railway	1904	1915 to 17 April 1917	
Dongola	Peninsular & Oriental	1905	25 May 1915 to July 1919	505
Dover Castle	Union Castle	1904	August 1915 to 26 May 1917	630
Drina	Royal Mail	1912	1 August 1914 to 1915	220
Dunluce Castle	Union Castle	1904	July 1915 to March 1919	755
Dunvegan Castle	Union Castle	1896	6 October 1915 to 20 April 1916	400
Ebani	Elder Dempster	1912	13 August 1915 to October 1919	510
Egypt	Peninsular & Oriental	1897	2 August 1915 to 1 June 1919	460
Ellora	Peninsular & Oriental	1911	12 November 1915 to 10 January 1920	475
Erinpura	British India	1911	August 1916 to June 1919	475
Essequibo	Royal Mail	1914	2 September 1915 to 12 September 1919	590
Formosa	*Société Générale des Transports Maritimes á Vapeur*	1906	23 June 1915 to 7 July 1919	415
Galeka	Union Castle	1899	June 1915 to 28 October 1916	365
Garth Castle	Union Castle	1910	4 November 1914 to 1919	250
Gascon	Union Castle	1897	25 November 1914 to 15 February 1920	435
Glenart Castle	Union Castle	1900	30 September 1914 to 26 February 1918	455
Glengorm Castle/ German	Union Castle	1898	10 September 1914 to 1921	420
Gloucester Castle	Union Castle	1911	24 September 1914 to 30 March 1917	410
Goorkha	Union Castle	1897	20 October 1914 to 10 October 1917	410
Grantala	Adelaide	1904	7 August 1914 to 1915	300
Grantully Castle	Union Castle	1910	22 June 1915 to 11 March 1919	520
Grianaig	Private yacht		1916 to February 1919	

Guildford Castle	Union Castle	1911	22 September 1914 to 19 November 1918	425
Herefordshire	Bibby	1905	25 July 1916 to 1 January 1918	380
Hindoo	Wilson & North Eastern Railway	1906	1915	
Jan Breydal	Belgian Government Mail		27 August 1915 to 1 August 1919	160
Kalyan	Union Castle	1914	4 May 1917 to 29 November 1919	820
Kanowna	Australian United	1902	26 August 1915 to 8 July 1919	450
Karanowna				
Karapara	British India	1915	27 August 1915 to 20 February 1916	340
Karoola	McIwraith, McEachern	1909	11 August 1915 to 6 November 1918	465
Kildonan Castle	Union Castle	1899	6 October 1915 to 10 March 1916	600
Kyarra	Australian United	1903	6 November 1914	
Liberty	Lord Tredegar's steam yacht	1908	1915 to January 1919	
Llandovery Castle	Union Castle	1914	26 July 1916 to 27 June 1918	405
Lanfranc	Booth	1906	6 October 1915 to 17 April 1917	405
Leasowe Castle	Union Castle management	1917		
Letitia	Donaldson	1912	18 November 1914 to 1 August 1917	550
Loyalty, former				
Empress of India	Maharajah of Gwailor	1890	2 October 1914 to 30 November 1918	325
Madras former				
Tanda	British India	1914	2 October 1914 to 30 November 1919	450
Magic II				
Maheno	New Zealand	1905	26 May 1915 to 2 June 1919	515
Maine	See Panama			
Marama	New Zealand	1907		550
Massalia	Anchor	1902	12 May 1915 to March 1916	375
Mauretania	Cunard	1907	22 October 1915 to 1 March 1916	1,950
Morea	Peninsular & Oriental	1908	8 October 1915 to 28 March 1916	750
Neuralia	British India	1912	12 June 1915 to 31 July 1919	630
Nevassa	British India	1913	8 January 1915 to 25 March 1918	660
Newhaven	London Brighton & South Coast	1911	7 May 1915 to 5 March 1919	165
Ophir	Orient	1891	1918	
Oxfordshire	Bibby	1912	15 September 1914 to 24 March 1918	560
Panama	Royal Fleet Auxilliary	1902	25 July to 23 November 1919	485
Pieter de Connick	Belgian Government Mail		16 March 1917 to 28 March 1919	375
Plassy	Peninsular & Oriental	1900		
Princess Elizabeth	Belgian Government		8 November 1916 to 3 September 1919	300
Queen Alexandria	Royal National Mission			
	Deep Sea Fishermen		February 1915 to January 1919	
Rewa	British India	1906	29 January 1915 to 4 January 1918	280
Rohilla	British India	1906	6 August 1914 to 29 October 1914	
Saint Andrew	Fishguard & Rossclare Rail	1908	19 August 1914 to 29 May 1919	195
St David	Fishguard & Rossclare Rail		19 August 1914 to 16 January 1919	195
St George	Canadian Pacific Railway	1906	7 May 1915 to 4 December 1917	275
St Margaret of	Royal Mail management	1909	1916 onwards	
Scotland				
St Patrick	Fishguard & Rossclare Rail	1908	19 August 1914 to 29 May 1919	195
Salta	*Société Générale des Transports*			
	Maritimes á Vapeur	1911	3 December 1914 to 9 April 1917	460
Seang Choon,				
former Cheshire	Lim Chin Tsong. Ex Bibby Line	1891	Late 1915 to middle of 1916	
Sheelah	Rear Admiral D Beatty's yacht		August 1914 to February 1919	
Sicilia	Peninsular & Oriental	1900	10 September 1914 to 11 September 1918	336

Simla	Peninsular & Oriental	1894		
St Denis, ex Munich	Great Eastern Railway	1908	12 October 1914 to 18 October 1919	230
Somali	Peninsular & Oriental	1901	1915	
Soudan	Peninsular & Oriental	1901		200
Stad Antwerpen	Belgian Government Mail		2 October 1915 to 12 December 1919	165
Sunbeam	Private yacht		1914 onwards	
Syria	Peninsular & Oriental	1901	2 October 1914 to 10 February 1920	395
Tagus	Royal Mail	1899	24 August 1915 to 31 March 1916	415
Takada	Peninsular & Oriental	1914	10 August 1915 to 29 April 1919	450
Tanda	Peninsular & Oriental	1914	September 1914 onwards	
Tigris	India Gift			
Valdivia	*Société Générale des Transports Maritimes á Vapeur*	1911	29 November 1914 to 22 December 1919	550
Varela	British India	1914	2 October 1915 to October 1920	450
Varsova	Peninsular & Oriental	1914	8 October 1914 to 8 May 1920	475
Vasna	British India	1917	29 May 1917 to 1919	615
Ville de Liege	Belgian Government Mail		13 June 1917 to 30 December 1918	170
Vita		1914	27 October 1915 to 24 February 1920	405
Wandilla	Adelaide	1912	5 August 1916 to 15 March 1918	550
Warilda	Adelaide	1912	25 July 1916 to 3 August 1918	546
Western Australia	Admiralty managed by Union Castle	1901	21 October 1915 to 6 December 1918	305

War Memorials and Cemeteries

A sample of the Commonweath War Graves Commision War Memorials referred to in the following appendix.

The Halifax Memorial, Nova Scotia, is a Cross of Sacrifice erected by the Commonwealth War Graves Commission to commemorate men and women of the Commonwealth who died in both world wars, and have no known grave. It commemorates particularly those Canadian sailors, merchant seamen, soldiers and nursing sisters who have lost their lives at sea, and also bears the names of men of the Canadian Army stationed in Canada who have no known grave. The memorial commemorates 274 First World War casualties and 2,847 from the Second World War.

The Hollybrook Memorial is situated in Southampton Cemetery which is located off Tremona Road, opposite the Accident and Emergency Hospital. The Hollybrook Memorial commemorates almost 1,900 servicemen and women of the Commonwealth land and air forces whose graves are not known, many of whom were lost in transports or other vessels torpedoed or mined in home waters. The memorial also bears the names of those lost or buried at sea, or who died at home but whose bodies could not be recovered for burial.

The Tower Hill Memorial stands on the south side of Trinity Square, close to the Tower of London. The Tower Hill Memorial commemorates the men and women of the Merchant Navy and Fishing Fleets who died in both world wars and who have no known grave. By the end of the Great War 3,305 merchant ships had been lost with a total of 17,000 lives. As a result of the Second World War 4,786 merchant ships were lost along with 32,000 lives.

NAME	RANK	NUMBER	UNIT	COMMEMORATED
	ANGLIA		**Lost 19 November 1915**	
Bassett, William Edward	Seaman		MM	Tower Hill Memorial, London
Callaway, William Henry	Steward		MM	Tower Hill Memorial, London
Campbell, NJ	Purser		MM	Tower Hill Memorial, London
Evans, R	Fireman		MM	Tower Hill Memorial, London
Hughes, J	Cook		MM	Tower Hill Memorial, London
Hughes, Lewis D	Engineer's Boy		MM	Tower Hill Memorial, London
Jones, John	Fireman		MM	Tower Hill Memorial, London
Jones, Owen	Fireman	Both on	MM	Tower Hill Memorial, London
Jones, Owen	Fireman	CWGC	MM	Tower Hill Memorial, London
Lewis, John	Fireman		MM	Tower Hill Memorial, London
Lewis, William	Quartermaster		MM	Tower Hill Memorial, London
Owen, Thomas H	Galley Boy		MM	Tower Hill Memorial, London
Parry, Thomas Richard	Seaman		MM	Tower Hill Memorial, London
Pritchard, Robert	Trimmer		MM	Tower Hill Memorial, London
Redmond, James	Fireman		MM	Tower Hill Memorial, London
Roberts, RD	Chief Steward		MM	Holyhead [Maeshyfryd] Burial Board Cemetery. 2. 879
Stuart, R	Fireman		MM	Tower Hill Memorial, London
Thomas, Owen	Stoker		MM	Tower Hill Memorial, London
Thomas, Richard	Deck Boy		MM	Tower Hill Memorial, London
Wallace, Alfred	Steward		MM	Tower Hill Memorial, London
Williams, George E	Chief Engineer		MM	Tower Hill Memorial, London
Williams, Joseph	Third Engineer		MM	Tower Hill Memorial, London
Williams, Meredith	Second Steward		MM	Tower Hill Memorial, London
Williams, Robert	Cabin Boy		MM	Tower Hill Memorial, London
Allen, Robert Henry	Private	76124	29 Canadian Inf.	Hollybrook Memorial, Southampton
Allen, William Andrew	Corporal	14010	8 South Lancashire Regt.	Hollybrook Memorial, Southampton
Armstrong, William	Private	S/8918	Seaforth High	Hollybrook Memorial, Southampton
Ashley, Charles Willis	Private	4669	8 Lincolnshire Regt.	Hollybrook Memorial, Southampton
Baker, Charles	Driver	T1/2411	ASC	Hollybrook Memorial, Southampton
Baldwin, John Jackson	Sergeant	G/12	R. Sussex Regt.	Hollybrook Memorial, Southampton
Barber, Albert	Private	8660	Suffolk Regt.	Hollybrook Memorial, Southampton
Barlas, John	Private	22721	11 Royal Scots	Hollybrook Memorial, Southampton
Bell, Christopher W	Private	13724	Yorkshire Regt.	Hollybrook Memorial, Southampton
Biddlestone, Richard	Private	14415	E Yorkshire Reg	Hollybrook Memorial, Southampton
Biggins, James	L/Cpl	18223	Notts Derby Reg	Hollybrook Memorial, Southampton
Billot, Stanley	Private	8880	RAMC	Hollybrook Memorial, Southampton
Bird, William	Private	19768	Grenadier Gds	Hollybrook Memorial, Southampton
Bishop, Lawrence Irwin	Private	11055	2 Royal Scots	Hollybrook Memorial, Southampton
Black, Robert	Private	413009	26 Canadian Inf.	Hollybrook Memorial, Southampton
Bolding, Alfred William	Private	1464	13 London Regt.	Hollybrook Memorial, Southampton
Bradbury, William	Private	21959	Notts Derby Reg	Hollybrook Memorial, Southampton
Bruce, William	Sapper	79663	R. Engineers	Hollybrook Memorial, Southampton
Bycroft, William	Private	14379	Yorkshire Regt.	Hollybrook Memorial, Southampton
Campbell, Arthur	Private	18106	Highland L.I.	Hollybrook Memorial, Southampton
Capen, Arthur Henry	Private	3222	22 London Regt.	Nunhead [All Saints] Cemetery

Capps, Alfred Hanley	Private	TF/2511	Middlesex Regt.	Hollybrook Memorial, Southampton
Carey, Patrick	Gunner	19790	RGA	Hollybrook Memorial, Southampton
Chapman, Albert James	Gunner	25633	RFA	Hollybrook Memorial, Southampton
Chorlton, Owen	Private	4963	10 Hussars	Hollybrook Memorial, Southampton
Clarkson, George	Private	17238	W Yorkshire Regt.	Hollybrook Memorial, Southampton
Coleman, John	Private	55803	19 Canadian Inf.	Hollybrook Memorial, Southampton
Collins, John	Pioneer	120181	R. Engineers	Hollybrook Memorial, Southampton
Colwell, Frederick	Private	18616	Devonshire Regt.	Hollybrook Memorial, Southampton
Cox, John Herbert	Sapper	45	Canadian Engrs	Hollybrook Memorial, Southampton
Curson, George	Private	7620	Canadian Inf.	Hollybrook Memorial, Southampton
Daltrey, Harry	Corporal	4998	RAMC	Hollybrook Memorial, Southampton
Davies, Charles	Sergeant	G/4594	Royal Fusiliers	Hollybrook Memorial, Southampton
Dobson, Stanley	Private	3164	N. Staffs Regt.	Hollybrook Memorial, Southampton
Doran, Edward C	Private	57953	RAMC	Hollybrook Memorial, Southampton
Drewery, Cornelius	Private	6500	A. Cyclist Corps	Hollybrook Memorial, Southampton
Drewitt, William	Private	16674	R. Berkshire Regt.	Hollybrook Memorial, Southampton
Duncan, Robert	Gunner	12899	RFA	Hollybrook Memorial, Southampton
Dunlop, James	Private	S/8243	Seaforth High	Hollybrook Memorial, Southampton
Dymond, William Henry	Gunner	72164	RFA	Hollybrook Memorial, Southampton
Eades, Joseph	Private	18836	S Staffordshire Regt.	Hollybrook Memorial, Southampton
Eastwick, Harry	Private	MS/1520	ASC	Hollybrook Memorial, Southampton
Eborell, Wilfred	Private	10617	Wiltshire Regt.	Hollybrook Memorial, Southampton
Edgar, Elizabeth	Staff Nurse		QAIMNS	Hollybrook Memorial, Southampton
Ellis, Edward	Rifleman	S/10169	3 Rifle Brigade	Hollybrook Memorial, Southampton
Evans, Walter	Private	2160	KOYLI	Hollybrook Memorial, Southampton
Fletcher, Henry	Lance Corporal	20126	Grenadier Grds	Hollybrook Memorial, Southampton
Frame, Robert	Gunner	903	RFA	Hollybrook Memorial, Southampton
Frankland, Arthur	Private	13079	W Yorkshire Reg	Hollybrook Memorial, Southampton
Fullwood, Emmanuel	Private	13931	Royal Scots	Hollybrook Memorial, Southampton
Garrett, John	Private	24600	13 Canadian Inf.	Hollybrook Memorial, Southampton
Geddes, Percy M	Private	9642	3 Canadian Inf.	Hollybrook Memorial, Southampton
Gilday, John Michael	Lance Corporal	7688	Coldstream Gds	Hollybrook Memorial, Southampton
Gines, William H	Private	18747	Worcestershire Regt.	Hollybrook Memorial, Southampton
Goodwin, Thomas	Private	3978	Lancashire Fusil	Hollybrook Memorial, Southampton
Gower, Francis	Private	SS/8728	ASC	Hollybrook Memorial, Southampton
Griffiths, John	Private	26315	Royal Scots	Hollybrook Memorial, Southampton
Griffiths, Tom	Gunner	96686	RFA	Hollybrook Memorial, Southampton
Hales, Henry	Sapper	22340	R. Engineers	Hollybrook Memorial, Southampton
Hardy, Frank Albert	Private	7647	RAMC	Hollybrook Memorial, Southampton
Harris, Henry Thomas J	Sergeant	TF/2142	Middlesex Regt.	Hollybrook Memorial, Southampton
Heaton, Thomas	Private	11218	RAMC	Hollybrook Memorial, Southampton
Hodgkins, Ernest V G	Private	18703	RAMC	Hollybrook Memorial, Southampton
Holmes, Ernest	Lance Corporal	17270	KOSB	Hollybrook Memorial, Southampton
Hurwitz, Mark	Private	2999	Notts Derby Reg	Hollybrook Memorial, Southampton
Ingham, E	Private	M2099447	ASC	Hollybrook Memorial, Southampton
Janin, George A F R	Major	H.Q. 2	Canadian Engineers	Hollybrook Memorial, Southampton
Joly, Leonidas	Private	61477	22 Canadian Inf.	Hollybrook Memorial, Southampton
Jones, Ellis	Sapper	61477	R. Engineers	Hollybrook Memorial, Southampton
Knight, George Ebenezer	Private	53350	18 Canadian Inf	Hollybrook Memorial, Southampton
Knox, George E	Private	53350	18 Canadian Inf.	Hollybrook Memorial, Southampton
Leathers, Cyril Robert	Sergeant	15077	9 Norfolk Regt.	Hollybrook Memorial, Southampton
Leggett, John Rupert	Private	69510	26 Canadian Inf.	Hollybrook Memorial, Southampton

MacKay, James	Corporal	19817	Highland L.I.	Hollybrook Memorial, Southampton
Mackenzie, John	Private	67548	25 Canadian Inf.	Hollybrook Memorial, Southampton
Mann, John	Private	312652	York & Lancs.	Hollybrook Memorial, Southampton
Marsh, William C	Corporal	T/19969	ASC	Hollybrook Memorial, Southampton
McCormack, John	Private	16628	KOSB	Hollybrook Memorial, Southampton
McDonald, Archie	Lance Corporal	18221	1 Canadian Inf.	Hollybrook Memorial, Southampton
McEachern, Archibald	Private	227	Canadian Motor M.G. Brigade	Hollybrook Memorial, Southampton
Miller, John	Private	22678	Royal Scots	Hollybrook Memorial, Southampton
Miller, Richard	Corporal	10869	W. Yorkshire Regt.	Hollybrook Memorial, Southampton
Milton, Arthur	Private	74018	28 Canadian Inf.	Hollybrook Memorial, Southampton
Mooney, William	Private	680	Northumberland Hussars	Hollybrook Memorial, Southampton
Moore, John	Private	12674	Lancashire Fusil	Hollybrook Memorial, Southampton
Morrison, Robert	Private	12204	W. Riding Regt.	Hollybrook Memorial, Southampton
Mortimer, Edward G	Private	4996	RAMC	Hollybrook Memorial, Southampton
Moss, Herbert James	Gunner	780	RFA	Hollybrook Memorial, Southampton
Myers, Kenneth	Gunner	33307	RFA	Hollybrook Memorial, Southampton
Myson, Ernest	Sergeant	3/8400	Bedfordshire Regt.	Hollybrook Memorial, Southampton
Napier, Henry Lennox	Major		Notts Derby Reg	Hollybrook Memorial, Southampton
Nicholson, Henry J	Driver	5724	Canadian Engrs	Hollybrook Memorial, Southampton
Orton, Elias	Private	22139	Notts Derby Reg	Hollybrook Memorial, Southampton
Pain, George William	Driver	2877	R. Engineers	Hollybrook Memorial, Southampton
Palmer, William R served as Cann	Private	A/14404	13 Canadian Inf.	Hollybrook Memorial, Southampton
Parden, Frank	Private	23255	King's Liverpool	Hollybrook Memorial, Southampton
Pearson, James	Private	2208	Durham L.I.	Hollybrook Memorial, Southampton
Pearson, Robert W	Private	M2/076062	ASC	Hollybrook Memorial, Southampton
Perry, George M	Private	56140	19 Canadian Inf.	Hollybrook Memorial, Southampton
Ponton, Maitland A	Private	66128	24 Canadian Inf.	Hollybrook Memorial, Southampton
Priestley, Trueman	Private	53840	18 Canadian Inf.	Hollybrook Memorial, Southampton
Pyper, David	Private	430187	31 Canadian Inf.	Hollybrook Memorial, Southampton
Reid, William David	Driver	61019	R. Engineers	Strathmiglo Parish Churchyard
Ridichan, Patrick	Private	24477	Highland L.I.	Hollybrook Memorial, Southampton
Robinson, Harry	Private	3807	W Yorkshire Regt.	Hollybrook Memorial, Southampton
Rodwell, Mary	Staff Nurse		QAIMNS	Hollybrook Memorial, Southampton
Rumble, Hubert William	Private	6395	RAMC	Hollybrook Memorial, Southampton
Ryan, Michael	Private	4482	Leinster Regt.	Hollybrook Memorial, Southampton
Shelley, John Archibald	Driver	1194	RFA	Hollybrook Memorial, Southampton
Shepherd, George	Rifleman	2077	W Yorkshire Regt.	Hollybrook Memorial, Southampton
Simpson, Charles W	Private	1341	A Cyclist Corps	Hollybrook Memorial, Southampton
Smith, Arthur J	Corporal	10529	Highland L.I.	Hollybrook Memorial, Southampton
Smith, Harry	Private	L/6303	East Kent Regt.	Hollybrook Memorial, Southampton
Smith, James	Private	12175	Cameronians	Hollybrook Memorial, Southampton
Southam, William G	Private	12024	Dorsetshire Regt.	Hollybrook Memorial, Southampton
Spinks, Joseph	Sapper	47404	Canadian Engrs	Hollybrook Memorial, Southampton
Steers, WA	Private	438555	3 Canadian Inf.	Hollybrook Memorial, Southampton
Stiff, TI	Lance Corporal	11274	Yorkshire Regt.	Boosbeck [St Aidan] Churchyard
Sullivan, Samuel	Driver	28631	RFA	Hollybrook Memorial, Southampton
Taylor, Charles Harry	Lieutenant		W. Yorkshire Regt.	Hollybrook Memorial, Southampton
Taylor, James	Private	G/7272	Middlesex Regt.	Hollybrook Memorial, Southampton
Tharrat, George Vanes	Lieutenant		Kings Liverpool	Hollybrook Memorial, Southampton

Turpin, Richard Dawson	Corporal	9926	York Lancs Reg	Hollybrook Memorial, Southampton
Turton, Frederick	Private	2690	KOYLI	Hollybrook Memorial, Southampton
Twist, William Edward	Lance Corporal	8688	Yorkshire Regt.	Hollybrook Memorial, Southampton
Walker, George V	Private	12425	Ox & Bucks L.I.	Screen Wall K 644 Epsom Cemetery
White, Henry Richard	Corporal	9620	Berkshire Regt.	Hollybrook Memorial, Southampton
White, William	Private	11874	E Yorkshire Reg	Hollybrook Memorial, Southampton
Williams, John	Private	2009	Kings Liverpool	Hollybrook Memorial, Southampton
Williams, Robert	Rifleman	S/4050	Rifle Brigade	Hollybrook Memorial, Southampton
Wood, Joshua	Private	2519	W Yorkshire Regt.	Hollybrook Memorial, Southampton
Worster, Walter Ernest	Private	1738	RAMC	Hollybrook Memorial, Southampton
Wright, John Thomas	Private	5675	5 Lancers	Hollybrook Memorial, Southampton
Wynne, James	Private	4056	Notts Derby Reg	Hollybrook Memorial, Southampton
Youngs, Arthur Ernest	Private	15698	9 Norfolk Regt.	Hollybrook Memorial, Southampton

	ASTURIAS	Lost 21 March 1917	
Anderson, John Aitken	Sixth Engineer	MM	Tower Hill Memorial, London
Andrews, Arthur Charles	Waiter	MM	Tower Hill Memorial, London
Brown, Arthur Edward	Trimmer	MM	Tower Hill Memorial, London
Crook, William Henry	Fireman	MM	Tower Hill Memorial, London
Cross, Stanley Henry	Greaser	MM	Tower Hill Memorial, London
Cross, William H	Fireman	MM	Tower Hill Memorial, London
Doncom, Edward T	Ordinary Seaman	MM	Tower Hill Memorial, London
Earl, James William	Trimmer	MM	Tower Hill Memorial, London
Flux, Henry Charles	Fireman	MM	Tower Hill Memorial, London
Glasspool, Edwin A	Assistant Baker	MM	Tower Hill Memorial, London
Gosney, Thomas Henry	Trimmer	MM	Tower Hill Memorial, London
Green, Orlando William	Fireman	MM	Tower Hill Memorial, London
Hall, Charles Henty	Fireman	MM	Tower Hill Memorial, London
Harvey, George Bevis	Engineer	MM	Tower Hill Memorial, London
Humby, Arthur Edward	Fireman	MM	Tower Hill Memorial, London
Hunt, Reginald Ernest	Assistant Pantryman	MM	Tower Hill Memorial, London
Jones, George Robert	Scullion	MM	Tower Hill Memorial, London
Kimber, Herbert George	Assistant Cook	MM	Tower Hill Memorial, London
Kneller, Albert Isaac	Mate of Hold	MM	Tower Hill Memorial, London
Lawes, Randolph Blair	Waiter	MM	Tower Hill Memorial, London
Manger, Charles Robert	Waiter	MM	Tower Hill Memorial, London
Munson, Charles Robert	Trimmer	MM	Tower Hill Memorial, London
Orman, Victor C M	Boy	MM	Tower Hill Memorial, London
Paxton, George Edward	Sixth Engineer	MM	Tower Hill Memorial, London
Pitfield, J W	Fifth Engineer	MM	Tower Hill Memorial, London
Reeves, Ernest Henry	Butcher's Mate	MM	Tower Hill Memorial, London
Robinson, Ernest H	Butcher's Mate	MM	Tower Hill Memorial, London
Robinson, John B E	Assistant Laundryman	MM	Tower Hill Memorial, London
Seaborn, W D	Waiter	MM	Tower Hill Memorial, London
Seaborn, Walter W G	Fireman	MM	Tower Hill Memorial, London
Shaw, W D	Waiter	MM	Tower Hill Memorial, London
Shore, Harry E	Seaman	MM	Tower Hill Memorial, London
Stone, Harold T	Fireman	MM	Tower Hill Memorial, London
Stone, Robert	Fireman	MM	Tower Hill Memorial, London
Tillyer, James John	Able Seaman	MM	Tower Hill Memorial, London
Trenerry, Bridget	Stewardess	MM	Tower Hill Memorial, London
Tubb, Percy Newton	Fireman	MM	Tower Hill Memorial, London

West, Henry Seymour	Fifth Engineer		MM	Tower Hill Memorial, London
White, John Albert	Third Cook		MM	Tower Hill Memorial, London
Atkinson, George L	Captain		RAMC	Ford Park Cemetery Portsmouth L25.10
Blake, Edgar Arthur	Private	33221	RAMC	Lowestoft [Beccles Rd] Cemetery
Fletcher, George W	Sergeant	37339	RAMC	Torquay Cemetery & Extension D2. 8757
Folley, Henry J	Private	6863	RAMC	Torquay Cemetery & Extension M6. 14548
Hart, James Richard	Private	1532	RAMC	Ledgate [St Ives] Churchyard
Horsley, Harold	Private	7982	RAMC	Horsley [St Clement] Churchyard
Kingsland, Frank	Sergeant	116	RAMC	Torquay Cemetery & Extension M6. 14548
Lloyd, Albert	Private	62299	RAMC	Widnes Cemetery XC. CE. 3617
Mallett, Frederick Percy	Sergeant	7662	RAMC	Hollybrook Memorial, Southampton
Muir, Alexander	Private	31780	RAMC	Torquay Cemetery & Extension D2. 8757
Phillips, J J	Nursing Sister		QAIMNS	Hollybrook Memorial, Southampton
Rippon, Robert	Private	8051	RAMC	Hollybrook Memorial, Southampton
Wenman, Edwin	Private	52948	RAMC	Torquay Cemetery & Extension M6. 14548
	Braemar Castle		**Mined 23 November 1916**	
Bushill, Robert W M	Private	14764	Royal Fusiliers	Mikra Memorial, Greece
Doyle, Joseph	Private	27330	R. Dublin Fusil	Mikra Memorial, Greece
Holbeck, Gilbert S	Sub Lieutenant		RNR	Haslar R N Cemetery, Gosport. G5 18
	Britannic		**Lost 21 November 1916**	
Babey, Robert Charles	Trimmer		MM	Tower Hill Memorial, London
Blake, T	Fireman		MM	
Brown, Joseph	Fireman		MM	Piraeus Naval & Consular Cemetery
Crawford, Thomas A	Fourth Butcher		MM	Tower Hill Memorial, London
Culley, T	Steward		MM	
Dabey, R C	Trimmer		MM	
Dennis, Arthur	Trimmer		MM	Tower Hill Memorial, London
Earley, Frank Joseph	Leading Fireman		MM	Tower Hill Memorial, London
Garland, Charles Claude	Steward		MM	Tower Hill Memorial, London
George, Leonard	Scullion		MM	Tower Hill Memorial, London
Gillespie, Pownall	Second Electrician		MM	Tower Hill Memorial, London
Godwin, George William	Fireman		MM	Tower Hill Memorial, London
Goodwin, T	Fireman		MM	Tower Hill Memorial, London
Hite, T	Trimmer		MM	
Honeycutt, G	Lookout		MM	Piraeus Naval & Consular Cemetery
Jenkins, Walter	Second Baker		MM	Tower Hill Memorial, London
McDonald, Thomas, served as Taylor	Assistant Cook		MM	Tower Hill Memorial, London
McFeat, John George	Fireman		MM	Tower Hill Memorial, London
Phillips, Charles J D	Fireman Trimmer		MM	Piraeus Naval & Consular Cemetery
Philps, George Bradbury	Fireman		MM	Tower Hill Memorial, London
Rice, James Patrick	Steward		MM	Tower Hill Memorial, London
Sherrin, George	Greaser		MM	

Smith, William J	Fireman		MM	Tower Hill Memorial, London
Toogood, Henry James	Steward		MM	Tower Hill Memorial, London
Tully, Thomas Francis	Steward		MM	Tower Hill Memorial, London
Walton, H	Fireman		MM	
White, Percival W E	Trimmer		MM	Tower Hill Memorial, London
Wing, W	Fireman		MM	
Binks, A W	Private	33642	RAMC	
Bostock, George James	Private	81292	RAMC	Mikra Memorial, Thesssaloniki
Cropper, John	Captain		RAMC	Mikra Memorial, Thesssaloniki
Freebury, Henry	Private	52640	RAMC	Mikra Memorial, Thesssaloniki
Jones, Thomas	Private	84010	RAMC	Mikra Memorial, Thesssaloniki
King, George William	Private	41692	RAMC	Mikra Memorial, Thesssaloniki
Sharpe, William	Sergeant	12423	RAMC	Mikra Memorial, Thesssaloniki
Smith, Leonard	Private	40213	RAMC	Mikra Memorial, Thesssaloniki
Stone, William	Private	35188	RAMC	Mikra Memorial, Thesssaloniki
	CHINA		**Mined 10 August 1918**	
Chamberlain, Lousia C	Reserve Nursing Sister		QARNNS	31 Chatham Naval Memorial
Marshall, Herbert Myers	Dental Surgeon		RNVR	31 Chatham Naval Memorial
Martin, Lionel Arthur	Surgeon		RN	31 Chatham Naval Memorial
	DONEGAL		**Lost 17 April 1917**	
Clifford, William John	Greaser		MM	Tower Hill Memorial, London
Cowley, Andrew	Fireman		MM	Tower Hill Memorial, London
Dawkins, Charles James	Fireman		MM	Tower Hill Memorial, London
Farnan, John William	Fireman		MM	Tower Hill Memorial, London
Hammond, Thomas	Able Seaman		MM	Tower Hill Memorial, London
Hill, Nelson	Able Seaman		MM	Tower Hill Memorial, London
Hughes, Robert	Carpenter		MM	Tower Hill Memorial, London
Jewell, Archie	Able Seaman		MM	Tower Hill Memorial, London
Macfadyen, Peter	Leading Deckhand		RNR	Tower Hill Memorial, London
Richards, Samuel	Fireman		MM	Tower Hill Memorial, London
Threlfall, Thomas	Fireman		MM	Tower Hill Memorial, London
Allworthy, Alfred James	Private	G/8013	R W Surrey Reg	Hollybrook Memorial, Southampton
Arnold, Stanley Richard	Private	28206	11 Border Regt.	Hollybrook Memorial, Southampton
Button, Albert John	Lance Corporal	24851	Suffolk Regt.	Hollybrook Memorial, Southampton
Chambers, Robert	Private	59303	MGC	Hollybrook Memorial, Southampton
Chapman, Arthur	Lance Corporal	38860	Northum'd Fusil	Hollybrook Memorial, Southampton
Corbett, Alfred James	Private	200446	Royal Fusiliers	Hollybrook Memorial, Southampton
France, Alonza	Private	28186	9 KOYLI	Hollybrook Memorial, Southampton
Hardon, Thomas	Private	16372	R Dublin Fusil	Hollybrook Memorial, Southampton
Hayes, John	Private	265633	Northum'd Fusil	Hollybrook Memorial, Southampton
Horner, Frederick	Rifleman	473513	12 London Regt.	Hollybrook Memorial, Southampton
Kirby, John	Private	201987	Royal Fusiliers	Hollybrook Memorial, Southampton
Knott, William	Private	43144	Northampt Regt.	Hollybrook Memorial, Southampton
Lazarus, Arthur	Private	5240	HAC	Hollybrook Memorial, Southampton
Logan, Harold Alexander	Sapper	185	Canadian Engrs	Hollybrook Memorial, Southampton
McCall, John Sharp	Private	22675	6 KOSB	Hollybrook Memorial, Southampton
McDonald, Alexander	Private	241484	5 Gordon High	Hollybrook Memorial, Southampton
Milne, Andrew	Private	925620	Canadian Inf'try	Hollybrook Memorial, Southampton

Nelson, Leonard	Private	9525	East Yorks Regt.	Hollybrook Memorial, Southampton
Newdick, George Elijah	Private	41568	Essex Regiment	W532 King's Lynn Cemetery
Raitt, Robert	Private	22/817	Northum'd Fusil	Hollybrook Memorial, Southampton
Sharp, John	Private	30130	10 KOYLI	Hollybrook Memorial, Southampton
Spaven, George	Gunner	152750	RFA	Hollybrook Memorial, Southampton
Tudor, William Henry	Private	11161	R Berkshire Regt.	Hollybrook Memorial, Southampton
Walker, David	Private	19123	E Yorkshire Regt.	Hollybrook Memorial, Southampton
Warren, Horace	Sapper	388233	R. Engineers	Hollybrook Memorial, Southampton
Webster, John	Private	G/40176	R W Surrey Regt.	Hollybrook Memorial, Southampton
Willett, Albert	Lance Corporal	16797	7 Norfolk Regt.	Hollybrook Memorial, Southampton
Williams, Frederick C	Private	41568	1 Essex Regt.	Hollybrook Memorial, Southampton

	DOVER CASTLE		**Lost 26 May 1917**	
Barret, Owen William	Fireman Trimmer		MM	Tower Hill Memorial, London
Bartley, Charles T	Fireman		MM	Tower Hill Memorial, London
Brand, George Charles	Fireman		MM	Tower Hill Memorial, London
Kentchen, William G	Trimmer		MM	Tower Hill Memorial, London
Munday, Walter	Trimmer		MM	Tower Hill Memorial, London
Taylor, Henry George	Trimmer		MM	Tower Hill Memorial, London
Isham, J E	Gunner	87313	RGA	Winslow [St Lawrence] Churchyard

	GALEKA		**Mined 28 October 1916**	
Black, John V Watson	Captain		MM	Died on war service date unknown
Barnes, George Edward	Private	58913	RAMC	Galeka Memorial St Marie Cemetery
Barron, Daniel	Private	45202	RAMC	St Marie Cemetery DIV.3.0.6
Bevan, William Charles	Private	44508	RAMC	Galeka Memorial St Marie Cemetery
Cairns, Ernest G	Private	59172	RAMC	Galeka Memorial St Marie Cemetery
Davies, Nathan	Private	51397	RAMC	Galeka Memorial St Marie Cemetery
Dutton, Thomas William	Private	56225	RAMC	Galeka Memorial St Marie Cemetery
Hodkinson, Jesse	Private	1376	RAMC	Galeka Memorial St Marie Cemetery
Holden, Harold	Private	43247	RAMC	Galeka Memorial St Marie Cemetery
Hughes, Harold	Private	43248	RAMC	Galeka Memorial St Marie Cemetery
Lake, Frank Melton	Private	4726	RAMC	Galeka Memorial St Marie Cemetery
Lanham, Glenis Alfred, served as Lanham-Gower	Private		RAMC	Galeka Memorial St Marie Cemetery
McLuskie, John	Private	59254	RAMC	Galeka Memorial St Marie Cemetery
Philp, George Charles L	Private	1815	RAMC	Galeka Memorial St Marie Cemetery
Roberts, John Henry	Private	52483	RAMC	Galeka Memorial St Marie Cemetery
Rolfe, John	Private	14560	RAMC	Galeka Memorial St Marie Cemetery
Saunders, Horace James	Private	36737	RAMC	Galeka Memorial St Marie Cemetery
Toogood, Joseph	Private	52913	RAMC	Galeka Memorial St Marie Cemetery
Wilkinson, Harry	Private	58609	RAMC	Galeka Memorial St Marie Cemetery
Wilson, William B	Private	71957	RAMC	Galeka Memorial St Marie Cemetery
Young, Henry	Private	5746	RAMC	Galeka Memorial St Marie Cemetery

	GLENART CASTLE		**Lost 26 February 1918**	
Andrews, Reginald John	Ordinary Seaman		MM	Tower Hill Memorial, London
Angus, Alexander Noble	Third Engineer		MM	Tower Hill Memorial, London

Attwood, William C J	Able Seaman	MM	Tower Hill Memorial, London
Bale, A	Fireman	MM	
Barnes, Alfred	Assistant Seaman	MM	Tower Hill Memorial, London
Bartlett, Leonard	Trimmer	MM	Tower Hill Memorial, London
Bates, Frederick	Assistant Pantryman	MM	Tower Hill Memorial, London
Beavis, Joseph Hector M	Ordinary Seaman	MM	Tower Hill Memorial, London
Belcher, Reginald H W	Assistant Pantryman	MM	Tower Hill Memorial, London
Black, W H	Fourth Engineer	MM	Tower Hill Memorial, London
Bristow, Alfred	Second Class Waiter	MM	Tower Hill Memorial, London
Bull, Jabez George	Wireless Operator	MM	Tower Hill Memorial, London
Burt, Bernard	Captain/Master	MM	Tower Hill Memorial, London
Cecil, Robert Buller	Scullion	MM	Tower Hill Memorial, London
Chadwick, James	Assistant Cook	MM	Tower Hill Memorial, London
Clasby, George Wilfred	Painter	MM	Tower Hill Memorial, London
Clifford, Frederick	Launch Man	MM	Tower Hill Memorial, London
Cousens, Arthur Henry	Barman	MM	Tower Hill Memorial, London
Cox, Clemens Leslie	Ordinary Seaman	MM	Tower Hill Memorial, London
Cumming, Albert Isaac	Chief Steward	MM	Tower Hill Memorial, London
D'Arcy, John Henry C	Ordinary Seaman	MM	Tower Hill Memorial, London
Dear, William T	Trimmer	MM	Tower Hill Memorial, London
Doe, William	Fireman Trimmer	MM	Tower Hill Memorial, London
Dove, Donald Clapham	Captain's Steward	MM	Tower Hill Memorial, London
Doyle, William Henry	Quartermaster	MM	Tower Hill Memorial, London
Elbra, Elizabeth	Stewardess	MM	Tower Hill Memorial, London
Farrow, Charles	Carpenter	MM	Tower Hill Memorial, London
Francis, Thomas Joseph	Assistant Steward	MM	Tower Hill Memorial, London
Gale, Frank George	Ordinary Seaman	MM	Tower Hill Memorial, London
German, Walter Fred	Linen Steward	MM	Tower Hill Memorial, London
Good, Alfred Ernest	Pantryman	MM	Tower Hill Memorial, London
Grant, Arthur Thomas	Assistant Storekeeper	MM	Tower Hill Memorial, London
Hamilton, James K	Electrician	MM	Tower Hill Memorial, London
Handford, Hudson	Fireman Trimmer	MM	Tower Hill Memorial, London
Herring, John Dewdney	Third Officer	MM	Tower Hill Memorial, London
Hopkins, Edgar	Wardroom Attendant	MM	Tower Hill Memorial, London
Hutchings, Samuel	First Officer	MM	Tower Hill Memorial, London
Inwood, William Ewart	Ward Attendant	MM	Tower Hill Memorial, London
Jackson, John R	Able Seaman	MM	Tower Hill Memorial, London
Jane, Simon Archibald	Ward Steward	MM	Tower Hill Memorial, London
Jenkins, William John	Fireman Trimmer	MM	Tower Hill Memorial, London
Joachim, Harold Emile	Ordinary Seaman	MM	Tower Hill Memorial, London
Johnson, Walter James	Assistant Steward	MM	Tower Hill Memorial, London
Jones, Louis William	Purser	MM	Tower Hill Memorial, London
Kelly, W J	Laundryman	MM	
Kennedy, Patrick K	Fireman Trimmer	MM	Tower Hill Memorial, London
Kennie, J	Quartermaster	MM	Tower Hill Memorial, London
Kilford, Charles	Greaser	MM	Tower Hill Memorial, London
Lane, Albert Harold	Fireman	MM	Tower Hill Memorial, London
Larbalestier, William J	Fireman	MM	Tower Hill Memorial, London
Lockhart, Alexander F	Lamps	MM	Tower Hill Memorial, London
Long, James Edward	Quartermaster	MM	Tower Hill Memorial, London
Mabey, Cyril Edward	Wardroom Attendant	MM	Tower Hill Memorial, London
MacAllen, Henry Walter	Second Cook	MM	Tower Hill Memorial, London

MacGregor, Alfred P	Ship's Cook		MM	Tower Hill Memorial, London
Matcham, Harold George	Boots		MM	Tower Hill Memorial, London
McCauley, George	Able Seaman		MM	Tower Hill Memorial, London
McCauley, Thomas	Able Seaman		MM	Tower Hill Memorial, London
McFarlane, Humphrey	Second Engineer		MM	Tower Hill Memorial, London
McQuay, William James	Boy		MM	Tower Hill Memorial, London
Miller, Alfred Gilbert	Trimmer		MM	Tower Hill Memorial, London
Moore, Albert Henry	Second Baker		MM	Tower Hill Memorial, London
Osman, Thomas John	Greaser		MM	Tower Hill Memorial, London
Parrett, Reginald John	Engineer's Steward		MM	Tower Hill Memorial, London
Petley, Frederick W	Fireman		MM	Tower Hill Memorial, London
Phillips, John James	Assistant Laundryman		MM	Tower Hill Memorial, London
Pope, William John	Boatswain		MM	Tower Hill Memorial, London
Punter, William Thomas	Scullion		MM	Tower Hill Memorial, London
Rankine, John Henry G	Deck Boy		MM	Tower Hill Memorial, London
Ratcliff, William Charles	Fireman		MM	Tower Hill Memorial, London
Rice, Frederick Charles	Able Seaman		MM	Tower Hill Memorial, London
Rickman, Frederick C	Ordinary Seaman		MM	Tower Hill Memorial, London
Rilford, C	Greaser		MM	
Rowe, John	Able Seaman		MM	Tower Hill Memorial, London
Rowley, J	Assistant Steward		MM	Tower Hill Memorial, London
Sheath, William	Fireman Trimmer		MM	Tower Hill Memorial, London
Sinclair, Victor George	Ward Steward		MM	Tower Hill Memorial, London
Sinnott, Michael Peter	Wireless Operator		MM	6 RC Penzance Cemetery
Sizeland, Herbert W	Ward Steward		MM	Tower Hill Memorial, London
Smith, Alfred Ernest	Assistant Steward		MM	Tower Hill Memorial, London
Smith, James Thomas	Second Steward		MM	Tower Hill Memorial, London
Stephenson, George	Able Seaman		MM	Tower Hill Memorial, London
Stimpson, Ernest Walter	Assistant Steward		MM	Tower Hill Memorial, London
Taylor, Percival John	Ward Attendant		MM	Tower Hill Memorial, London
Thompson, Walter	First Engineer		MM	Tower Hill Memorial, London
Toms, Frank Herbert	Trimmer		MM	Tower Hill Memorial, London
Wendes, Charles	Trimmer		MM	Tower Hill Memorial, London
Wey, Alfred Douglas	Fifth Engineer		MM	Tower Hill Memorial, London
White, Jesse	Fireman		MM	Tower Hill Memorial, London
Wilkins, Harry	Storekeeper		MM	Tower Hill Memorial, London
Wilkins, Harry Charles	Donkeyman		MM	Tower Hill Memorial, London
Wishart, R	Able Seaman		MM	Tower Hill Memorial, London
Wood, H George	Able Seaman		MM	Tower Hill Memorial, London
Woodlett, Ralph	Second Officer		MM	Tower Hill Memorial, London
Wyatt, Wilfred Sidney	Fireman Steward		MM	Tower Hill Memorial, London
Young, Ernest Edward	Fireman		MM	Tower Hill Memorial, London
Young, Walter John J	Fireman		MM	Tower Hill Memorial, London
Abrahamson, Alexander	Private	123992	RAMC	Hollybrook Memorial, Southampton
Adams, George William	Private	482	RAMC	Hollybrook Memorial, Southampton
Bamford, Ernest	Private	123854	RAMC	Hollybrook Memorial, Southampton
Beaufoy, Katy	Acting Matron		QAIMNS	Hollybrook Memorial, Southampton
Benham, Harry	Private	123869	RAMC	Hollybrook Memorial, Southampton
Beresford, Rebecca Rose	Staff Nurse		QAIMNS	Hollybrook Memorial, Southampton
Birch, Thomas	Private	84908	RAMC	Hollybrook Memorial, Southampton
Blake, Edith	Staff Nurse		QAIMNS	Hollybrook Memorial, Southampton
Blench, William	Private	123911	RAMC	Hollybrook Memorial, Southampton

Breakell, George	Private	122531	RAMC	Hollybrook Memorial, Southampton
Brice, Alfred	Private	120410	RAMC	Hollybrook Memorial, Southampton
Brown, Arthur George	Private	119131	RAMC	Hollybrook Memorial, Southampton
Clamp, Charle	Private	123997	RAMC	Hollybrook Memorial, Southampton
Cumber, William Saul	Staff Sergeant	27745	RAMC	Hollybrook Memorial, Southampton
Daniel, Llewellyn	Private	27002	RAMC	Hollybrook Memorial, Southampton
Donnelly, Henry	Private	123999	RAMC	Hollybrook Memorial, Southampton
Duncan, Andrew	A/ LCpl	42850	RAMC	Hollybrook Memorial, Southampton
Edgar, Elizabeth	Staff Nurse		QAIMNS	Hollybrook Memorial, Southampton
Edinger, Frank Harrison	Reverend		Army Chaplains	Hollybrook Memorial, Southampton
Evans, Jane	Nursing Sister		QAIMNS	Hollybrook Memorial, Southampton
Ferguson, John	Private	42846	RAMC	Hollybrook Memorial, Southampton
Furness, James Collins	Lieutenant Colonel		RAMC	Hollybrook Memorial, Southampton
Gerdes, Samuel	A.L/Cpl	58627	RAMC	Hollybrook Memorial, Southampton
Goldsworthy, John.	Private	8810	RAMC	Hollybrook Memorial, Southampton
Grimsley, William T	Private	123710	RAMC	Hollybrook Memorial, Southampton
Hay, William	Private	124833	RAMC	Hollybrook Memorial, Southampton
Henry, Charlotte E	Staff Nurse		QAIMNS	Hollybrook Memorial, Southampton
Hutson, George Thomas	Private	123711	RAMC	Hollybrook Memorial, Southampton
Hyatt, Thomas	Private	36053	RAMC	Hollybrook Memorial, Southampton
Jacobs, Jacob	Private	122319	RAMC	Hollybrook Memorial, Southampton
Jardine, Joseph	Private	123940	RAMC	Hollybrook Memorial, Southampton
Kelsey, Arthur Edward	Captain		RAMC	Hollybrook Memorial, Southampton
Kelso, David	Corporal	44314	RAMC	Hollybrook Memorial, Southampton
Kendal, Rose Elizabeth	Nursing Sister		QAIMNS	Hollybrook Memorial, Southampton
Last, Albert Victor	Private	12560	RAMC	Hollybrook Memorial, Southampton
Lyon, Gilchrist	Private	123943	RAMC	Hollybrook Memorial, Southampton
MacKinnon, Mary	Staff Nurse		TFNS	Hollybrook Memorial, Southampton
Mavor, George	Private	42013	RAMC	Hollybrook Memorial, Southampton
McIlvaine, John Joseph	Reverend		Chaplains Dept	Hollybrook Memorial, Southampton
McMeekin, James	Private	124010	RAMC	Hollybrook Memorial, Southampton
Moysey, Lewis	Captain		RAMC	Hollybrook Memorial, Southampton
Norton, John	Private	130530	RAMC	Hollybrook Memorial, Southampton
Parry, John	Private	124014	RAMC	Hollybrook Memorial, Southampton
Richmond, William	Private	122370	RAMC	Hollybrook Memorial, Southampton
Ritchie, John	Staff Sergeant	42828	RAMC	Hollybrook Memorial, Southampton
Rogers, Percy	Private	123979	RAMC	Hollybrook Memorial, Southampton
Simpson, Frederick	Private	119032	RAMC	Hollybrook Memorial, Southampton
Small, William	Private	65546	RAMC	Hollybrook Memorial, Southampton
Smith, William Albert	Private	124045	RAMC	Hollybrook Memorial, Southampton
Stainsby, John Addison	Lieutenant		RAMC	Hollybrook Memorial, Southampton
Turner, Edward Corben	A.Sgt/Major	18391	RAMC	Hollybrook Memorial, Southampton
Underhill, Reuben	Private	113660	RAMC	Hollybrook Memorial, Southampton
Vine, Frederick Thomas	Acting Corporal	1177	RAMC	Hollybrook Memorial, Southampton
Wadsworth, Harold	Private	122276	RAMC	Hollybrook Memorial, Southampton
Wright, John	Private	123950	RAMC	Hollybrook Memorial, Southampton
Wright, Thomas Henry	Private	123987	RAMC	Hollybrook Memorial, Southampton
Young, George William	Captain		RAMC	Hollybrook Memorial, Southampton

	GLOUCESTER CASTLE		**Torpedoed 30 March 1917**	
Lamb, Alexander	Fourth Engineer		MM	Aberdeen [Nellfield] Cemetery 2.393
White, Henry William	Greaser		MM	Tower Hill Memorial, London

Williams, William John	Greaser		MM	Sholing [St Mary] Cemetery A.32.8
	GRANTULLY CASTLE			
Ellis, E G	Purser		MM	Died 17 July 1915. Lancashire Landing Cemetery Gallipoli A.51
	LANFRANC		**Lost 19 April 1917**	
Boyce, Sidney Herbert	Trimmer		MM	Tower Hill Memorial, London
Crutcher, John	Able Seaman		MM	Tower Hill Memorial, London
Dewey, William	Greaser & Fireman		MM	Tower Hill Memorial, London
Friend, William	Assistant Steward		MM	Row 6 Grave 9 Fecamp [Le Val Aux Clercs] Communal Cemetery
Hawton, Bernard Cecil	Assistant Cook		MM	Tower Hill Memorial, London
Alexander, James M	Sergeant	265048	Black Watch	Hollybrook Memorial, Southampton
Burrows, Harry James	Private	203377	Notts Derby Reg	Hollybrook Memorial, Southampton
Edwards, Lawrence W	Private	23307	RAMC	Hollybrook Memorial, Southampton
Franklin, Edgar John	Captain		RFA	Hollybrook Memorial, Southampton
King, Harry	Private	18671	Devonshire Regt.	Hollybrook Memorial, Southampton
Knox, John T	Private	45753	Durham L.I.	Hollybrook Memorial, Southampton
MacPhee, Murdock Neil	Captain		Canadian Engrs	Hollybrook Memorial, Southampton
May, George Henry	Private	110368	5 Canadian M.Rifles	Hollybrook Memorial, Southampton
Moody, Ernest	Sapper	160470	Royal Engineers	Hollybrook Memorial, Southampton
Orman, Thomas	Private	S/15441	Cameron High	Hollybrook Memorial, Southampton
Penny, John	Private	14261	Devonshire Regt.	Hollybrook Memorial, Southampton
Ribbans, William A	Private	G/8686	Royal Fusiliers	Hollybrook Memorial, Southampton
Rowland, William T	Private	33393	Devonshire Regt.	Hollybrook Memorial, Southampton
Sadowski, Leo Jack	Private	183426	10 Canadian Inf.	Hollybrook Memorial, Southampton
Turner, Charles	Private	40666	Manchester Regt.	Hollybrook Memorial, Southampton
	LLANDOVERY CASTLE		**Lost 27 June 1918**	
Admans, Frederick C	Linen Steward		MM	Tower Hill Memorial, London
Allan, Thomas	Third Engineer		MM	Tower Hill Memorial, London
Allen, John	Fireman		MM	Tower Hill Memorial, London
Anderson, Allan John	Fourth Engineer		MM	Tower Hill Memorial, London
Anderson, Thomas	Assistant Cook		MM	Tower Hill Memorial, London
Baker, Alfred James	Ward Assistant		MM	Tower Hill Memorial, London
Barker, Frederick V	Laundryman		MM	Tower Hill Memorial, London
Barton, Andrew	Fireman		MM	Tower Hill Memorial, London
Batsford, William Arthur	Engineer's Steward		MM	Tower Hill Memorial, London
Beddows, Thomas	Trimmer		MM	Tower Hill Memorial, London
Bracken, George	Able Seaman		MM	Tower Hill Memorial, London
Bradley, Bruce	Fireman		MM	Tower Hill Memorial, London
Bray, Albert	Able Seaman		MM	Tower Hill Memorial, London
Brennan, Michael	Trimmer		MM	Tower Hill Memorial, London
Broadbent, George	Trimmer		MM	Tower Hill Memorial, London
Brown, Frederick	Donkeyman		MM	Tower Hill Memorial, London
Campbell, Harry	Captain's Steward		MM	Tower Hill Memorial, London
Carey, George M C	Able Seaman		MM	Tower Hill Memorial, London
Clarke, Clifford Hartley	Assistant Steward		MM	Tower Hill Memorial, London
Clements, William J	Deck Boy		MM	Tower Hill Memorial, London
Cocks, Harry Robert	Assistant Steward		MM	Tower Hill Memorial, London

Coe, Ernest P	Chief Steward	MM	Tower Hill Memorial, London
Collier, William John	Ordinary Seaman	MM	Tower Hill Memorial, London
Cook, Ernest H	Able Seaman	MM	Hartland [St Nectan] Church, Stoke
Coulson, Robert	Seventh Engineer	MM	Tower Hill Memorial, London
Crellin, William Elliot	Able Seaman	MM	Tower Hill Memorial, London
Cumiskey, John	Trimmer	MM	Tower Hill Memorial, London
Curry, William John	Assistant Steward	MM	Tower Hill Memorial, London
Curtis, George	Able Seaman	MM	Tower Hill Memorial, London
Davey, William Stephen	Greaser	MM	Tower Hill Memorial, London
Davies, Edgar Allan	Wireless Operator	MM	Tower Hill Memorial, London
Doyle, Patrick	Able Seaman	MM	Tower Hill Memorial, London
Earl, Percy Lionel	Fireman	MM	Tower Hill Memorial, London
Edwards, Edward James	Assistant Steward	MM	Tower Hill Memorial, London
Farley, Algie Victor	Deck Boy	MM	Tower Hill Memorial, London
Ferguson, William	Greaser	MM	Tower Hill Memorial, London
Findlay, William	Night Watchman	MM	Tower Hill Memorial, London
Fox, William John	Able Seaman	MM	Tower Hill Memorial, London
Franklin, George	Engrs Storeman	MM	Tower Hill Memorial, London
Fry, William Richard	Trimmer	MM	Tower Hill Memorial, London
Fullbrook, George	Fireman	MM	Tower Hill Memorial, London
Fulton, Charles W A	Assistant Cook	MM	Tower Hill Memorial, London
Gard, Charles Edward	Greaser	MM	Tower Hill Memorial, London
Giorgis, Gioranni	Chef	MM	Tower Hill Memorial, London
Grima, Angelo	Trimmer	MM	Tower Hill Memorial, London
Hagan, Thomas	Fireman	MM	Tower Hill Memorial, London
Hawker, Albert John	Butcher	MM	Tower Hill Memorial, London
Hawkes, George Ernest	Wireless Operator	MM	Tower Hill Memorial, London
Heath, Alfred James	Assistant Butcher	MM	Tower Hill Memorial, London
Heath, George	Greaser	MM	Tower Hill Memorial, London
Heney, William	Fireman	MM	Tower Hill Memorial, London
Hill, William Ernest	Able Seaman	MM	Tower Hill Memorial, London
Hitchens, John	Quartermaster	MM	Tower Hill Memorial, London
Hobbs, Benjamin	Deck Boy	MM	Tower Hill Memorial, London
Hodge, Arthur	Greaser	MM	Tower Hill Memorial, London
Hogan, Madin	Assistant Baker	MM	Tower Hill Memorial, London
Hooper, Frederick	Fireman	MM	Tower Hill Memorial, London
Hopley, John Holland	Deck Boy	MM	Tower Hill Memorial, London
Johnson, Burton Thomas	Electrician	MM	Tower Hill Memorial, London
Johnson, Francis William	Assistant Steward	MM	Tower Hill Memorial, London
Jones, Edwin John	Fireman	MM	Tower Hill Memorial, London
Jones, John	Able Seaman	MM	Tower Hill Memorial, London
Joseph, Harry	Fireman	MM	Tower Hill Memorial, London
Justice, James	Fireman	MM	Tower Hill Memorial, London
Kadrewell, Martin A W	Second Cook	MM	Tower Hill Memorial, London
Kelly, John Frederick	Quartermaster	MM	Tower Hill Memorial, London
Kelly, William	Fireman	MM	Tower Hill Memorial, London
Kentfield, William	Assistant Steward	MM	Tower Hill Memorial, London
King, Thomas Inman	Able Seaman	MM	Tower Hill Memorial, London
Kinloch, John Frederick	Carpenter's Mate	MM	Tower Hill Memorial, London
Lacey, Raymond Edgar	Assistant Steward	MM	Tower Hill Memorial, London
Lamb, Henry	Assistant Steward	MM	Tower Hill Memorial, London
Lane, B	Second Baker	MM	Tower Hill Memorial, London

Lee, Lawrence	Fireman	MM	Tower Hill Memorial, London
Leighton, William	Second Engineer	MM	Tower Hill Memorial, London
Le Marechal, Alfred W	Second Class Waiter	MM	Tower Hill Memorial, London
Lodge, Alfred Thomas	Fireman	MM	Tower Hill Memorial, London
Long, James Gilbert	Deck Boy	MM	Tower Hill Memorial, London
MacKenzie, John	Able Seaman	MM	Tower Hill Memorial, London
Manley, Frederick L	Kitchen Porter	MM	Tower Hill Memorial, London
Manley, W C	Assistant Cook	MM	
Marechal, A L	Second Waiter	MM	
Mathews, Sydney	Pantry Boy	MM	
Mayes, T	Able Seaman	MM	Tower Hill Memorial, London
Maynard, Samuel John	Head Waiter	MM	Tower Hill Memorial, London
McAllen, Sidney	Assistant Steward	MM	Tower Hill Memorial, London
McAllister, William	Ship's Cook	MM	Tower Hill Memorial, London
McCann, W	Greaser	MM	
McCombe, Charles	Ward Room Attendant	MM	Tower Hill Memorial, London
	Also commemorated on a headstone at Llysfaen Churchyard nr Colwyn Bay		
McInerney, Edmond	Fireman	MM	Tower Hill Memorial, London
McIver, James Murdock	Carpenter	MM	Tower Hill Memorial, London
McMahon, J	Trimmer	MM	Tower Hill Memorial, London
Mills, Albert James	Scullion	MM	Tower Hill Memorial, London
Moir, William	Greaser	MM	Tower Hill Memorial, London
Moorey, Herbert Joseph	Baker	MM	Tower Hill Memorial, London
Morgan, Francis John	Assistant Cook	MM	Tower Hill Memorial, London
Mulcahy, James	Bosun's Mate	MM	Tower Hill Memorial, London
Murphy, Robert Henry G	Assistant Pantryman	MM	Tower Hill Memorial, London
Nicholson, James	Quartermaster	MM	Tower Hill Memorial, London
Obee, Richard	Able Seaman	MM	Tower Hill Memorial, London
Ogden, James	Fireman	MM	Tower Hill Memorial, London
Owen, John	Able Seaman	MM	Tower Hill Memorial, London
Owens, William	Able Seaman	MM	Tower Hill Memorial, London
Paines, Thomas W J	Able Seaman	MM	Tower Hill Memorial, London
Parsons, Walter Henry L	Ward Attendant	MM	Tower Hill Memorial, London
Pay, Leonard John	First Assistant Cook	MM	Tower Hill Memorial, London
Pearce, Arthur Charles	Ward Attendant	MM	Tower Hill Memorial, London
Powell, Edgar Atheling	First Assistant Cook	MM	Tower Hill Memorial, London
Purcell, Thomas James	Fireman Trimmer	MM	Tower Hill Memorial, London
Richardson, John Henry	Storekeeper	MM	Tower Hill Memorial, London
Rolston, Thomas	Fireman's Steward	MM	Tower Hill Memorial, London
Rowland, Joseph	Chief Steward	MM	Tower Hill Memorial, London
Sharp, Robert	Boatswain	MM	Tower Hill Memorial, London
Sharrock, George F	Trimmer	MM	Tower Hill Memorial, London
Shead, Clara Harriet	Stewardess	MM	Tower Hill Memorial, London
Sherwood, G	Trimmer	MM	
Short, Raymond Cyril	Quartermaster	MM	Tower Hill Memorial, London
Sinden, F	Ward Attendant	MM	Tower Hill Memorial, London
Slater, Harry Glenco	Baker's Boy	MM	Tower Hill Memorial, London
Smith, Alfred James	Fireman	MM	Tower Hill Memorial, London
Smith, George Henry	First Pantryman	MM	Tower Hill Memorial, London
Sneddon, John	Assistant Storeman	MM	Tower Hill Memorial, London
Starmer, Ernest	Assistant Baths Steward	MM	Tower Hill Memorial, London
Start, Reuben Henry	Able Seaman	MM	Tower Hill Memorial, London

Strachan, H W	Baths Steward		MM	Tower Hill Memorial, London
Summers, Owen Edward	Engineer's Steward		MM	Tower Hill Memorial, London
Sumner, Harold	Sixth Engineer		MM	Tower Hill Memorial, London
Sutton, William George	Chief Engineer		MM	Tower Hill Memorial, London
Sweet, Thomas	Trimmer		MM	Tower Hill Memorial, London
Taylor, Charles	Fireman		MM	Tower Hill Memorial, London
Taylor, Murray C	Fifth Engineer		MM	Tower Hill Memorial, London
Thomas, George	Trimmer		MM	Tower Hill Memorial, London
Thomas, Kenneth A	Able Seaman		MM	Tower Hill Memorial, London
Travis, R	Trimmer		MM	
Tunks-Clarke, Victor	Assistant Steward		MM	Tower Hill Memorial, London
Turner, Benjamin Harold	Third Mate		MM	Tower Hill Memorial, London
Vance, Walter French	Assistant Storeman		MM	Tower Hill Memorial, London
Vincent, Walter Henry	Officers' Steward			MM Tower Hill Memorial, London
Walker, Thomas J	Trimmer		MM	Tower Hill Memorial, London
Walsh, Francis Charles	Trimmer		MM	Tower Hill Memorial, London
Watkins, John	Laundryman		MM	Tower Hill Memorial, London
Watson, W	Boatswain's Mate		MM	Tower Hill Memorial, London
Way, Arthur	Ward Attendant		MM	Tower Hill Memorial, London
Weedon, Thomas	Assistant Steward		MM	Tower Hill Memorial, London
Weller, Archibald A	Assistant Steward		MM	Tower Hill Memorial, London
White, Ernest Evelyn	Assistant Cook		MM	Tower Hill Memorial, London
Whitty, Percy John	Second Steward		MM	Tower Hill Memorial, London
Wyatt, James	Ward Attendant		MM	Tower Hill Memorial, London
Yeeles, Frederick T	Fireman		MM	Tower Hill Memorial, London
Zahra, Emanuelle	Second Cook		MM	Tower Hill Memorial, London
Anderson, J	Private	536451	CAMC	Halifax Memorial, Nova Scotia
Angus, Hubert Tyndall	Private	421053	CAMC	Halifax Memorial, Nova Scotia
Baker, A	Private	536234	CAMC	Halifax Memorial, Nova Scotia
Barker, Frank	Private	33281	CAMC	Halifax Memorial, Nova Scotia
Bentley, John Arthur	Private	02568	CAMC	Halifax Memorial, Nova Scotia
Bloomfield, John W B	Private	524309	CAMC	Hollybrook Memorial, Southampton
Bonnell, H	L/Cpl	50972	CAMC	Halifax Memorial, Nova Scotia
Bristow, James F W	Private	524507	CAMC	Halifax Memorial, Nova Scotia
Brown, D	Sergeant	2098951	CAMC	Halifax Memorial, Nova Scotia
Campbell, Christina	Nursing Sister		CAMC	Halifax Memorial, Nova Scotia
Carter, N R S	Private	526511	CAMC	Halifax Memorial, Nova Scotia
Cates, William Frederick	Private	962	CAMC	Halifax Memorial, Nova Scotia
Clark, F	Private	536231	CAMC	Halifax Memorial, Nova Scotia
Clark, W	Private	536448	CAMC	Halifax Memorial, Nova Scotia
Cowie, Walter	Private	536023	CAMC	Halifax Memorial, Nova Scotia
Curtis, John Henry	Private	526671	CMGC	Halifax Memorial, Nova Scotia
Daly, Kenneth	Private	536282	CAMC	Halifax Memorial, Nova Scotia
Davis, Gustavus Mitchell	Major		CAMC	Halifax Memorial, Nova Scotia
Dawson, William Albert	Lance Corporal	823269	CMGC	Halifax Memorial, Nova Scotia
Douglas, Carola J	Nursing Sister		CAMC	Halifax Memorial, Nova Scotia
Duffie, D W	Private	536338	CAMC	Halifax Memorial, Nova Scotia
Dunlop, Alexander L	Private	418883	CAMC	Halifax Memorial, Nova Scotia
Dussault, Alexina	Nursing Sister		CAMC	Halifax Memorial, Nova Scotia
Eaton, J C	Private	50379	CAMC	Halifax Memorial, Nova Scotia
Elsley, Harley Clifton	Private	523837	CAMC	Halifax Memorial, Nova Scotia
Enright, William James	Major		CAMC	Les Baraques Military Cemetery

	Recovered from the sea on 14 October 1918.			Sangatte VG 8
Evans, Herbert Harold	Staff Sergeant	34408	CMGC	Halifax Memorial, Nova Scotia
Falconer, R D	Private	645609	CAMC	Halifax Memorial, Nova Scotia
Foley, James Benedict	Private	50946	CAMC	Halifax Memorial, Nova Scotia
Follette, Minnie A	Nursing Sister		CAMC	Halifax Memorial, Nova Scotia
Fortescue, Margaret J	Nursing Sister		CAMC	Halifax Memorial, Nova Scotia
Fraser, Margaret M	Acting Matron		CAMC	Halifax Memorial, Nova Scotia
Gallagher, Minnie K	Nursing Sister		CAMC	Halifax Memorial, Nova Scotia
Gemmel, W H	Private	522922	CAMC	Halifax Memorial, Nova Scotia
Goldberg, M P	Private	535505	CAMC	Halifax Memorial, Nova Scotia
Hannah, J	Private	70053	CAMC	Halifax Memorial, Nova Scotia
Harlock, Mathew Henry	Private	33354	CAMC	Halifax Memorial, Nova Scotia
Harris, B D	Private	33079	CAMC	Halifax Memorial, Nova Scotia
Harrison, H	Private	536276	CAMC	Halifax Memorial, Nova Scotia
Harvey, George Edward	Private	524248	CAMC	Halifax Memorial, Nova Scotia
Hoskins, Clifford Hugh	Private	40310	CAMC	Halifax Memorial, Nova Scotia
Isaac, S	Private	T/815	CAMC	Halifax Memorial, Nova Scotia
Jackson, William	Corporal	33653	CAMC	Halifax Memorial, Nova Scotia
James, Wilfred Lawrence	Private	535449	CAMC	Halifax Memorial, Nova Scotia
Kelly, R C		195880	CAMC	Halifax Memorial, Nova Scotia
Leonard, Arthur Vincent	Captain		CAMC	Halifax Memorial, Nova Scotia
MacDonald, T H	Lieutenant Colonel		CAMC	Halifax Memorial, Nova Scotia
MacPherson, E M	Private	536277	CAMC	Halifax Memorial, Nova Scotia
McAnally, F L	Private	5/6674	CAMC	Halifax Memorial, Nova Scotia
McDermott, James H. served as Murray	Private	526600	CAMC	Halifax Memorial, Nova Scotia
McDiarmuid, Jessie M	Nursing Sister		CAMC	Halifax Memorial, Nova Scotia
McDonald, Leonard H	Private	2098858	CAMC	Halifax Memorial, Nova Scotia
McGarry, John, served as Rogers	Private	525169	CAMC	Halifax Memorial, Nova Scotia
McKenzie, Mary Agnes	Nursing Sister		CAMC	Halifax Memorial, Nova Scotia
McLean, Rena Maud	Nursing Sister		CAMC	Halifax Memorial, Nova Scotia
MacPhail, Donald G, Rev	Chaplain	Chaplains Department		Lampaul Churchyard, Ile D' Ouessant off the coast of Brittany
McPherson, E M	Private	536277	CAMC	Halifax Memorial, Nova Scotia
Nash, George Edward	Private	644511	CAMC	Halifax Memorial, Nova Scotia
O'Neil, Norman Robert	Private	213383	CAMC	Halifax Memorial, Nova Scotia. Hollybrook Memorial, Southampton
Pateman, John Cooper	Private	467562	CAMC	Halifax Memorial, Nova Scotia
Patton, Herbert Arthur	Private	81693	CAMC	Halifax Memorial, Nova Scotia
Pollard, F D	Private	1390	CAMC	Halifax Memorial, Nova Scotia
Porter, John	Private	525545	CAMC	Halifax Memorial, Nova Scotia
Purcell, John Arthur	Private	50089	CAMC	Halifax Memorial, Nova Scotia
Renyard, Alfred	Private	524579	CAMC	Halifax Memorial, Nova Scotia
Richards, Percy	Private	523324	CAMC	Halifax Memorial, Nova Scotia
Roseboro, K	Private	910940	CAMC	Halifax Memorial, Nova Scotia
Sacre, Walter Bramwell	Private	536477	CAMC	Halifax Memorial, Nova Scotia
Sampson, Mary Belle	Nursing Sister		CAMC	Halifax Memorial, Nova Scotia
Sanders, Victor	Private	644708	CAMC	Halifax Memorial, Nova Scotia
Sanders, W H	Private	527999	CAMC	Halifax Memorial, Nova Scotia
Sanderson, R A	Private	536403	CAMC	Halifax Memorial, Nova Scotia
Sare, Gladys Irene	Nursing Sister		CAMC	Halifax Memorial, Nova Scotia

Sayyae, F J O	Private	826726	CAMC	Halifax Memorial, Nova Scotia
Scribner, C G	Private	536249	CAMC	Halifax Memorial, Nova Scotia
Shipman, L	Private	524307	CAMC	Halifax Memorial, Nova Scotia
Sills, George Luther	Captain		CAMC	Halifax Memorial, Nova Scotia
Smith, E C	Private	527654	CAMC	Halifax Memorial, Nova Scotia
Smuck, David Radcliffe	Private	3676	CAMC	Halifax Memorial, Nova Scotia
Spittal, John	Private	536315	CAMC	Halifax Memorial, Nova Scotia
Stamers, Anna Irene	Nursing Sister		CAMC	Halifax Memorial, Nova Scotia
Steen, Robert Alexander	Private	400171	CAMC	Halifax Memorial, Nova Scotia
Sutherland, H	Private	51098	CAMC	Hollybrook Memorial, Southampton
Templeman, Jean	Nursing Sister		CAMC	Halifax Memorial, Nova Scotia
Williams, Frank	Private	536236	CAMC	Halifax Memorial, Nova Scotia
Williams, Robert	Private	530063	CAMC	Halifax Memorial, Nova Scotia
Wilson, Andrew	Private	527674	CAMC	Halifax Memorial, Nova Scotia
	REWA		**Lost 4 January 1918**	
Ali Ahmad Umar	Fireman		IMS	Bombay 1914–18 Memorial Bombay
Said Ahmad Umar	Fireman		IMS	Bombay 1914–18 Memorial Bombay
Sultan Shah Azad	Paniwallah		IMS	Bombay 1914–18 Memorial Bombay
Usman Ghulam Qadir	Lascar		IMS	Bombay 1914–18 Memorial Bombay
	ROHILLA		**Lost 30 October 1914**	
Barron, W	Pantryman		MM	Trench grave plot 4C Whitby Cem.
Bleakly, John	Storeman		MM	
Brain, George	Carpenter	M/2729	RN	1620 Tamworth [Bolehall & Glascote] Cemetery
Brown, John	Third Engineer		MM	West panel of the Rohilla memorial
Burney, Albert Howard	Shipwrt 2nd Cl.	M/7774	RN	6 Chatham Naval Memorial
Gover, G	Asst Storekeeper		MM	Trench grave 4C Whitby Cemetery
Hare, J			MM	Trench grave 4C Whitby Cemetery
McBride, Henry Thomas	Ships Cpl [Pen]	149592	RN	6 Chatham Naval Memorial
McDonald, Stewart			RNR	
Morgan, Frederick W	Master at Arms	350008	RN	Screen Wall 103.31628 Nunhead [All Saints] Cemetery
Morris, Sidney	Sick Berth Stwd.	351357	RN	Trench grave 4C Whitby Cemetery
Nicolson, L	A/S & Quartermaster		MM	Trench grave 4C Whitby Cemetery
Nisbet, David	Able Seaman		MM	Trench grave 4C Whitby Cemetery
Page, Alfred	Sick Berth Stwd	350882	RN	Trench grave 4C Whitby Cemetery
Patton, D	Fireman		MM	Trench grave 4C Whitby Cemetery
Patton, J	Fireman		MM	Trench grave 4C Whitby Cemetery
Perrin, William	Electrician		MM	Cove [St John] Churchyard 101
Robbins, Harry	Master at arms	104323	RN	5 Portsmouth Naval Memorial
Rose, C E	Carpenter's mate		MM	Trench grave 4C Whitby Cemetery
Ross, George Inglesby	Sick Berth Att	M/4881	RN	Trench grave 4C Whitby Cemetery
Smith, John	Fireman		MM	Trench grave 4C Whitby Cemetery
Tarbet, Mathew	General servant		MM	Trench grave 4C Whitby Cemetery
Weatherstone, Henry W	General servant		MM	Trench grave 4C Whitby Cemetery
Anderson, Thomas	Private	CH/8742	RMLI	7 Chatham Naval Memorial
Anderson, William E	Sr Reserve Att	M/10066	RNASBR	8 Chatham Naval Memorial
Barter, Henry James	Jr Reserve Att	M/10069	RNASBR	6958 Worcester [Astwood] Cemetery

Birtwistle, Milton	Sr Reserve Att	M/10068	RNASBR	8 Chatham Naval Memorial
Daly, William John	Sr Reserve Att	M/10072	RNSBR	8 Chatham Naval Memorial
Dunkley, Frank	Jr Reserve Att	M/10073	RNASBR	8 Chatham Naval Memorial
Elsworth, Alred Carr	Sr Reserve Att	M/10074	RNASBR	8 Chatham Naval Memorial
Gwydir, Robert Basil	Reverend	RN Chaplain		Belmont Abbey [St Michael] R/C Churchyard
Harrison, Frederick W	Sr Reserve Att	M/10074	RNASBR	8 Chatham Naval Memorial
Hodkinson, Harold	Sr Reserve Att	M/10079	RNASB	8 Chatham Naval Memorial
Horsfield, Thomas	Jr Reserve Att	M/10081	RNASBR	8 Chatham Naval Memorial
Horsfield, Walter	Jr Reserve Att	M/10098	RNASBR	8 Chatham Naval Memorial
Mardell, Charles Henry	S/Berth Att	M/3908	RN	6 Chatham Naval Memorial
Milner, Charles W M	S/Berth Att 1/C	M/5060	RN	6 Chatham Naval Memorial
Neville, Maurice Alfred	Sen/Reserve Att	M/10087	RNASBR	8 Chatham Naval Memorial
Parsons, George Edgar	S/Berth Att	M/3515	RN	Sedgeford [St Mary] Churchyard Ext
Petty, Arthur	Sr Reserve Att	M/10088	RNSBR	8 Chatham Naval Memorial
Petty, Thomas	Sr Reserve Att	M/10099	RNSBR	8 Chatham Naval Memorial
Pickles, John Thomas	Sr Reserve Att	M/10089	RNASBR	8 Chatham Naval Memorial
Sellars, James	Sr Reserve Att	M/10095 [CH]	RNASBR	B43 Little Marsden [St Paul] Churchyard
Shute, Albert Edmund	S/Berth Steward	358759	RN	4.24J. Harwich Cemetery

Commemorated on the Rohilla Memorial further details are unavailable

Ambrose, A	West panel of the memorial
Burney, A H	East panel of the memorial
Burns, J J	West panel of the memorial
Cain, J	West panel of the memorial
Cameron, G	North panel of the memorial
Cowie, J G	West panel of the memorial
Cribb, H J	West panel of the memorial
Currell, J	West panel of the memorial
Dawson, F	North panel of the memorial
Dawson, W	West panel of the memorial
Duffy, M J	West panel of the memorial
Fogarty, J J	West panel of the memorial
Gibson, G B	West panel of the memorial
Gibson, W	West panel of the memorial
Gillies, A	North panel of the memorial
Graham, J	North panel of the memorial
Henderson, S	West panel of the memorial
Horsburgh, J	North panel of the memorial
Kelly, J	North panel of the memorial
Kerr, J	North panel of the memorial
Kirk, G	North panel of the memorial
MacKenzie, J	North panel of the memorial
McCloud, N	North panel of the memorial
McCullam, A	North panel of the memorial
McDonald, D	North panel of the memorial
McDonald, W	West panel of the memorial
McGlasham, G	North panel of the memorial
McMillan, A	West panel of the memorial
McNaughtan, D	North panel of the memorial

	McNaughtan, J		North panel of the memorial
	Muir, W		North panel of the memorial
	Murphy, J		West panel of the memorial
	Nichol, J		West panel of the memorial
	Ogilvie, W		North panel of the memorial
	Queenan, J		North panel of the memorial
	Rafferty, P		North panel of the memorial
	Reid, A		North panel of the memorial
	Reid, J		West panel of the memorial
	Reid, W		West panel of the memorial
	Scott, A		West panel of the memorial
	Scott, R D		North panel of the memorial
	Smith, B		East panel of the memorial
	Stewart, A		North panel of the memorial
	Stewart, J		West panel of the memorial
	Tinney, J		West panel of the memorial
	Torrance, D		North panel of the memorial
	Watson, R		East panel of the memorial
	Watts, H		North panel of the memorial
	White, W		North panel of the memorial
	SALTA	**Lost 10 April 1917**	
Abdullah, Ali	Greaser	MM	Salta Memorial St Marie Cemetery
Abduz, Zamin	Fireman Trimmer	MM	Salta Memorial St Marie Cemetery
Ahmad, Ali	Fireman Trimmer	MM	Salta Memorial St Marie Cemetery
Ahmad, Ali	Fireman Trimmer	MM	Salta Memorial St Marie Cemetery (Two on CWGC)
Ahmad, Nagi	Fireman Trimmer	MM	Salta Memorial St Marie Cemetery
Ahmad, Saleh	Fireman Trimmer	MM	Salta Memorial St Marie Cemetery
Akerman, Alfred Henry	Seaman	MM	Salta Memorial St Marie Cemetery
Ali, Hasan	Fireman Trimmer	MM	Salta Memorial St Marie Cemetery
Ali, Muhammad	Greaser	MM	Salta Memorial St Marie Cemetery
Ali, Muhammad	Fireman & Greaser	MM	Salta Memorial St Marie Cemetery
Antania, Ismail	Fireman & Greaser	MM	Salta Memorial St Marie Cemetery
Baker, F W	Night watchman	MM	St Marie Cemetery Div. 62.I
Benford, William T	Pantryman	MM	Salta Memorial St Marie Cemetery
Cable, Sidney George	First Bedroom Steward	MM	Salta Memorial St Marie Cemetery
Castle, Charles T	Assistant Storekeeper	MM	Salta Memorial St Marie Cemetery
Cox, Frederick John	Assistant Bed Steward	MM	Salta Memorial St Marie Cemetery
Eastaway, Benjamin T	Master	MM	St Marie Cemetery Div. 62.I
England, F J	Stewardess	MM	Salta Memorial St Marie Cemetery
Foster, George Alfred N	Kitchen Porter	MM	Salta Memorial St Marie Cemetery
Frailey, William J	Baker	MM	Salta Memorial St Marie Cemetery
Geard, Charles Henry	Assistant Cook	MM	Salta Memorial St Marie Cemetery
Gimblett, Sydney	Assistant Steward	MM	Salta Memorial St Marie Cemetery
Glaves, John Edward	Marconi Operator	MM	Salta Memorial St Marie Cemetery
Graham, Wilfred Henry	Junior Engineer	MM	Salta Memorial St Marie Cemetery
Haley, Charles Thomas	Second Steward	MM	Salta Memorial St Marie Cemetery
Hansen, Henry Beecher	Chief Officer	MM	Salta Memorial St Marie Cemetery
Hasan, Al	Fireman Trimmer	MM	Salta Memorial St Marie Cemetery
Heath, A	Assistant Sculleryman	MM	St Marie Cemetery Div. 62.I
Henderson, Gordon	Carpenter	MM	Salta Memorial St Marie Cemetery

Holden, D	Able Seaman	MM	Salta Memorial St Marie Cemetery
Ibne, Hasan	Fireman Trimmer	MM	Salta Memorial St Marie Cemetery
Imeson, Thomas John	Assistant Steward	MM	Salta Memorial St Marie Cemetery
Jackson, Arthur	Junior Engineer	MM	Salta Memorial St Marie Cemetery
James, Joseph Selwyn	Quartermaster	MM	Salta Memorial St Marie Cemetery
Justen, John Hjalmar	Lamp Trimmer	MM	Salta Memorial St Marie Cemetery
Khalid, Bin Muhammad	Fireman Trimmer	MM	Salta Memorial St Marie Cemetery
Lain, John William	Assistant Bed Steward	MM	Salta Memorial St Marie Cemetery
Levene, Mendel E	Wardroom Attendant	MM	Salta Memorial St Marie Cemetery
Light, Ernest Edward	Writer	MM	Salta Memorial St Marie Cemetery
Lucas, C	Assistant Steward	MM	St Marie Cemetery Div. 62.I
MacKenzie, Charles H	Able Seaman	MM	Salta Memorial St Marie Cemetery
Manning, A	Head Waiter	MM	Salta Memorial St Marie Cemetery
Martin, Albert John	Assistant Cook	MM	Salta Memorial St Marie Cemetery
McCulloch, John M	Electrician	MM	Salta Memorial St Marie Cemetery
McDougal, J E	Quartermaster	MM	Salta Memorial St Marie Cemetery
McNulty, James Edward	Assistant Steward	MM	Salta Memorial St Marie Cemetery
Mintram, Alfred George	Plumber	MM	Salta Memorial St Marie Cemetery
Mooney, P	Able Seaman	MM	Salta Memorial St Marie Cemetery
Muhammed, Ali	Mess Man	MM	Salta Memorial St Marie Cemetery
Muhammed, Nagi	Fireman Trimmer	MM	Salta Memorial St Marie Cemetery
Muhammed, Saleh	Fireman Trimmer	MM	Salta Memorial St Marie Cemetery
Muhammed, Saleh	Fireman Trimmer	MM	Salta Memorial St Marie Cemetery (Two on CWGC database)
Musa, Saleh	Fireman Trimmer	MM	Salta Memorial St Marie Cemetery
Nedrett, J	Able Seaman	MM	St Marie Cemetery Div. 62.I
Nicholas, G	Steward	MM	Salta Memorial St Marie Cemetery
Nixon, Arthur Joseph	Assistant Cook	MM	Salta Memorial St Marie Cemetery
Oakley, Arthur Hartop	Third Officer	MM	Salta Memorial St Marie Cemetery
Payne, Horace James	Marconi Operator	MM	Salta Memorial St Marie Cemetery
Raff, G	Fireman	MM	St Marie Cemetery Div. 62.I
Rees, John James	Quartermaster	MM	Salta Memorial St Marie Cemetery
Rogers, A	Assistant Pantry Steward	MM	Salta Memorial St Marie Cemetery
Saleh, Yahya	Fireman Trimmer	MM	Salta Memorial St Marie Cemetery
Salem, Saleh	Fireman Trimmer	MM	Salta Memorial St Marie Cemetery
Salik, Muhammed	Fireman Trimmer	MM	Salta Memorial St Marie Cemetery
Sharp, Edward James	Storekeeper	MM	St Marie Cemetery Div. 62.I
Siebert, Henry George	Assistant Baker	MM	Salta Memorial St Marie Cemetery
Stride, Harry	Assistant Cook	MM	Salta Memorial St Marie Cemetery
Taylor, Edgar Charles	Wardroom Attendant	MM	St Marie Cemetery Div. 62.I
Tensan, N	Sailor	MM	Salta Memorial St Marie Cemetery
Tillyard, E	Steward	MM	Salta Memorial St Marie Cemetery
Timson, Joseph John	Assistant Butcher	MM	St Marie Cemetery Div. 62.I
Turner, William Reginald	Assistant Steward	MM	Salta Memorial St Marie Cemetery
Waht, Harry	Sailor	MM	Salta Memorial St Marie Cemetery
Watt, Frank Ernest	Purser	MM	Salta Memorial St Marie Cemetery
White, Edgar Harry	Wardroom Attendant	MM	Salta Memorial St Marie Cemetery
White, P J	Barman	MM	Salta Memorial St Marie Cemetery
Wright, F H	Wardroom Attendant	MM	Salta Memorial St Marie Cemetery
Yasin, Ali	Fireman Trimmer	MM	Salta Memorial St Marie Cemetery
Youngs, Alfred James	Linen Keeper	MM	St Marie Cemetery Div. 62.I
Zucchi, Camillo	Second Cook	MM	Salta Memorial St Marie Cemetery

Barnsley, Walter William	Private	36560	RAMC	Salta Memorial St Marie Cemetery
Bigwood, John Robert	Private	1603	RAMC	Salta Memorial St Marie Cemetery
Birt, Ernest Arthur	Private	9981	RAMC	Salta Memorial St Marie Cemetery
Brennan, Thomas M	Private	75306	RAMC	Salta Memorial St Marie Cemetery
Brosky, Arthur	Private	8673	RAMC	Salta Memorial St Marie Cemetery
Clark, Donald	Private	6307	RAMC	Salta Memorial St Marie Cemetery
Cowan, Archiebald	Private	9767	RAMC	Salta Memorial St Marie Cemetery
Cruickshank, Isabelle	Nursing Sister		QAIMNS	Salta Memorial St Marie Cemetery
Dawson, Eveline Maud	Matron		QAIMNS	Etaples Military Cemetery XVII D24
Driver, Bertie	Private	66331	RAMC	Salta Memorial St Marie Cemetery
Foyster, Ellen Lucy	Nursing Sister		QAIMNS	Salta Memorial St Marie Cemetery
Gilman, William Richard	Private	38599	RAMC	Salta Memorial St Marie Cemetery
Gould, John William	Private	61574	RAMC	Salta Memorial St Marie Cemetery
Gurney, Elizabeth S	Staff Nurse		QAIMNS	Salta Memorial St Marie Cemetery
Gyllencreutz, James R	Major		RAMC	Salta Memorial St Marie Cemetery
Harris, Ernest Henry	Private	72143	RAMC	Salta Memorial St Marie Cemetery
Hawes, Godfrey C B	Captain		RAMC	St Marie Cemetery Div. 62.I
Herbert, William Antony	Private	5215	RAMC	St Marie Cemetery Div. 62.I
Hicks, Wilfred	Private	65144	RAMC	Salta Memorial St Marie Cemetery
Hill, James Henry	Private	10014	RAMC	Salta Memorial St Marie Cemetery
Hingerton, William	Private	810	RAMC	Salta Memorial St Marie Cemetery
Hodkinson, Frederick	Private	44363	RAMC	Salta Memorial St Marie Cemetery
Hodson, Thomas G S	Captain		RAMC	Salta Memorial St Marie Cemetery
Johnstone, Donald M	Corporal	4835	RAMC	Salta Memorial St Marie Cemetery
Jones, Ernest Newton	Sergeant	18920	RAMC	Salta Memorial St Marie Cemetery
Jones, Gertrude Eileen	Nursing Sister		QAIMNS	Salta Memorial St Marie Cemetery
Kinder, Mark	Sergeant Major	17555	RAMC	Salta Memorial St Marie Cemetery
King, Thomas Edward	Private	97182	RAMC	Salta Memorial St Marie Cemetery
Mann, Agnes Greig	Staff Nurse		QAIMNS	St Marie Cemetery Div. 62.I
Mason, Fanny	Staff Nurse		QAIMNS	Salta Memorial St Marie Cemetery
McAlister, Clara	Staff Nurse		QAIMNS	Salta Memorial St Marie Cemetery
McGee, Hugh	Private	5742	RAMC	Salta Memorial St Marie Cemetery
Millward, William B	Private	37554	RAMC	Salta Memorial St Marie Cemetery
Naylor, Joseph	Lieutenant		RAMC	Salta Memorial St Marie Cemetery
Pollard, Paul	Private	5975	RAMC	Salta Memorial St Marie Cemetery
Prowse, Russel B M	Private	10901	RAMC	Salta Memorial St Marie Cemetery
Purdie, John	Private	79027	RAMC	Salta Memorial St Marie Cemetery
Roberts, Jane	Staff Nurse		QAIMNS	Salta Memorial St Marie Cemetery
Runciman, James Lornie	Private	43977	RAMC	Salta Memorial St Marie Cemetery
Seymour, William	Private	65534	RAMC	Salta Memorial St Marie Cemetery
Sherman, Henry Bert	Private	6902	RAMC	Salta Memorial St Marie Cemetery
Snelson, J C	Private	68751	RAMC	Salta Memorial St Marie Cemetery
Sole, Gerald Ernest	Private	97281	RAMC	Salta Memorial St Marie Cemetery
Taylor, John G	Sergeant	54832	RAMC	St Marie Cemetery Div. 62.I
Wallace, Michael Joseph	Private	4953	RAMC	Salta Memorial St Marie Cemetery
Wheeler, George Robert	Private	6455	RAMC	Salta Memorial St Marie Cemetery
White, Leonard	Corporal	5327	RAMC	Salta Memorial St Marie Cemetery
Wooldridge, George C	Private	65094	RAMC	Salta Memorial St Marie Cemetery
Wright, Thomas Henry	Private	14994	RAMC	Salta Memorial St Marie Cemetery

	WARILDA		Lost 3 August 1918	
Courtney, Albert Henry	Steward		MM	Tower Hill Memorial, London
Harris, Victor	Steward		MM	Tower Hill Memorial, London
Jordan, Edward	Fireman		MM	Tower Hill Memorial, London
Maidment, Frederick	Greaser		MM	Tower Hill Memorial, London
Milne, John	Third Engineer		MM	Tower Hill Memorial, London
Newnham, Bernard G	Saloon Steward		MM	Tower Hill Memorial, London
Phillips, Douglas W	Third Cook		MM	Tower Hill Memorial, London
Abbott, Norman	Private	3263	33/AIF	Hollybrook Memorial, Southampton
Annat, William	Private	S/41656	Seaforth High	Hollybrook Memorial, Southampton
Becker, Albert	Private	139506	RGA	Hollybrook Memorial, Southampton
Bellamy, Arthur Edward	Private	669792	Canadian Engrs	Halifax Memorial, Nova Scotia
Bennett, Christopher J	Rifleman	B201992	Rifle Brigade	Hollybrook Memorial, Southampton
Benton, Frederick	Rifleman	742337	London Regt.	Hollybrook Memorial, Southampton
Beveridge, Alexander	Private	250430	A & S High	Hollybrook Memorial, Southampton
Biddle, Henry	Bombardier	94759	RFA	Hollybrook Memorial, Southampton
Boggis, William A	Private	39857	East Surrey Regt.	Hollybrook Memorial, Southampton
Boyack, William	Private	22153	A & S High	Hollybrook Memorial, Southampton
Boyle, William	Private	16378	R. Irish Rifles	Hollybrook Memorial, Southampton
Brown, Hugh	Private	201408	A & S High	Hollybrook Memorial, Southampton
Browning, Harry MM	Sergeant	13610	Norfolk Regt.	Hollybrook Memorial, Southampton
Buck, Albert	Private	11436	RWF	Hollybrook Memorial, Southampton
Buckman	Corporal		American E F	
Burns, George	C/Sgt Mjr	325457	Royal Scots.	Hollybrook Memorial, Southampton
Chaplin, Walter	Private	T206619	R. West Surrey	Hollybrook Memorial, Southampton
Claridge, Robert O J	Private	2912	41/AIF	Hollybrook Memorial, Southampton
Clayton, Maurice	Private	241251	KOSB	Hollybrook Memorial, Southampton
Clements, Frederick G	Private	422864	London Regt.	Hollybrook Memorial, Southampton
Cliff, Bernard served as Collins	Private	141385	MG Corps	Hollybrook Memorial, Southampton
Collins, John	Private	21966	Coldstream Gds	Hollybrook Memorial, Southampton
Cooper, Archibald	Private	S/20809	A & S High	Hollybrook Memorial, Southampton
Coult, Bertram	Rifleman	370798	London Regt.	Hollybrook Memorial, Southampton
Cox, Fredrick MM	Gunner	311273	RGA	Hollybrook Memorial, Southampton
Coyle, J	Lance Corporal	260030	Gordon High	Hollybrook Memorial, Southampton
Craven, Bernard	Private	11871	R. Irish Fusiliers	Hollybrook Memorial, Southampton
Crossman, John	Private	32007	Somerset LI	Hollybrook Memorial, Southampton
Doran, James	Private	23418	W. Sussex Regt.	Hollybrook Memorial, Southampton
Everett, John	Private	58994	Otago Regt. N.Z.	Otago Provincial Memorial. NZ
Faulks, Thomas	Private	3231	29/AIF	Hollybrook Memorial, Southampton
Fletcher, George M	Private	43115	Cameronians	Hollybrook Memorial, Southampton
Gallagher, Robert	Private	241045	KOSB	Hollybrook Memorial, Southampton
Giddings, Henry	Private	G/22179	Sussex Regt.	Hollybrook Memorial, Southampton
Gilooley, J	Gunner	71782	RGA	Hollybrook Memorial, Southampton
Harding, Archibald	Corporal	T206672	R. West Surrey	Hollybrook Memorial, Southampton
Harris, Patrick	Private	42014	S. Staffordshires	Hollybrook Memorial, Southampton
Hart, James	Private	M/371712	ASC	Hollybrook Memorial, Southampton
Haslam, Arnold	Private	201693	KOSB	Hollybrook Memorial, Southampton
Henderson, Gilbert R	Private	20882	R. Scots Fusilier	Hollybrook Memorial, Southampton
Herbert, Gilbert R	Private	20882	R. Scots Fusilier	Hollybrook Memorial, Southampton
Holland, Thomas H	Private	354758	London Regt.	Hollybrook Memorial, Southampton

Hopwood, Henry	Private	52613	West Yorkshire	Hollybrook Memorial, Southampton
Hossell, John W	Private	240702	York & Lancs Regt.	Hollybrook Memorial, Southampton
Hume, Hugh	Private	S/32190	Cameronians	Hollybrook Memorial, Southampton
Hurst, William Charles	Corporal	M2/019767	Army Service Corps	Hollybrook Memorial, Southampton
Hynett, Albert Arthur	Sapper	478712	Royal Engineers	Hollybrook Memorial, Southampton
Illingworth, John B	Private	53157	Lincolnshire Regt.	Hollybrook Memorial, Southampton
Jackson, Walter John	Private	103764	MGC	Hollybrook Memorial, Southampton
Jakeman, Arthur	Corporal	M2/ 053475	ASCorps	Hollybrook Memorial, Southampton
Jones, Reginald Arthur	Private	39015	Loyal N. Lancs	Hollybrook Memorial, Southampton
Kerr, John Peter	Private	277274	A & S High	Hollybrook Memorial, Southampton
Kinniburgh, James	Private	8908	Scots Guards	Hollybrook Memorial, Southampton
Laidlaw, Eric Leslie	Private	3581	31/AIF	Hollybrook Memorial, Southampton
Lawson, Arthur	Private	13732	Australian ASC	Hollybrook Memorial, Southampton
Leppard, George Francis	Gunner	15120	RFA	Hollybrook Memorial, Southampton
Long, Violet A, OBE	Chief Controller		QMAAC	Hollybrook Memorial, Southampton
Lowe, Tom	Shoeing Smith	L/23238	RFA	Hollybrook Memorial, Southampton
Lowson, Herbert	Private	45860	York & Lancs Regt.	Hollybrook Memorial, Southampton
MacKenzie, Charles	Private	200714	A & S High	Hollybrook Memorial, Southampton
MacKenzie, Frederick W	Private	S/41221	Cameronians	Hollybrook Memorial, Southampton
MacLean, John	Private	201726	KOSB	Hollybrook Memorial, Southampton
Maley, Martin	Private	S/20533	A & S High	Hollybrook Memorial, Southampton
Marples, Walter	Private	58702	West Yorks Reg	Hollybrook Memorial, Southampton
Martin, James	Private	201137	A & S High	Hollybrook Memorial, Southampton
McDougall, D	Private	290685	Cameronians	Hollybrook Memorial, Southampton
McIntosh, James	Private	201588	Seaforth High	Hollybrook Memorial, Southampton
McIntosh, John	Corporal	S/40651	Seaforth High	Hollybrook Memorial, Southampton
McIntyre, Donald	Private	3206	37/AIF	Hollybrook Memorial, Southampton
McKie, John	Private	241117	KOSB	Hollybrook Memorial, Southampton
McKinnie, James	Private	42734	Cameronians	Hollybrook Memorial, Southampton
McMichael, John	Private	128631	M G Corps	Hollybrook Memorial, Southampton
McRae, Robert	Private	201776	KOSB	Hollybrook Memorial, Southampton
McVittie, George H	Second Lieutenant		Border Regt.	Hollybrook Memorial, Southampton
Milgate, Henry C	Private	5024	12/Lancers	Hollybrook Memorial, Southampton
Millson, George Andrew	Sergeant	9417	Loyal N. Lancs	Hollybrook Memorial, Southampton
Moss, Albert Hubert	Lieutenant		Australian F A	Hollybrook Memorial, Southampton
Murphy, James	Private	5626	Connaught Rangers	Hollybrook Memorial, Southampton
Myers, James	Coy Q/M Sgt	5502	Lancashire Fusiliers	Hollybrook Memorial, Southampton
Nolan, James	Private	39023	Loyal N. Lancs	Hollybrook Memorial, Southampton
Norris, William	Private	42572	Yorkshire Regt.	Hollybrook Memorial, Southampton
Ogden, Joseph A	Private	353103	Royal Scots	Hollybrook Memorial, Southampton
Owen, Sidney Ernest	Private	11509	9 Lancers	Hollybrook Memorial, Southampton
Parker, John	Private	42198	KOSB	Hollybrook Memorial, Southampton
Paterson, William	Private	201518	A & S High	Hollybrook Memorial, Southampton
Pierce, John	L/Cpl	153893	Royal Engineers	Hollybrook Memorial, Southampton
Pike, Victor Hugo	Private	2654	Australian Pioneers	Hollybrook Memorial, Southampton
Power, Charles Norman	Private	3066	Australian Inf.	Hollybrook Memorial, Southampton
Purcell, Robert Henry	Private	6118	Australian Inf.	Hollybrook Memorial, Southampton
Rae, L	Private	201168	Gordon High	Hollybrook Memorial, Southampton
Reid, John	Sergeant	200042	A & S High	Hollybrook Memorial, Southampton
Retell, Paul	Private	3191	Australian Pioneers	Hollybrook Memorial, Southampton
Richardson, Urbane C	Driver	38387	RHA	Hollybrook Memorial, Southampton
Richardson, William M	Private	201246	Durham L.I.	Hollybrook Memorial, Southampton

Roberts, William	Private	9518	Somerset L.I.	Hollybrook Memorial, Southampton
Robinson, Arthur	Private	21479	RAMC	Hollybrook Memorial, Southampton
Robinson, John	Private	200676	Cheshire Regt.	Hollybrook Memorial, Southampton
Roxburgh, John	Private	2631	38/AIF	Hollybrook Memorial, Southampton
Royle, Thomas Wright	Gunner	37634	RFA	Hollybrook Memorial, Southampton
Shine, James Frederick	Private	T/4096447	Army Service Corps	Hollybrook Memorial, Southampton
Smith, John	Private	350567	Royal Scots	Hollybrook Memorial, Southampton
Stimson, Albert	Rifleman	372808	London Regt.	Hollybrook Memorial, Southampton
Sutherland, Thomas	Sergeant	7716	Seaforth High	Hollybrook Memorial, Southampton
Swain, Walter	Gunner	95622	RFA	Hollybrook Memorial, Southampton
Tait, Alexander	Private	S/18113	Gordon High	Hollybrook Memorial, Southampton
Temple, Thomas Young	Sergeant	10497	Durham L.I.	Hollybrook Memorial, Southampton
Truscott, Thomas H	Private	21756	Duke Cornwall L.I.	Hollybrook Memorial, Southampton
Watson, Walter Kerr	Private	S/22781	Gordon High	Hollybrook Memorial, Southampton
Whomack, Arthur	Rifleman	17175	West York Regt.	Hollybrook Memorial, Southampton
Wilkins, Ernest	Private	4239	32/AIF	Hollybrook Memorial, Southampton
Wilson, Joseph	Gunner	676048	RFA	Hollybrook Memorial, Southampton
Wilson, William Robert	Corporal	47013	RGA	Hollybrook Memorial, Southampton
Wood, C K	Lieutenant		ASC	Hollybrook Memorial, Southampton

1. Casualties either walked or were carried to an Advanced Dressing Station sited a few miles from the front.

2. Stretcher bearers transferring wounded to an adapted light railway wagon for medical evacuation.

3. Another stage closer to Blighty.

4. Royal Navy hospital train with hammock cots and fitted carpets.

5. A hospital ship receiving wounded personnel.

6. Below: One of the *Saint Margaret of Scotland* hospital wards.

7. Bottom: HMHS *Vasna*

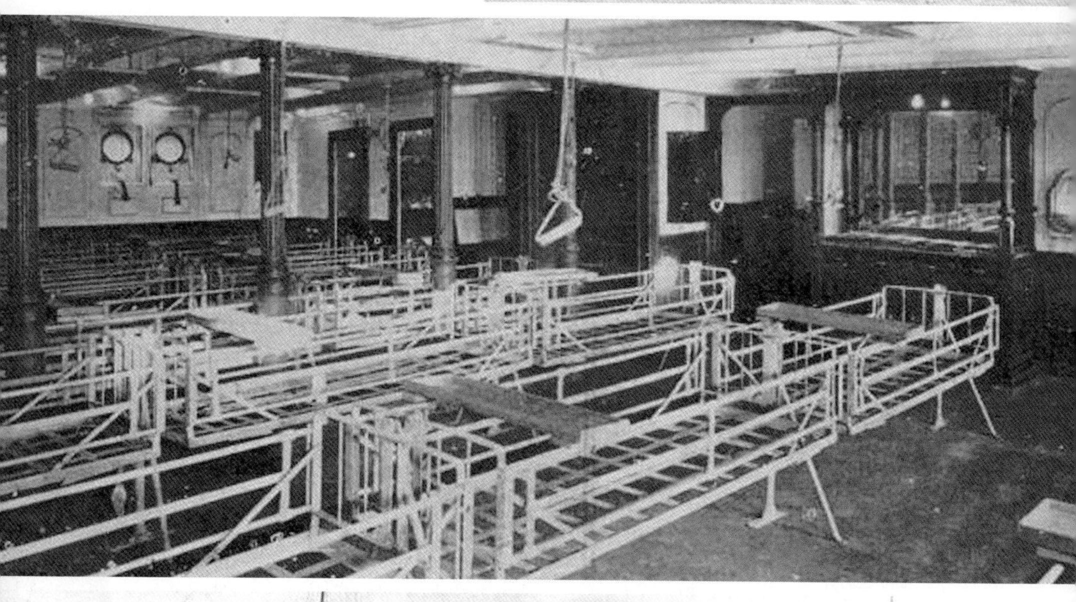

8. Officers reclining in steamer chairs take in the sea breeze as an orderly sees to their comfort and an angel of mercy passes by.

9. Contrasting with the above, hospital ship patients belonging to the other ranks raise a smile for the camera.

10. Bottom: Nurses in life jackets muster on the boat deck for life boat drill.

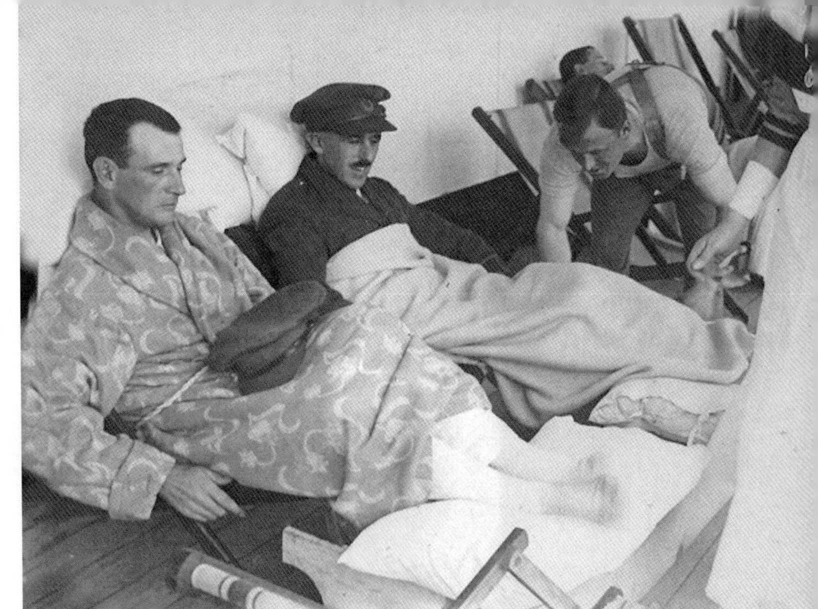

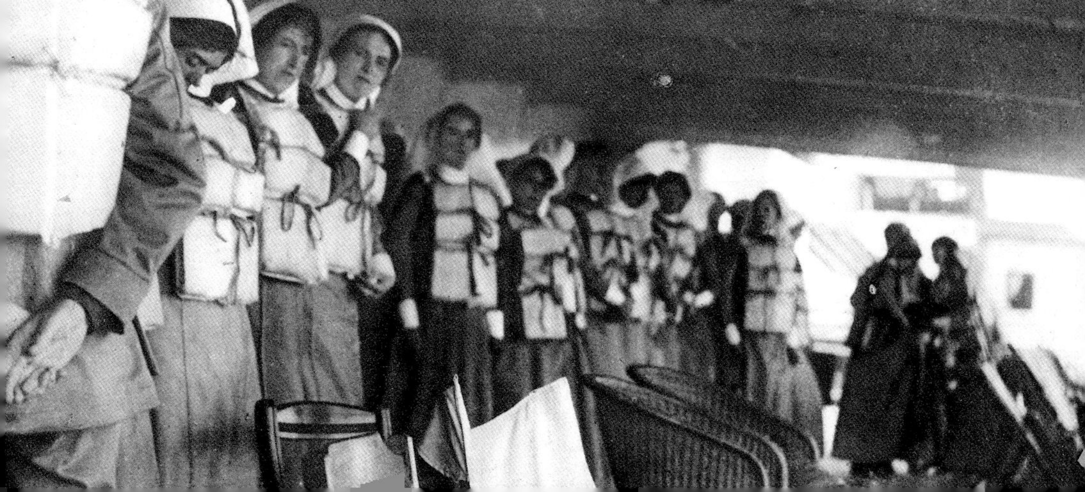

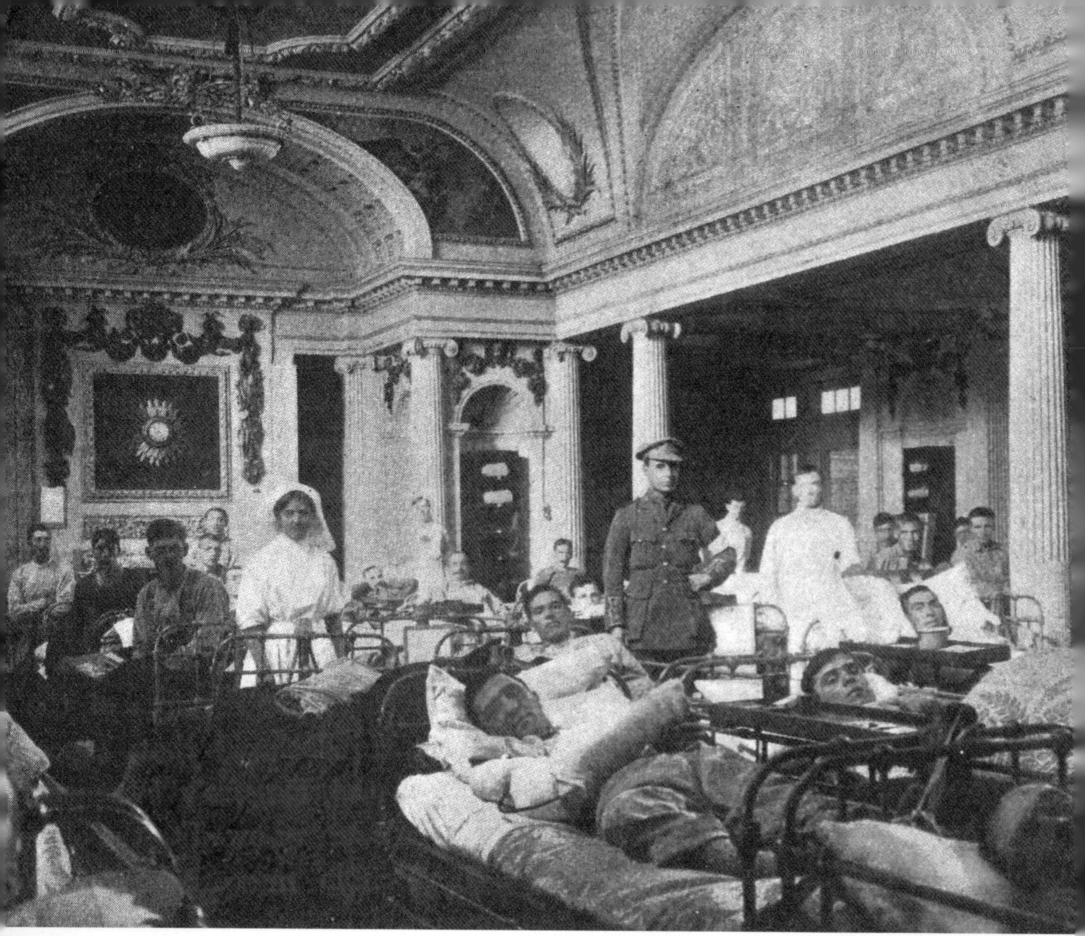

11. The opulent lounge of the *Aquitania* utilised as a hospital ward.

12. HMHS *Garth Castle* dwarfs an unconfirmed *St Margaret* of Scotland.

13. A postcard indicating a wounded patient's high regard for the nursing staff.

14. A surfaced U-boat searching for prey.

15. 'Full speed ahead' confirmed as a U-boat manoeuvres for the kill.

16. Quadruple torpedo tubes to dispense death and destruction.

17. A crowded lifeboat pulls clear of a torpedoed and sinking vessel. Note the screw is not turning; when a ship went down with engines still driving its propellers everything in the water in the vicinity could be sucked in and destroyed.

18. HMHS *Soudan* at Malta.

19. A hospital nurse looks with compassion on a severely mutilated patient.

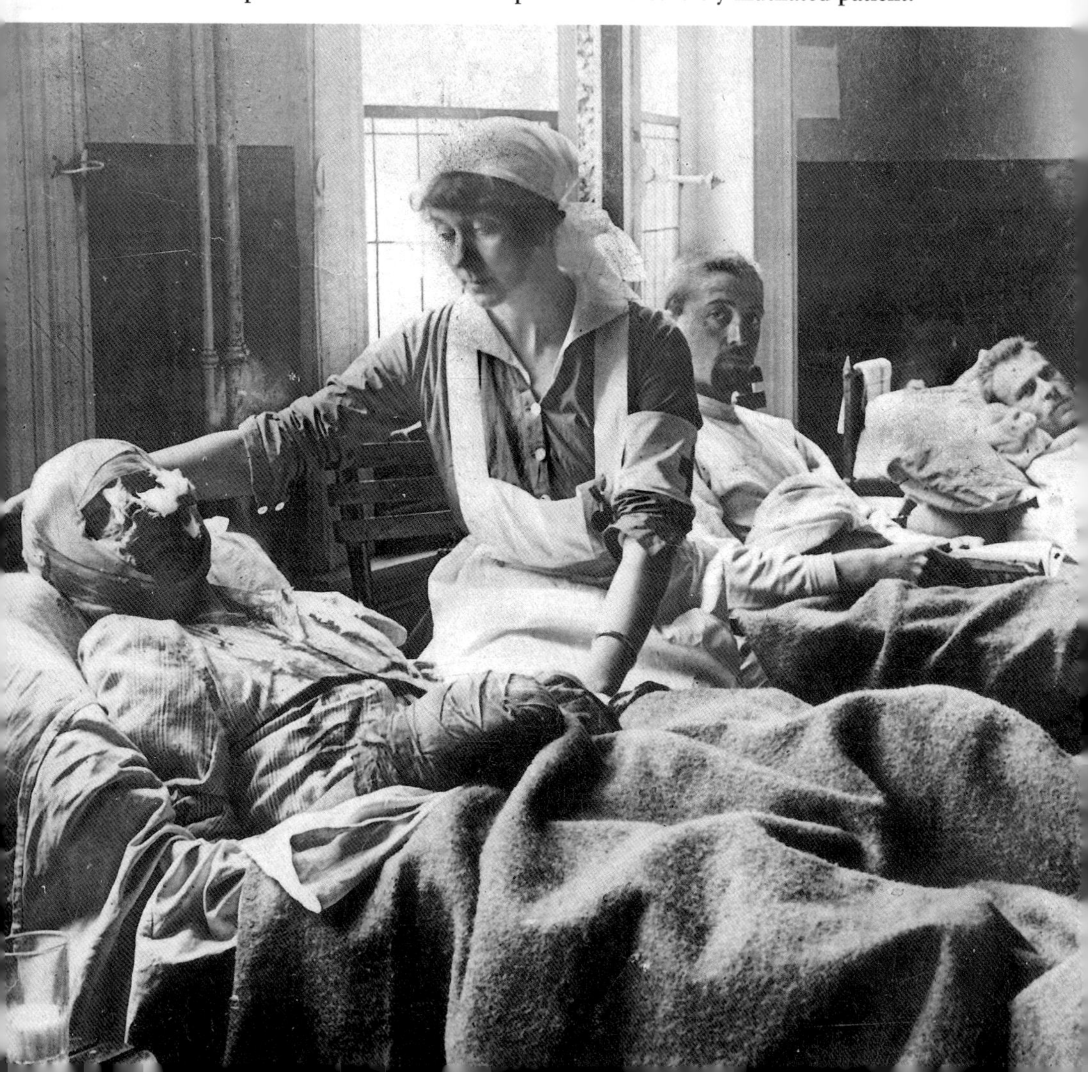

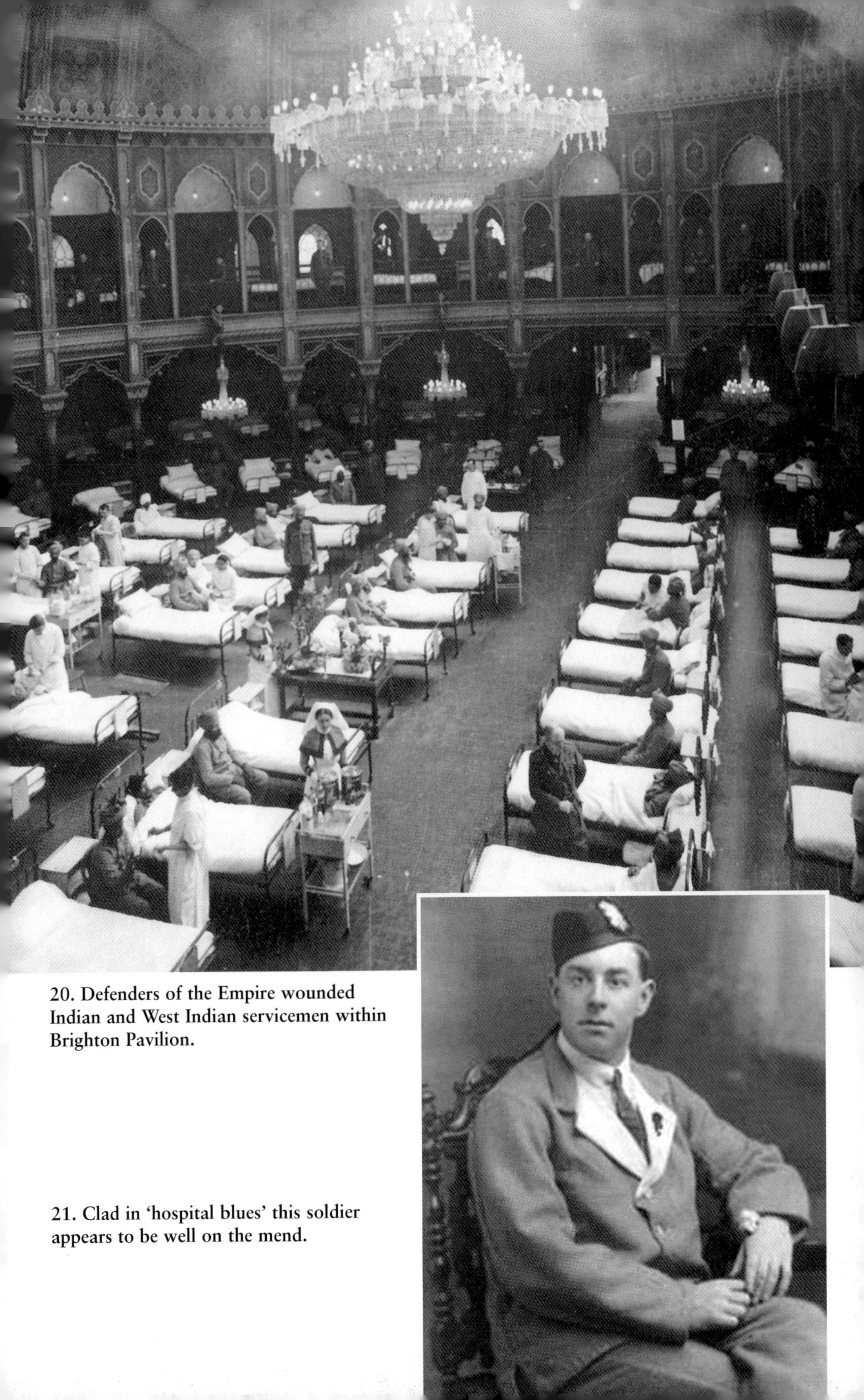

20. Defenders of the Empire wounded Indian and West Indian servicemen within Brighton Pavilion.

21. Clad in 'hospital blues' this soldier appears to be well on the mend.

22. Red Cross and St Johns Ambulance staff with patients dated 12 August 1916.

23. For those fortunate enough to make a full recovery...

Bibliography

Barnaby, K C. Some ship disasters and their causes. Hutchinson & Co. London. 1970.
Carver, Field Marshal Lord. Turkish Front 1914-18. Pan Books. London. 2004.
Coles, Alan. Slaughter at sea. Robert Hale, London. 1986.
Haws, Duncan. Merchant Fleets, Royal Mail Line. Planet Press Ltd, Sussex. 1982.
Hoehling, A. A. The Great War at sea. Arthur Baker Ltd, London. 1965.
Jarvis, SD & DB. The cross of sacrifice Vol IV. Roberts, Reading 1996.
Keegan, John. The face of battle. Barrie & Jenkins, London 1988.
Knight, E F. Union Castle & the war 1914-19. Union Castle Mail SS Co. Ltd. London, 1920.
Laffin. John. Damn the Dardenelles. Osprey Publishing Limited, Stroud, Glos. 1980.
Massie, Robert K. Castles of steel. Pimlico, London. 2005.
McDonald, Lynne. The Roses of No Mans Land. McMillan Publishing. London. 1984.
McGreal Stephen. Zeebrugge & Ostend Raids. Pen & Sword Books. Barnsley, S. Yorks. 2007.
Mollet, Joyce. With a camera in my pocket. Baddeley Books, Wales. 2005.
Mullins, Claude. The Leipzig trials. London, H F & G Witherby London 1921.
Pratt, E A. British Railways and the Great War. Official History, 1916 Volume One. J E Edmonds.
Smith, Eugene W. Passenger ships of the world, Past and present. 1963.
Tennent A. J. British merchant ships sunk by U Boats in the 1914-1918 war. Starling Press, Gwent. 1990.
Woodward Llewellyn, Sir. Great Britain & the war of 1914-1918. Methuen & Co Ltd, London. 1967.
Plumridge John H. Hospital ships and ambulance trains. Seeley, Service & Co Ltd. London. 1975.

Newspapers and Periodicals

Times history of the war, The.
Daily Mirror.
Birmingham Weekly Post, The.
Liverpool Daily Post and Courier.
Birkenhead News. Wallasey News.
Liverpool Echo.
New York Times, The.

National Archives.

3 Wing Records. Air 1/115/15/39/51 and Air 1/648/17/122/397.
Foreign Office Prisoner of War and Aliens Department. FO383/281 FO383/280 and 1906 FO383/149.
Inquiry into the loss of HMHS *Glenart Castle*. ADM 137/3253 and ADM 137/3424.
Admiralty Transport Department conveyance of personnel and stores onboard HMHS *Britannic*. MT 23/593.
Explanation of the difference between a hospital carrier and hospital ship. MT 23/446.
Admiralty and Supreme Court prize papers concerning the seized *Ophelia*.
Admiralty Transport Department. Correspondence relating to ship and crew of HMHS *Garth Castle*. MT 23/472.
Admiralty Transport Department. Statement of Master and crew regarding the enemy torpedo fired at HMHS *Asturias*. MT23/364. Several more files were consulted however their index numbers were omitted by the researcher.
Baralong Papers, The. ADM 137/385

Other Archives

Letitia File, The. RG 42 Wreck Commissioners Court. Department of Marine & Fisheries. RG 42 Series C 3A, Volume 595.

Monuments and Memorials

Tower Hill Memorial, London. Hollybrook Memorial, Southampton.
The Commonwealth War Graves Commission. [CWGC]

Museums

Imperial War Museum. For the extracts from the Diary of Nurse Ada Garland.

Index

Allied Warships

The Kaisers' Warships

German Merchant Vessels

Miscellaneous Hospital Ships.

Male Allied Individuals